Grammar Sense 3

Teacher's Book

Katharine Sherak

198 Madison Avenue
New York, NY 10016 USA

Great Clarendon Street
Oxford OX2 6DP England

Oxford New York
Auckland Bangkok Buenos Aires Cape Town Chennai Dar es Salaam
Delhi Hong Kong Istanbul Karachi Kolkata Kuala Lumpur Madrid
Melbourne Mexico City Mumbai Nairobi São Paulo Shanghai Taipei
Tokyo Toronto

OXFORD is a trademark of Oxford University Press

ISBN 0-19-436629-4

Copyright © 2004 Oxford University Press

No unauthorized photocopying.

All rights reserved. No part of this publication may be reproduced, stored in a retrieval system, or transmitted, in any form or by any means, electronic, mechanical, photocopying, recording, or otherwise, without the prior written permission of Oxford University Press.

This book is sold subject to the condition that it shall not, by way of trade or otherwise, be lent, resold, hired out, or otherwise circulated without the publisher's prior consent in any form of binding or cover other than that in which it is published and without a similar condition including this condition being imposed on the subsequent purchaser.

Editorial Manager: Janet Aitchison
Senior Editor: Stephanie Karras
Associate Editor: Daria Ruzicka
Art Director: Lynn Luchetti
Design Project Manager: Mary Chandler
Production Manager: Shanta Persaud
Production Coordinator: Eve Wong
Designer: Michael Steinhofer
Compositor: Compset, Inc.
Cover design: Lee Anne Dollison

Printing (last digit): 10 9 8 7 6 5 4 3 2 1

Printed in Hong Kong

Contents

Introduction v

Chapter 1 The Present 1

Chapter 2 The Past 6

Chapter 3 Future Forms 11

Chapter 4 The Present Perfect 15

Chapter 5 The Present Perfect Continuous 20

Chapter 6 The Past Perfect and the Past Perfect Continuous 24

Chapter 7 Modals of Possibility 28

Chapter 8 Past Modals 32

Chapter 9 Passive Sentences (Part 1) 36

Chapter 10 Passive Sentences (Part 2) 40

Chapter 11 Contrasting Gerunds and Infinitives 44

Chapter 12 Indefinite and Definite Articles; Review of Nouns 49

Chapter 13 Relative Clauses with Subject Relative Pronouns 54

Chapter 14 Relative Clauses with Object Relative Pronouns 58

Chapter 15 Real Conditionals, Unreal Conditionals, and Wishes 63

Chapter 16 Past Unreal Conditionals and Past Wishes 68

Chapter 17 Noun Clauses 72

Chapter 18 Reported Speech 76

Student Book Tapescript 81

Student Book Answer Key 91

Series Introduction

Series Director: Susan Kesner Bland

Grammar Sense: A Discourse-Based Approach

Grammar Sense is a comprehensive three-level grammar series based on the authentic use of English grammar in discourse. The grammar is systematically organized, explained, and practiced in a communicative, learner-centered environment, making it easily teachable and learnable.

Many people ask, why learn grammar? The answer is simple: meaningful communication depends on our ability to connect form and meaning appropriately. In order to do so, we must consider such factors as intention, attitude, and social relationships, in addition to the contexts of time and place. All of these factors make up a discourse setting. For example, we use the present continuous not only to describe an activity in progress *(He's working.)*, but also to complain *(He's always working.)*, to describe a planned event in the future *(He's working tomorrow.)*, and to describe temporary or unusual behavior *(He's being lazy at work.)*. It is only through examination of the discourse setting that the different meanings and uses of the present continuous can be distinguished from one another. A discourse-based approach provides students with the tools for making sense of the grammar of natural language by systematically explaining *who, what, where, when, why,* and *how* for each grammatical form.

SYSTEMATICALLY ORGANIZED SYLLABUS

Learning grammar is a developmental process that occurs gradually. In *Grammar Sense* the careful sequencing, systematic repetition, recycling, review, and expansion promote grammatical awareness and fluency.

Level 1 (basic level) focuses on building an elementary understanding of form, meaning, and use as students develop basic oral language skills in short conversations and discussions. Level 1 also targets the grammar skills involved in writing short paragraphs, using basic cohesive devices such as conjunctions and pronouns.

At **Level 2 (intermediate level)** the focus turns to expanding the basic understanding of form, meaning, and use in longer and more varied discourse settings and with more complex grammatical structures and academic themes. Level 2 emphasizes grammar skills beyond the sentence level, as students begin to initiate and sustain conversations and discussions, and progress toward longer types of writing.

Finally, at **Level 3 (high intermediate to advanced level)** the focus moves to spoken and written grammar in academic discourse settings, often in contexts that are conceptually more challenging and abstract. Level 3 emphasizes consistent and appropriate language use, especially of those aspects of grammar needed in extended conversations and discussions, and in longer academic and personal writing.

INTRODUCTION OF FORM BEFORE MEANING AND USE

Form is introduced and practiced in a separate section before meaning and use. This ensures that students understand what the form looks like and sounds like at the sentence level, before engaging in more challenging and open-ended activities that concentrate on meaning and use.

FOCUS ON NATURAL LANGUAGE USE

Grammar Sense uses authentic reading texts and examples that are based on or quoted verbatim from actual English language sources to provide a true picture of natural language use. To avoid unnatural language, the themes of the introductory reading texts are only subtly touched upon throughout a chapter. The focus thus remains on typical examples of the most common meanings and uses.

Exposure to authentic language helps students bridge the gap between the classroom and the outside world by encouraging awareness of the "grammar" all around them in daily life: in magazines, newspapers, package instructions, television shows, signs, and so on. Becoming language-aware is an important step in the language learning process: Students generalize from the examples they find and apply their understanding to their independent language use in daily living, at work, or as they further their education.

SPECIAL SECTIONS TO EXTEND GRAMMATICAL KNOWLEDGE

Understanding grammar as a system entails understanding how different parts of the language support and interact with the target structure. *Grammar Sense* features special sections at strategic points throughout the text to highlight relevant lexical and discourse issues.

- **Beyond the Sentence** sections focus on the structure as it is used in extended discourse to help improve students' writing skills. These sections highlight such issues as how grammatical forms are used to avoid redundancy, and how to change or maintain focus.

- **Informally Speaking** sections highlight the differences between written and spoken language. This understanding is crucial for achieving second language fluency. Reduced forms, omissions, and pronunciation changes are explained in order to improve aural comprehension.

- **Vocabulary Notes** provide succinct presentations of words and phrases that are commonly used with the target structure, such as time expressions associated with the simple past, or the use of *say*, *tell*, and *ask* in reported speech.

STUDENT-CENTERED PRESENTATION AND PRACTICE

Student-centered presentation and practice allow learners at all levels to discover the grammar in pairs, groups, and individually, in both the Form and in the Meaning and Use sections of each chapter. Numerous inductive activities encourage students to use their problem-solving abilities to gain the skills, experience, and confidence to use English outside of class and to continue learning on their own.

FLEXIBILITY TO SUIT ANY CLASSROOM SITUATION

Grammar Sense offers teachers great flexibility with hundreds of intellectually engaging exercises to choose from. Teachers may choose to skip chapters or sections within chapters, or teach them in a different order, depending on student needs and time constraints. Each Student Book is self-contained so teachers may choose to use only one book, or the full series, if they wish.

Components at Each Level

- The **Student Book** is intended for classroom use and offers concise charts, level-appropriate explanations, and thorough four-skills practice exercises. Each Student Book is also a useful reference resource with extensive Appendices, a helpful Glossary of Grammar Terms, and a detailed Index.

- The **Audio Cassettes** and **CDs** feature listening exercises that provide practice discriminating form, understanding meaning and use, and interpreting non-standard forms.

- The **Workbook** has a wealth of additional exercises to supplement those in the Student Book. It is ideal for homework, independent practice, or review. The Answer Key, on easily removable perforated pages, is provided at the back of the book.

- The **Teacher's Book** has many practical ideas and techniques for presenting the Form and the Meaning and Use charts. It also includes troubleshooting advice, cultural notes, and suggestions for additional activities. The Answer Key for the Student Book and the complete Tapescript are also provided.

- **TOEFL®-Style Tests** and Answer Keys, along with advice on conducting the tests and interpreting the results, are available for teachers to download from the Internet. (See www.oup.com/elt/teacher/grammarsense)

Tour of a Student Book Chapter

Each chapter in *Grammar Sense* follows this format:

The **Grammar in Discourse** section introduces the target structure in its natural context via a high-interest authentic reading text.

• Authentic reading texts show how language is really used.

• Structured reading tasks help students read and understand the text.

viii   Introduction

The **Form** section(s) provides clear presentation of the target structure, detailed notes, and thorough practice exercises.

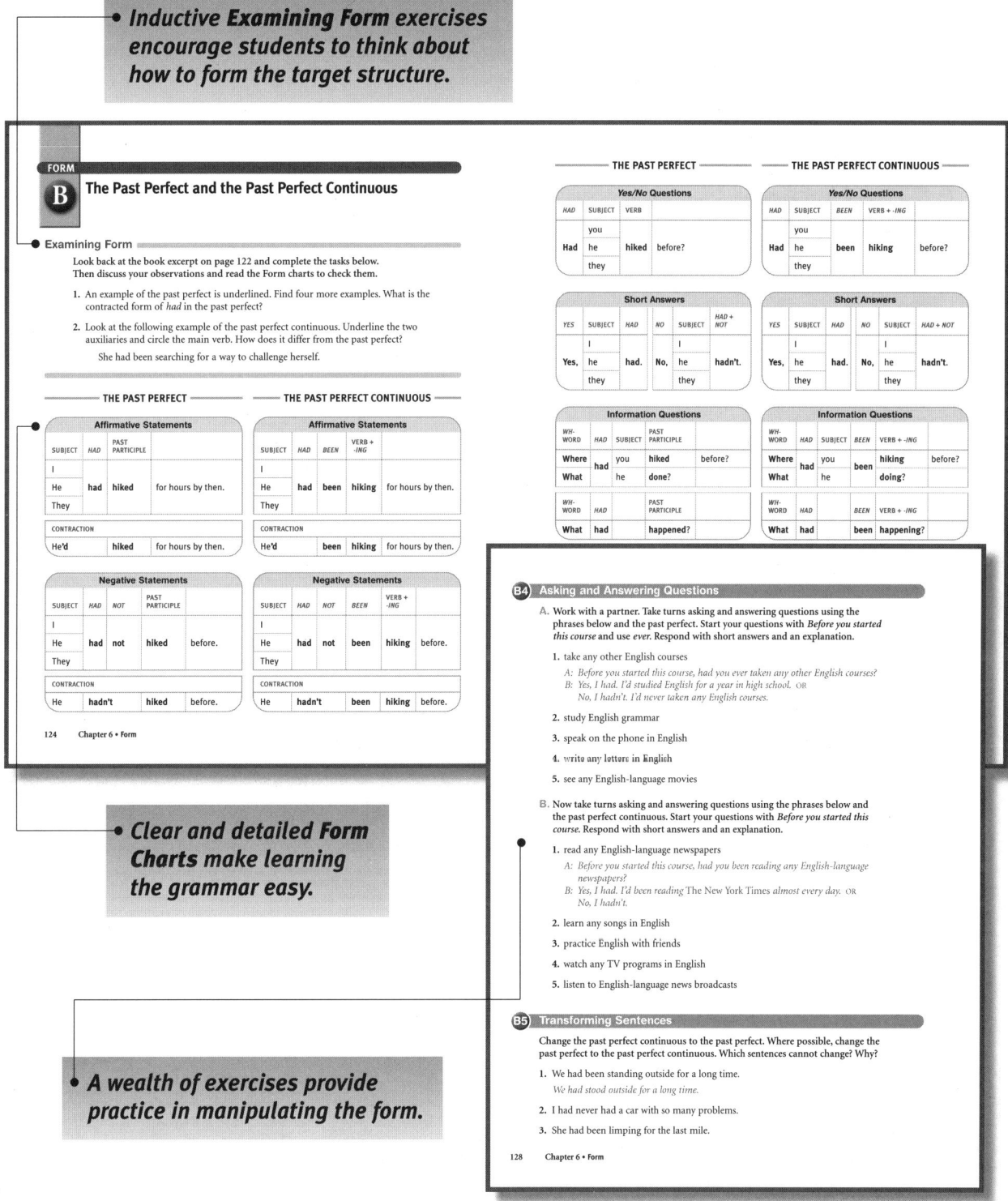

The **Meaning and Use** section(s) offers clear and comprehensive explanations of how the target structure is used, and exercises to practice using it appropriately.

Inductive Examining Meaning and Use exercises encourage students to analyze how we use the target structure.

Succinct explanations and authentic examples illustrate the various meanings and uses of the structure.

Practice exercises enable students to use the structure appropriately and fluently.

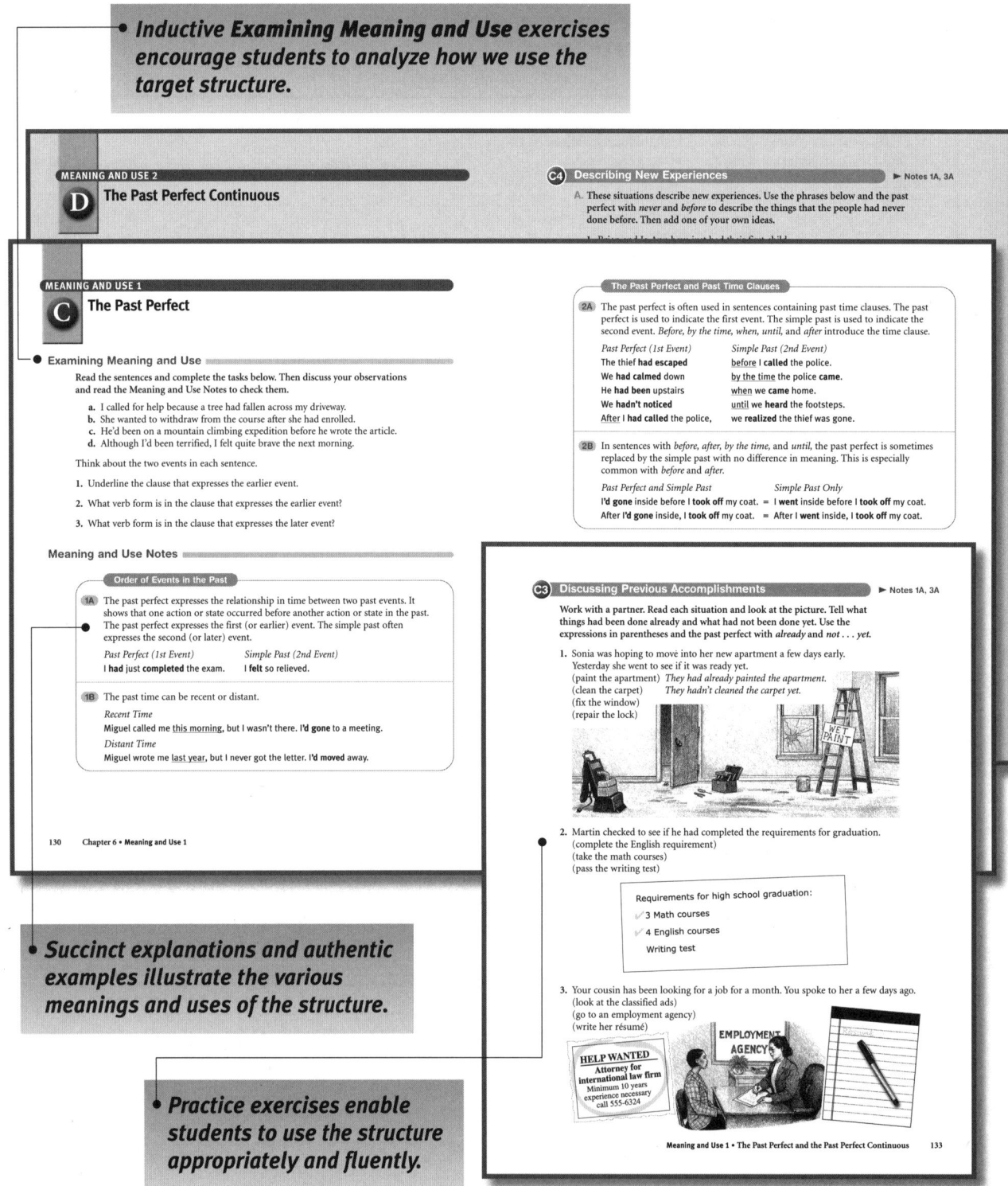

Introduction

The **Review** section allows students to demonstrate their mastery of all aspects of the structure. It can be used for further practice or as a test.

> **Thinking about Meaning and Use** exercises consolidate students' understanding of all aspects of the structure.

> **Editing** exercises teach students to correct their own writing.

REVIEW

E Combining Form, Meaning, and Use

E1 Thinking About Meaning and Use

Read each sentence and the statements that follow. Write *T* if the statement is true, *F* if it is false, or *?* if you do not have enough information to decide. Then discuss your answers in small groups.

1. After he had eaten a sandwich, he ate a salad.
   - _F_ a. He ate the salad first. Then he ate the sandwich.
   - _F_ b. He ate the salad and sandwich together.

2. He had left before the play ended.
   - ___ a. The play ended. Then he left.
   - ___ b. He was gone by the end of the play.

3. He had known her for many years when they started to work together.
   - ___ a. He met her at work.
   - ___ b. He knew her a long time.

4. Tom didn't lose weight until he went on a diet.
   - ___ a. Tom didn't lose weight.
   - ___ b. Tom went on a diet.

5. It was lunchtime. I looked out the window, and I saw that it had rained.
   - ___ a. It had rained just before I looked out the window.
   - ___ b. I looked out the window after the rain stopped.

6. He left his job because he had found a better one.
   - ___ a. He left his job. Then he looked for a better job.
   - ___ b. He left his job after he found another job.

7. The hospital didn't lose power, although there had been a power failure in the city.
   - ___ a. The hospital had a power failure.
   - ___ b. The city lost power.

8. The two men had been working on a project together when I met them.
   - ___ a. They worked together before I met them.
   - ___ b. They finished the project.

E2 Editing

Find the errors in these paragraphs and correct them, using either the simple past or the present perfect.

In 1953, Edmund Hillary and Tenzing Norkay ~~had been~~ *were* the first climbers to reach the top of Mount Everest. Since then, many people had climbed Mount Everest, especially in recent years. Before 1953, no human had ever stood on top of the world's highest peak, although some had tried. George Mallory and Sandy Irvine, for example, had died almost 30 years earlier on a perilous path along the North Ridge.

Since 1953, many more people had set world records. In 1975, Junko Tabei of Japan had become the first woman on a mountaineering team to reach the top. In 1980, Reinhold Messner of Italy had become the first person to make the climb to the top alone, without other people and without oxygen. In 1995, Alison Hargreaves of Scotland had duplicated Messner's triumph. She became the first

---

▶ Beyond the Classroom

Searching for Authentic Examples

Find examples of English grammar in everyday life. Choose one of the tasks below. Be prepared to discuss your findings.

A. Look in a newspaper, in a magazine, or on the Internet. Write down five examples of the past perfect and the past perfect continuous and bring them to class. Why do you think the past perfect or the past perfect continuous was used? Where in the article did you find the examples? Could you substitute the simple past instead?

B. Find examples of the past perfect and the past perfect continuous in a short story and bring them to class. Why do you think the past perfect and the past perfect continuous were used? Where in the story did you find the examples? Could you substitute the simple past instead?

Speaking

In small groups, follow these steps to prepare a description of a famous "mystery person."

1. Think of a famous person in history or sports who accomplished something that had never been done before. You are going to role-play that person by describing yourself and your accomplishment without revealing your identity to your group. You may wish to find out more about this person in the library or on the Internet.

2. Prepare a description of your mystery person using the first person. Give background information using the past perfect, the past perfect continuous, time clauses, and other tenses, where appropriate.

3. Present your description to your group and ask them to guess who you are. The group may wish to ask more questions.

> **Beyond the Classroom** activities offer creative suggestions for further practice in new contexts.

Special Sections appear throughout the chapters, with clear explanations, authentic examples, and follow-up exercises.

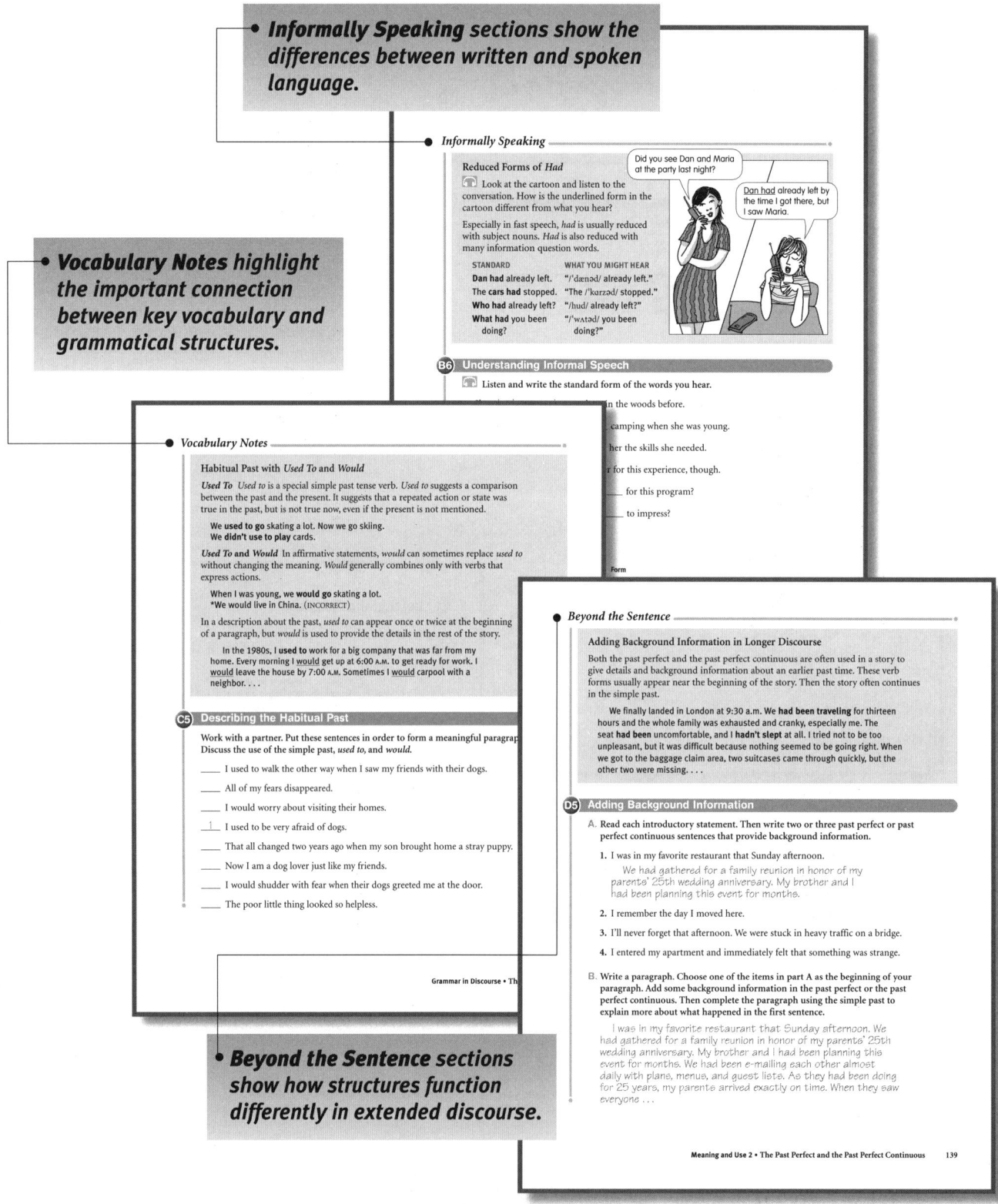

- **Informally Speaking** sections show the differences between written and spoken language.

- **Vocabulary Notes** highlight the important connection between key vocabulary and grammatical structures.

- **Beyond the Sentence** sections show how structures function differently in extended discourse.

Teacher's Book Introduction
Susan Iannuzzi

About the Teacher's Book

THE CHAPTERS

- **Overview:** Each chapter of the Teacher's Book begins with an overview of the grammar presented in the Student Book chapter. It enables the teacher to focus on the main points covered in the chapter, and highlights difficulties students may have with the structures.

- **Grammar in Discourse:** This section provides directions to help the teacher effectively teach the Before You Read, Read, and After You Read activities in the Student Book. It suggests creative ways to activate background knowledge, offers innovative reading strategies, and gives tips on checking comprehension.

- **Form:** This section offers two alternative ways to teach the inductive Examining Form exercises: Method 1 for students who are unfamiliar with the structure and may need extra support, and Method 2 for students who are already familiar with the structure and may be able to work more independently. The section also contains step-by-step instructions for presenting the Form Charts, and directions for utilizing the Special Sections such as Informally Speaking.

- **Meaning and Use:** This section offers advice on teaching the inductive Examining Meaning and Use exercises. It also provides step-by-step instructions for presenting the Meaning and Use Notes and directions for using the Special Sections such as Vocabulary Notes and Beyond the Sentence.

- **Trouble Spots:** These notes, placed at strategic points throughout the Teacher's Book, alert the teacher to problems that students may have with the grammar. They suggest how to address these problems effectively, and, where relevant, direct the teacher to parts of the Student Book that clarify or offer practice of the grammar point.

- **Cultural Notes:** These occasional notes give background about American culture that students typically do not know, and that may help their understanding of the topic in the Student Book. The teacher can relay this information to students as appropriate.

- **Additional Activities:** The Student Book provides extensive practice of each grammatical structure. However, for teachers who want to give further practice, each Teacher's Book chapter contains at least one additional writing or speaking activity. In most chapters there is also an activity called Returning to Grammar in Discourse, which has students return to the Grammar in Discourse reading at the beginning of each chapter and demonstrate their understanding of key meanings and uses of the target structures in the chapter.

AT THE BACK OF THE BOOK

- **Student Book Tapescript:** A complete tapescript is available for every listening activity in the Student Book.

- **Student Book Answer Key:** The Teacher's Book contains the answers to all the Student Book exercises. (The answers are not available in the Student Book.)

Teaching Techniques for the Grammar Classroom

TEACHING STUDENTS AT THE HIGH-INTERMEDIATE TO ADVANCED LEVEL

Students at this level will have already been exposed to most of the forms as well as some of the meanings and uses of the structures presented in the Student Book. They may still need to focus on form issues in more complex clauses and verb phrases, such as word order, agreement, and multiple auxiliary verbs. They may also be interested in the finer details of meaning and use, such as the distinction between the present perfect and present perfect continuous, the use of stative verbs in continuous forms, or the subtle differences in meaning and use between gerunds and infinitives. *Grammar Sense 3* provides students at this level with the necessary guidance and a wealth of exercises to practice and expand their grammar knowledge.

PRESENTING THE FORM SECTIONS

Examining Form Exercises

One of the most challenging aspects of teaching grammar is finding clear and concise ways to present new forms to students. The Examining Form exercise in each chapter is a series of inductive tasks in which students work on *identifying* the target structure and its most important structural features. In these exercises, students are asked to return to the reading text in the Grammar in Discourse section of the chapter, and follow the steps to recognize or systematically analyze key aspects of the form (such as the number of different parts in a structure, the addition of suffixes, word order, agreement, and so on). This serves as an introduction to the structural features illustrated and explained in the Form Charts, which students may then consult to check their answers.

Form Charts

In chapters with particularly challenging structures, you may need to help students work through and internalize the information in the Form Charts before they start on the form exercises. The following is a compilation of some of the most successful techniques for guiding students through this section. Choose appropriate techniques based on your teaching style, class size, class level, and students' previous experience with the grammar point. Most importantly, vary the techniques you use to accommodate the different learning styles of your students—some students may prefer to read and discuss every example in the chart before moving on to the exercises, while others may need to study the material less intensively.

Whole Class Techniques

1. After students have finished the Examining Form exercise, ask them to close their books. Elicit examples of the target grammar from the reading text by asking questions that will produce the target grammar. When possible, personalize your questions. For example, to elicit possessive pronouns, hold up a book and ask, *Whose book is this?* with the aim of eliciting responses such as *It's his. It's mine.* When students answer, write their responses on the board. If a student gives an incorrect response (e.g., *It is her.*), you should still write it on the board. Incorrect answers are as valuable as correct ones, because they can be used to focus students' attention on the structure. Likewise, if a student answers correctly but uses a different structure than the one you wish to focus on (e.g., *It's her book.*), write this answer on the board and ask if anyone knows an alternative response (e.g., *It's hers.*). Write students' responses on the board, then have them open their books to the Form Charts and find sentences that use the same structures as those on the board.

2. To focus more closely on the various parts of a structure, copy the chart headings onto the board, or construct other types of contrastive charts (e.g., *-s/-es/-ies*, or singular/plural, etc.). Elicit examples from the reading text to illustrate each point, or ask students to create

their own examples. Have individual students come to the board and fill in the charts. Then ask the rest of the class to decide if their examples are correct or not, and to explain why.

3. After students have finished the Examining Form exercise, ask them to silently review the Form Charts for a few minutes. Assess their understanding of the charts by asking questions about the form. For example, for *Yes/No* questions in the present tense, you might ask *Where is the subject? What word does the question begin with? How many* Yes/No *question forms are there?* In this way, you will be able to judge whether students have fully understood the form of the target grammar.

Pair or Group Work Techniques

1. Divide students into pairs or small groups. Assign each group a Form Chart and ask them to read and study the information. Then ask each group in turn to present the form in their chart to the rest of the class. Students can use their own example sentences to aid their presentation, in addition to those provided in the book.

2. Divide students into pairs or small groups. Write two correct sentences and one incorrect sentence on the board. (Make sure the error is one of *form*, not meaning and use.) Tell students that one sentence is incorrect. Ask them to work together to identify the incorrect sentence by looking at the Form Charts. Some students may know the answer without using the charts, but ask them to point to the information or example in the chart that shows why it is incorrect. This insures that they know how to interpret the charts.

PRESENTING THE MEANING AND USE SECTIONS

Examining Meaning and Use Exercises

Once students have grasped the form of a given structure, the next challenge is to find creative and engaging ways to help them understand the meaning and use. The Examining Meaning and Use exercises do just this by offering carefully constructed examples, often in the form of minimal pairs, and asking students to use contextual cues to draw inferences about key aspects of meaning and use. These inductive tasks serve as an introduction to the features of meaning and use that are further elucidated in the Notes that follow.

Meaning and Use Notes

Students need to read and absorb the Meaning and Use Notes before starting the exercises. What follows are some techniques for helping students work through the Meaning and Use Notes. Regardless of the technique you choose, it is important that you have a clear understanding of the scope of the Meaning and Use Notes before you present them. In some instances, a particular structure may have multiple meanings and uses, but the chapter will not address all of them. In Levels 1 and 2, certain meanings and uses of structures are omitted to avoid overwhelming the students with too much information, while in Level 3, basic meanings and uses may be de-emphasized in order to focus on more complex issues.

Whole Class Techniques

1. Give students an opportunity to read and ask questions about the Meaning and Use Notes. Check their understanding by writing several original sentences on the board and asking them to match the meaning and use in each sentence to the Meaning and Use Notes. With more advanced students you can include a few incorrect sentences among the examples and have students identify correct and incorrect meanings and uses. Before you do this, be sure you have a firm grasp of the meaning and use you are focusing on so you can clearly explain why the examples you provided are correct or incorrect.

2. If there are several Meaning and Use Notes, or if you think students will find the content challenging, have them read and demonstrate their understanding of one Note at a time. Once they have read the Note, elicit sentences that demonstrate the meaning and use of the

Note they just read. For example, to elicit examples of *must be* and *must feel* to show understanding of someone's feelings (Student Book 3, page 154, Note 4B), make up sentences such as *I didn't eat dinner last night. I ran ten miles yesterday.* Ask students to respond. This should elicit sentences such as *You must be hungry. You must feel exhausted!*

Pair or Group Work Techniques

1. Divide students into pairs or small groups. Assign each pair or group a Note and ask students to study it. Then ask each pair or group to present their Note to the rest of the class. Students can create their own example sentences to aid their presentation, in addition to those provided in the book. Again, be sure you fully understand the meaning and use in question so you can tell students whether their examples are correct or incorrect and, most importantly, *why* they are correct or incorrect.

2. Divide students into pairs or small groups. Have each pair or group read one Note and create two example sentences to illustrate the information presented in the Note. Ask each pair or group to come to the front of the class to explain the Note and write their example sentences on the board. Ask the class if the sentences are correct examples of the information in the Note. If not, call on individual students to suggest alternate correct sentences.

General Teaching Techniques

Grammar Sense contains a wealth of exercises covering all four skills areas: reading, writing, listening, and speaking. Depending on your students, curriculum, and time frame, these exercises can be taught in many ways. Successful grammar teaching requires skillful classroom management and teaching techniques, especially in the areas of elicitation (drawing information from students), grouping procedures (groups, pairs, or individuals), time management (lengthening or shortening exercises), and error correction (peer or teacher correction, correction of spoken or written errors).

ELICITATION

Elicitation is one of the most useful teaching techniques in the grammar classroom. In essence, elicitation draws information out of the students through the use of leading questions. This helps students to discover, on their own, information about grammar forms as well as meanings and uses. For example, to elicit the difference in meaning between a gerund and an infinitive when used after the verb *stop*, write the following sentences on the board: *Alan stopped to smoke. Alan stopped smoking.* Then, in order to elicit the difference in meaning between the two sentences, ask questions such as, *In which sentence are we talking about a smoker? Which sentence is about a reformed (or ex-) smoker?* These questions require students to analyze what they know about the grammar and make inferences about meaning.

Knowing when to elicit information can be difficult. Too much elicitation can slow the class and too little elicitation puts students in a passive position. Avoid asking students to judge whether something sounds natural or acceptable to them because, as non-native speakers, they will not have the same intuitions about English as native speakers.

GROUPING STUDENTS

Group work is a valuable part of language learning. It takes away the focus from the teacher as the provider of information and centers on the students, giving them the opportunity to work together and rely on each other for language acquisition. Shyer students who may be less likely to speak out in class have an opportunity to share answers or ideas. Your class level will inform how you approach group work. Be sure to circulate among groups to monitor the progress of an activity, particularly at lower levels, and to answer any questions students cannot resolve on their own. Although students at the higher levels are more independent and can often manage their own groups, be attentive to the activities at hand, ready to offer feedback and keep everyone on-task. In classes where the level of students is uneven, try varying the composition of the groups to make the learning process interesting for everybody. Sometimes you can pair up a higher-level student with a lower-level student to give him or her an opportunity to help another classmate. However, other times you may want to group all the higher-level students together and offer them additional, more challenging activities. It is useful, especially in discussion activities, to conclude with a culminating task in which one or more students report back something (results, a summary) to the rest of the class using the target structure. This helps to refocus the class on the structure and provide a conclusion to the activity.

TIME MANAGEMENT

Some exercises are divided into steps, making it possible to shorten an activity by assigning part of it for homework or by dividing the class into two groups and assigning half the items to each group. Similarly, exercises can be lengthened. Many of the exercises in *Grammar Sense* require students to ask for or offer real-life information. You can ask students to create additional sentences within these activities, or have them do an activity again with a different partner. If your class does an activity well, ask them to focus on other aspects of the form, for example, transforming their affirmative sentences into negative ones, and vice-versa.

CHECKING EXERCISES

How you check exercises with students will depend on the level you are teaching. Having students check their answers in pairs or groups can be an effective technique, because it makes students revisit their work and resolve with other students the mistakes they have made. With lower levels, this requires careful teacher supervision. It is also possible at all levels to check exercises as a class, elicit corrections from students, and offer necessary feedback. It is often useful, especially for correcting editing exercises, to use an overhead projector. Be careful not to single out students when correcting work. Aim instead to create a supportive atmosphere whereby the class learns through a group effort.

CORRECTING ERRORS

Students can often communicate effectively without perfect grammar. However, in order to succeed in higher education or the business world, they need to demonstrate a high level of grammatical accuracy, and to understand that even a small change in form can sometimes result in a significant change in meaning. As students become aware of this, they expect to be corrected. However, their expectations as to how and when correction should be offered will vary. Many teachers have difficulty finding the optimal amount of correction—enough to focus students on monitoring errors, but not so much as to demoralize or discourage them. It is important to target specific types of errors when correcting students, rather than aiming to correct everything they say or write. The focus of the current lesson and your knowledge of your students' strengths and weaknesses will dictate whether you focus on form, pronunciation, meaning, or appropriate use. Discuss error correction with your students and determine how *they* would like to be corrected. Aim to combine or vary your correction techniques depending on the focus of the lesson and the needs of your students.

Spoken Errors

There are a variety of ways to correct spoken errors. If a student makes an error repeatedly, stop him or her and encourage self-correction by repeating the error with a questioning (rising) tone, or by gesturing. Develop a set of gestures that you use consistently so students know exactly what you are pointing out. For example, problems with the past tense can be indicated by pointing backwards over your shoulder, future time can be indicated by pointing your hand ahead of you, and third person can be shown by holding up three fingers. (Be careful not to choose gestures that are considered offensive by some cultures.) If your students feel comfortable being corrected by their peers, encourage them to help each other when they hear mistakes. Another option is to keep track of spoken errors during an activity, and then at the end elicit corrections from the class by writing the incorrect sentences you heard on the board. This way, students are not singled out for their mistakes, but get the feedback they need.

Written Errors

It is important to encourage students to monitor their written errors and learn strategies to self-correct their writing. Establish a standard set of symbols to use when marking students' work. For example, *pl* for *plural, agr* for *agreement, s* for *subject, v* for *verb*. When you find an error, do not correct it, but instead mark it with a symbol. Students will have to work out the exact nature of their error and correct it themselves. This will reduce your correction time and encourage students to learn for themselves by reflecting on their errors. Peer correction is another useful technique by which students can provide feedback on a partner's work. In order for it to be effective, give students clear and limited objectives and do not expect them to identify all the errors in their classmate's work. Note that students may be resistant to peer correction at first, and nervous about learning others' mistakes. But once they develop a trust in one another, they will be surprised at how much they can learn from their classmates.

CHAPTER 1

The Present

Overview

The simple present is used to describe actions or states that have a general, habitual, and unchanging sense (e.g., *I work at the library.*). The present continuous is used to describe events that are happening now or around now and don't last forever (e.g., *They are eating lunch.*). Note that stative verbs (e.g., *know, believe, have*) are sometimes difficult for students because some of these verbs are not generally used in the present continuous (e.g., *know*), and others have a different meaning in the present continuous than in the present simple (e.g., *I have a car.* vs. *I am having a good time.*).

Form: The key challenges are remembering

- the *-s/-es* for third-person singular (*he, she,* and *it*) in the simple present.
- the *do* auxiliary in simple present questions and negatives (e.g., *Do you work on weekends? I don't sleep enough.*).
- the *be* auxiliary and the *-ing* ending of the main verb in the present continuous.

A GRAMMAR IN DISCOURSE

You Snooze, You Win at Today's Workplace

A1: Before You Read

- Give students five minutes to discuss the questions in their book in pairs.
- Call on several students to share their answers.
- Then ask *How do you feel when you don't get enough sleep?* Allow students to share their responses.
- Ask the class if they know the meaning of the expression "You snooze, you lose." If they don't ask them if they know the meaning of the word "snooze" (to sleep, to nap). Now have the students try to guess the meaning of the expression. If they still don't understand, explain that this is a saying that means if you sleep late or don't pay attention, you might miss an opportunity for success.
- Ask students why they think the title of the article is "You Snooze, You Win at Today's Workplace." (Sleeping at work can refresh people and make them more productive workers.)

A2: Read

- Before students start reading, ask them to scan the article to find the sentence that describes the average American company's attitude toward napping at work (paragraph 7, line 52 . . . *napping on the job is not yet acceptable.*).
- Ask students whether the title of the article seems to support this attitude. (It does not.)

Cultural Notes

Explain that the trend in the American workplace is to work more than the typical eight-hour day. Because of this, many employees are tired all the time.

La-Z-Boy is a well-known furniture company that specializes in recliners. The name La-Z-Boy is often used as a synonym for the word *recliner* (e.g., *My grandfather sits on his La-Z-Boy all day and watches TV.*).

A3: After You Read

- Have students answer the true/false questions individually and mark the places in the article where they found their answers.
- Ask them to compare answers with a partner.
- Circulate and note any problematic items; then go over these with the whole class.
- As a follow-up activity, write the following questions on the board and have students discuss them in pairs: *Should employers permit*

employees to nap at work? Do you ever nap at work? Do you know anybody who naps at work? (Students may have differing views of daytime resting.)
- Then bring the class together and have students share views.

B) FORM

The Simple Present and the Present Continuous

EXAMINING FORM

Method 1
(For students not familiar with the structure)

- **Question 1:** Tell students to look at the double-underlined verb in line 2 of the article (*You're sitting*). Elicit the form (the present continuous). Ask how many parts the verb has (two: *be* and verb + *-ing*). Have students go through the article to find six more verbs in the present continuous.
- Call on individual students for the present continuous verbs, and have them write these verbs in one column on the board. Remind students that some of the verbs are negative and some don't have the auxiliary right before the main verb, e.g., line 2, *You're sitting at your desk and plowing*. Ask one of the students to label the column *Present Continuous*.
- Have students find the simple present verb underlined in line 8 *(sounds)* and ask them to tell you how many parts this verb has (one: base form of verb + *-s* for third-person singular). Tell students to find six more verbs in the simple present and have them write them in another column on the board. Have one student label this column *Simple Present*.
- Ask students to examine the two lists of verbs on the board and tell you the differences in form. Students should notice the following: Present continuous consists of *be* in the simple present tense (*am*, *is*, or *are*) and verb + *-ing*, whereas the simple present consists of the base form of the verb for the entire conjugation except for third-person singular, which takes an *-s/-es* ending.

- **Question 2:** Ask students to find a negative simple present verb (*they're not*, line 50; *doesn't stop*, line 54). Elicit how many parts the verb has. (*They're not*, has two parts: *be* and *not*. *Doesn't stop* has three parts: *do* and *not* and verb.) Make sure students understand the difference in form by pointing out that *be* in the negative simple present consists of *be* and *not*, and other verbs consist of *do* and *not* and verb.
- Then ask students to find one negative present continuous verb (*are not getting*, lines 34–35). Elicit how many parts the verb has (three parts: *be* and *not* and verb + *-ing*).
- **Question 3:** Ask students to work in pairs to change the sentences to *Yes/No* questions. Have two students write their answers on the board (*a. Does the average American sleep six hours a night? b. Are Americans sleeping less?*). Elicit or offer feedback as necessary.
- Explain that the simple present verb *sleep* requires the *do* auxiliary as a helping verb to form a question. The present continuous verb *are sleeping* only requires inverting the subject and the auxiliary *be* to form a question.
- Point out that in the simple present the verb *be* only requires inverting the subject and *be* to form a question (e.g., *Maria is tired.* becomes *Is Maria tired?*). It does not need the *do* auxiliary like other verbs.

Method 2
(For students familiar with the structure)

- Have students work in pairs to answer the questions.
- Give students a few minutes to refer to the charts to check their answers and review the structures.
- Call on students to go over the exercise. Discuss any disagreements and have students make any necessary corrections.

FORM CHARTS

- Have students read the simple present charts. As they read, write the following on the board in a column: *Affirmative Statement, Negative Statement, Yes/No Question, Short Answer*, and *Information Question*. Leave room after each category for example sentences.

- Allow students to ask any questions. Then call on a student for a new affirmative statement in the simple present (e.g., *I email my sister every night.*). Write this sentence next to *Affirmative Statement* on the board and elicit the other forms listed.
- Have students read the present continuous charts and repeat the procedure above for a new present continuous affirmative statement.
- Then have students write two *Yes/No* questions in the simple present using the verbs *be* and *want*.
- Have some students share examples on the board. Make sure students remember to use the *do* auxiliary for sentences with *want* and to just invert the subject and the verb *be*.

Informally Speaking: Omitting Auxiliaries and *You* (p. 11)

- Choose two students to read the text in the speech bubbles. Then tell the class you will play the recording and that they should listen to how the underlined form in the cartoon is different from what they hear. If needed, play the recording more than once.
- Have students point out the differences. (The cartoon reads *Are you feeling OK?* and *Do you have any asprin?* whereas on the recording this is read *You feeling OK?* and *You have any asprin?*) Explain that the form on the recording is considered more informal spoken English. Point out that the form in the cartoon is standard English and students should use this form when writing and speaking, although they may hear native speakers using the informal form.

C MEANING AND USE 1

Contrasting the Simple Present and the Present Continuous

EXAMINING MEANING AND USE

- Have students answer questions 1 and 2.
- Call on individual students to explain the answers. (For question 1 the answer is b. The conversation is in the present continuous, describing something happening right now. The answer to question 2 is a. The conversation is in the simple present, describing a repeated action or a routine.)
- Ask the students to think of two more questions in the present continuous and simple present using the same verb (e.g., *What do you eat for breakfast? What are you eating?* or *What do you usually read? What are you reading?*). One sentence should be about something happening at the moment and another about a repeated action or a routine.
- Have students write their questions on the board, and then go over them as a class.

MEANING AND USE NOTES

- Divide the board into two columns and label them *Simple Present* and *Present Continuous*.
- Put the class into groups (or pairs if the class is small) and assign each group one of the Notes.
- Ask each group to read the Note and prepare to teach the explanation to the class. Tell each group to paraphrase the explanation and write original sentences, based on the examples, that clearly illustrate the particular aspect of meaning and use.
- For the group presentations, have one student present the explanation and another write the sentences in the correct columns. Have students check for any errors. Answer any questions.

Trouble Spots

Meaning and Use Note 2B explains a potentially challenging aspect of the present continuous: the extended present. Point out that with this usage, the activity is not happening right now but it is in progress over a period of time *around* now. Emphasize the underlying principle of the present continuous: The action is changing, not permanent. Direct students to the time expressions, such as *this week* and *these days*, which stress the temporary nature of the activity.

Beyond the Sentence: Introducing a Topic with the Simple Present (p. 16)

This section gives students practice with the meaning and use of grammar as it functions naturally in extended discourse such as paragraphs and conversations.

- Tell students to read the Note. Call on one student to summarize it.
- Have students examine the verbs in bold and tell you how many tenses were used in the passage (two—simple present and present continuous).
- Ask students which verbs refer to unchanging, habitual situations (*suffer, are, wake up, feel, can affect*) and which verb refers to a changing, "in progress" situation (*is becoming*).

D MEANING AND USE 2

Verbs with Stative Meanings vs. Verbs with Active Meanings

EXAMINING MEANING AND USE

- Have students underline the verb in each sentence.
- Then on the board make two columns titled *Actions* and *States/Conditions*. Ask students to tell you the two verbs that should go in the *Actions* column (*use* and *do*) and the three verbs that should go in the *States/Conditions* column (*have, be,* and *feel*). Write the verbs in the appropriate columns.

Trouble Spots

In general, because stative verbs express unchanging states or conditions, they do not typically occur in the continuous (e.g., *know, believe,* and *have*). However, avoid telling students that stative verbs *never* use the continuous or that they *always* use the simple present. There are times, as students will see later in the chapter, when we want to stress that a state or condition is temporary (e.g., *My kids are being so good today.*), when a stative verb is used actively (e.g., *I'm tasting the soup to see if it's too hot.*), or when we use stative verbs to stress emotion (e.g., *I'm just loving this book!*). (See Informally Speaking on page 22 of the Student Book for more information.) In these cases, the present continuous is used.

MEANING AND USE NOTES

By now, students should have begun to see that stative verbs express a more permanent meaning than active verbs because they refer to a condition or state and are therefore usually used in the simple present. However, students should also realize that some stative verbs can be used in the present continuous with active meanings that are different from the stative meaning (e.g., *I have a pen. I'm having lunch.*).

- Give students time to read through the Notes and ask questions.
- Then write the following verbs on the board: *know, taste, have, feel, weigh, sound*.
- Put students into pairs and have them write one sentence in the simple present for each of the verbs in the list above. Then tell them to write four new sentences putting the verbs in the present continuous. Point out that two of the verbs cannot be put in the present continuous.
- Combine the pairs into groups of four and have them compare their sentences. Put the following questions on the board and have the groups answer them:

  Which two verbs cannot be put into the present continuous? (*know, sound*)
  Why not? (These are stative verbs that cannot be used as action verbs.)
  Can you think of other examples of such stative verbs? (e.g., *mean, believe, need, seem, own, mind, appreciate*)
  Compare the meaning of the verbs in the present continuous sentences and the simple present sentences. Do they differ? (Yes, the meanings differ. Note that for the verb *feel*, if both sentences refer to physical sensations [e.g., *I feel OK. He is not feeling well today.*] then there is no difference in meaning. See Note 3. But if the sentence has an active verb, then the meaning of *feel* is different [e.g., *She is feeling the fabric to see if she likes it.*] *Feel* means *touch*.).

  Refer students to Notes 2A, 2B 2C, and 3 to check their answers.

- Bring the class together to go over the answers to the questions. Then call on students to read their sentences for the different verbs and tenses. Note any problematic ones and write them on the board. Try to elicit corrections from students. Answer any outstanding questions and discuss any disagreements.

Informally Speaking: Expressing Emotions in the Continuous (p. 22)

- Choose two students to read the text in the speech bubbles. Then tell the class you will play the recording and that they should listen to how the underlined form in the cartoon is different from what they hear. If needed, play the recording more than once.
- Have students point out the differences. (On the recording the present continuous is used for the stative verbs *love* and *hate*, and in the cartoon the present simple is used.) Explain that the form on the recording is considered more informal English. Point out that the form in the cartoon is standard English and students should use this form when writing and speaking, although they may hear native speakers using the informal form.

ADDITIONAL ACTIVITIES

Writing About a Trend

The purpose of this activity is to give students practice using the present continuous and the simple present together in the same context, while writing about a trend or recent change in their city or country.

- Begin by giving students a few minutes to make a list of three or four current trends in their country, city, or town. This might include more cell phone use or more fast-food restaurants. Explain that students will choose one of these trends and for homework they will write a one-paragraph description. They should describe both what is happening now and in the extended present (e.g., *More and more people are using cell phones these days.*) and give general information about the trend (e.g., *People think that cell phones are very convenient.*). Remind students to use the simple present and the present continuous.
- When students come to class, have them exchange their paragraphs with a partner. The partner will read the paragraph and tell the writer one thing he or she liked about it and two things he or she would like to learn more about. The partner should also check for correct use of the simple present and present continuous.
- Explain that for homework, students will revise their paragraphs using the feedback from their partners. Before they turn in their paragraphs, have students underline all the verbs and examine the context to be sure they used them correctly.
- Collect students' assignments to correct any errors in form, meaning, or use.

Returning to Grammar in Discourse

The purpose of this activity is to check students' understanding of key meanings and uses of the target structures in the chapter, by returning to the article at the beginning of the chapter and applying what they have learned.

- Write the following extracts from article on the board (or type them up and photocopy them before class) and have students work in pairs to find them in the article. Make sure they read the complete sentences these extracts come from.
    1. *The words on your computer are zooming in and out of focus . . .*
    2. *Each one contains a sleeping bag . . .*
    3. *Professor Anthony rarely misses a nap.*
    4. *. . . the workforce is aging.*
- Now write the following on the board:
    a. a state or condition
    b. a changing situation over time
    c. a habit or routine
    d. an activity in progress now
- Have students think about the use of the simple present and present continuous in the extracts, and match each one to the letter above that best describes it (1. d; 2. a; 3. c; 4. b).
- Bring the class together. Call on pairs for the answers and have them offer explanations. If students still have problems, revisit the Meaning and Use Notes.

CHAPTER 2

The Past

Overview

The simple past and the past continuous are often used together to clarify the order of past events. The past continuous can give background information to completed events in the simple past (e.g., *I was sleeping when the phone rang.*). The meaning and use of these verb forms can be confusing for students because the choice of form depends entirely on context. For example, to emphasize that an activity was completed, the simple past is used (e.g., *She drove home.*). However, in order to emphasize that the activity was in progress, the past continuous is used (e.g., *She was driving home.*).

Form: Students will likely continue to make errors with irregular simple past verb forms. Refer them to the list of irregular verbs in Appendix 6 of the student book.

A GRAMMAR IN DISCOURSE

A Night to Remember

A1: Before You Read

- Give students some examples of important recent news events (e.g., the collapse of the Berlin Wall in 1989, the death of Princess Diana in 1997, the terrorist attack on the World Trade Center in New York in 2001, etc.) and write them on the board.
- Elicit a few other important recent news events and write them on the board. Put students into groups. Have them discuss where they were and what they were doing at the time these events happened.

A2: Read

- Ask students if they have seen the movie or know the history of the *Titanic*. Ask if anyone can give a brief summary of what happened to the ship. If no one can, provide a summary yourself. (The *Titanic* was a luxury transatlantic passenger ship. The engineers who built the ship thought it was unsinkable, but on its first voyage from Britain to New York, it hit an iceberg and sank.)
- Explain key vocabulary such as *iceberg, crew, crash,* and *sink* as necessary.
- Tell students to read the excerpt individually. Have them note what each person or group of people was doing when the *Titanic* hit the iceberg.
- Divide students into small groups and have them compare their answers.
- Write the phrase *When the Titanic hit the iceberg* on the board. Call on each group to name one thing that was happening when the ship hit the iceberg. Write each answer on the board so that it completes the sentence (*one of the ship's officers was standing watch, the night baker was making rolls,* etc.).
- Ask a student to read the sentences on the board out loud.

A3: After You Read

- Have students do this exercise individually and mark the places in the text where they found the answers.
- Ask them to compare answers with a partner.
- Circulate and note any difficult or problematic items. Then go over these with the whole class.
- As a follow-up activity, write these questions on the board and have students discuss them in groups: *Do you think most of the passengers were frightened when the* Titanic *hit the iceberg? Why or why not? Do you think the crew was frightened? Why or why not? Do you know why so many of the passengers and crew of the* Titanic *died?* (They died because there weren't

enough lifeboats.) *What do you think people have learned from the* Titanic *disaster?* (Better engineering and construction methods, better emergency preparation.)

B) FORM

The Simple Past, the Past Continuous, and Time Clauses

EXAMINING FORM

Method 1
(For students not familiar with the structure)

- **Question 1:** Point out the underlined verb *banged* in the excerpt. Elicit how many parts this verb has (one: verb + *-d/-ed* for past tense). Explain that this is the regular form of the simple past.

- Ask students to call out three other regular simple past verb forms from the excerpt. Write them on the board in a column labeled *Regular Simple Past*.

- Point out the underlined word *was* in the excerpt. Elicit that *was* is the simple past of the verb *be*. Explain that *was* is an irregular simple past verb form. Tell students that irregular simple past verb forms must be memorized. Refer students to Appendix 6 in the Student Book for a list of irregular verbs.

- Call on students to find three irregular simple past verb forms in the excerpt and write them on the board in a column labeled *Irregular Simple Past*.

- **Question 2:** Tell students to look at the circled verb form in the excerpt *(were watching)*. Elicit the name of this form of the verb (the past continuous) and ask how many parts the verb has (two: *was/were* and verb + *-ing*). Explain that with the past continuous, only the verb *be* is in the past. Elicit the past forms of the verb *be (was, were)* and write them on the board with their appropriate subject pronouns *(I/he/she/it was; you/we/they were)*.

- Ask students to find six past continuous verb forms in the excerpt. Call on individual students for examples. Write them on the board in a column labeled *Past Continuous*.

Remind students that in some cases a single subject and auxiliary verb can be used for several main *-ing* verbs (e.g., line 29: *While they were playing and laughing*).

- Ask students to sort the verbs into two lists, singular and plural. Elicit that the verb *were watching* is plural—the subject is *they*; the verb *was standing watch* is singular—the subject is *George Thomas Rowe*.

- **Question 3:** If necessary, ask students *What is a clause?* (a group of words that has a subject and verb). Direct students to the clause, *while they were talking*, line 19–20. Explain that this is a time clause and that time clauses in this excerpt begin with *when*, *while*, and *before*.

- Ask students to find and mark some of the time clauses in the excerpt. Then elicit which form, the simple past or past continuous, is connected to each type of time clause. (*When* and *before* are connected to the simple past; *while* is connected to the past continuous.)

- Ask students if the time clauses come before or after the main clause they are connected to. (Some come before and some come after.)

Method 2
(For students familiar with the structure)

- Have students work in pairs to answer the questions.

- Give students a few minutes to refer to the charts to check their answers and review the structures.

- Call on students to go over the exercise. Discuss any disagreements and have students make any necessary corrections.

FORM CHARTS

- Read the simple past and past continuous example sentences in the charts out loud.

- Put students into groups and give each group a different set of four verbs (both regular and irregular, e.g., *sleep, walk, play, think*). Have each group write two sentences for each verb, one in the simple past and one in the past continuous (e.g., *Tamara slept on the couch. The baby was sleeping when we arrived.*). Each group should have a total of eight sentences.

- Circulate and offer feedback as necessary.

- Give students time to read through the remaining charts.
- Then have groups exchange sentences and put the other group's sentences into the negative (e.g., *Tamara didn't sleep on the couch. The baby was not sleeping when we arrived.*), and create information questions (e.g., *Where did Tamara sleep? Who was sleeping when you arrived?*) and *Yes/No* questions with short answers (e.g., *Did Tamara sleep on the couch? Yes, she did. No, she did not. Was the baby sleeping when you arrived? Yes, she was. No, she was not.*). Refer students to the charts to help them create the various structures.
- Have the groups exchange their questions again and check the structures the other group wrote. Answer any questions.
- If necessary, do a quick review of time clauses and main clauses. The main clause (also known as an independent clause) is a clause that can stand by itself (e.g., *My mother called me.*). A time clause is a dependent clause that cannot stand by itself. For example, the time clause *While you were sleeping* is not a complete sentence. It depends on the main clause for additional information. When you connect a time clause with a main clause, you get a complete sentence (e.g., *While you were sleeping, my mother called me.*).
- Have students read the sentences in the charts and note the time clauses, the main clauses, and the use of commas.
- Write several new sentences with time clauses on the board without commas:

    Before our teacher came into the room we were talking.
    While we were studying yesterday someone was listening to music outside.
    They were reading when someone turned off the light.

- Elicit the correct punctuation (commas are needed in the first two sentences: after *room* and after *yesterday*). Remind students that when the time clause precedes the main clause, there should be a comma after the time clause (e.g., *Before our teacher came into the room, we were talking.*).

Trouble Spots
Irregular past tense verbs are sometimes difficult even for more advanced students because their formation is not rule governed. The only way to learn the different forms of these verbs is to memorize them. Quizzes, spelling bee type games, and drills on these forms can help students remember them.

C) MEANING AND USE 1

Contrasting the Simple Past and the Past Continuous

EXAMINING MEANING AND USE

- Give students a minute to examine the two pairs of sentences and answer the question.
- Call on individual students to explain the difference between the sentences (Completed event: 1a and 2a; Unfinished event: 1b and 2b).
- Have students work in pairs to write a new pair of sentences, using a different verb, in the simple past and the past continuous.
- Call on several pairs to share their sentences with the class. Elicit the difference in meaning between the pairs of sentences.

MEANING AND USE NOTES

- Divide students into groups and assign one of the Notes to each group.
- Ask each group to read the Note and prepare to teach the explanation to the class. Tell each group to paraphrase the explanation and write new examples that clearly illustrate the particular aspect of meaning and use.
- Circulate as the groups work, answering questions and pointing out any problems in their example sentences.
- Ask one of the students in each group to present the explanation while another student writes the example sentences on the board. Ask the rest of the class if the paraphrase is accurate and if the example sentences are correct. If not, work together as a class to improve them.

Vocabulary Notes: Habitual Past with *Used To* and *Would* (p. 39)

These Notes remind students that both *used to* and *would* are used to talk about a repeated action that was true in the past but is no longer true now. The key difference between the two is that *would* is not used with states, but *used to* is.

- Tell students they are going to write sentences about things they used to do at different times in their lives, but no longer do. Write the following on the board: *When I was five, I . . . , When I was in high school, I . . . , etc.* Have students write four activities for each category. Remind students to start a description with *used to,* and then use *would* to provide details.
- Correct students if they use *would* with verbs that do not express action, and remind them to use *used to* instead.
- Finally have students write two sentences about things they didn't use to do. Remind students of the form change from *used to* to *use to* with negatives (e.g., *I didn't use to sleep late.*).

Beyond the Sentence: Using the Simple Past in Discourse (p. 40)

This section is intended to give your students practice with the meaning and use of grammar as it functions naturally in extended discourse such as paragraphs and conversations.

- Point out that a time expression indicates the verb tense. A time expression is usually necessary when there is a change in tense. For example, *I called Jill last weekend* shows past tense, and then, *She's back at work now* indicates a change to present.
- Ask students to read the two passages, paying close attention to the time expressions (*last week* in paragraph 1; *last weekend, this morning,* and *now* in paragraph 2). Talk about the tense changes in both paragraphs. (Paragraph 1 starts with the present and changes to the past. Paragraph 2 starts with the past and changes to the present.)
- Answer any outstanding questions.

D MEANING AND USE 2

The Simple Past and the Past Continuous in Time Clauses

EXAMINING MEANING AND USE

- Ask students to read the example sentences and questions in their book.
- Explain to students that before they answer the questions, they will show the meaning of the verbs in the example sentences with time lines.
- Draw a time line on the board like this:

- Copy sentence a on the board and underline the verbs. Mark on the time line where the verbs in the sentence would fall sequentially.

a.

- Ask two students to copy sentences b and c on the board, underline the verbs, and draw time lines beneath them. See the models below.

b.

c.

- Elicit corrections and suggestions from the class if the two students need help.
- Ask students to compare the three time lines and answer the three questions in the exercise.
- Come together as a class to check the answers and go over any problem areas (1. c; 2. a; 3. b).

MEANING AND USE NOTES

- Divide students into groups. Assign each group one Note to read and prepare to present to the class. Ask the students to draw a time line to accompany one of the sample sentences. Then have them write an original sentence and draw a time line to show its meaning.
- Ask each group to present the sample sentence with time line to the class, and then write the additional example sentence on the board. Have the group call a student from a different group to draw a time line for the new sentence. Allow the group to correct the time line if necessary. Offer assistance if students have any problems.
- Once every group has presented, offer additional examples if necessary, and answer any outstanding questions.

ADDITIONAL ACTIVITIES

Writing About Past Events

The purpose of this activity is to have students use the simple past, the past continuous, and time clauses in a writing assignment about an important past event.

- Have students brainstorm some important historical events, natural disasters, and other major news events that they remember occurring. (Refer them to your discussion from the beginning of the chapter if necessary.)
- Have students pick one topic to write about. Write the following questions on the board: *Where were you when the event happened? What were you doing? How did you hear about the event? How did you feel when you learned the news?* Have students answer these questions in writing.
- Then have students expand their answers to the questions and write a paragraph. Remind students to use the past continuous to describe background information and the simple past to describe events. Ask them to use time clauses where appropriate.
- Put students into pairs and have them read each other's papers. Have them note their partner's use of the simple past, the past continuous, and time clauses.
- Collect the assignments and correct any errors in form, meaning, and use.

Returning to Grammar in Discourse

The purpose of this activity is to check students' understanding of key meanings and uses of the target structures in the chapter, by returning to the excerpt at the beginning of the chapter and applying what they have learned.

- Write the following extracts from the excerpt on the board (or type them up and photocopy them before class) and have students work in pairs to find them in the excerpt. Make sure they read the complete sentences these extracts come from.
    1. *They were watching for icebergs when Fleet suddenly saw something directly ahead.*
    2. *Around one table, some men were enjoying a final cigar. At another table, the ship's younger passengers were enjoying a lively game of bridge.*
    3. *Before the watertight door slammed down, the two men leaped through the doorway . . .*
- Now write the following on the board:
    a. *One completed event followed by another completed event.*
    b. *One short event interrupting a longer event.*
    c. *Two events in progress at the same time.*
- Have students think about the use of the simple past and past continuous in the extracts, and match each one to the letter above that best describes it (1. b; 2. c; 3. a).
- Bring the class together. Call on pairs for the answers and have them offer explanations. If students still have problems, revisit the Meaning and Use Notes.

CHAPTER 3

Future Forms

Overview

Several future forms can be used to express future time. This chapter introduces the future continuous (e.g., *She will be working late.*) and reviews the four future forms: *will* (e.g., *I will do it tomorrow.*), *be going to* (e.g., *We are going to travel all summer.*), present continuous (e.g., *I am seeing a movie tonight.*), and simple present (e.g., *The bus leaves at 3:30.*). The choice of form depends on the context of the sentence. Frequently, more than one form is acceptable. Therefore, it is helpful to students to focus on areas where the choice of form indicates a clear difference in meaning and where specific rules for use exist.

Form: Students may find it confusing to use the simple present and the present continuous for future events (e.g., *My flight leaves at 6:00 tomorrow. Relatives are visiting me this weekend.*).

A GRAMMAR IN DISCOURSE

Trend Forecasters Predict Future

A1: Before You Read

- Elicit or explain the meaning of *fortune-tellers* (people who claim to predict the future). Then put the students into pairs and have them discuss the questions.
- Bring the class back together and have each pair of students share some of the predictions they came up with.

A2: Read

- Before students read, elicit or explain the meaning of *trend* (a currently popular idea or behavior). Then ask them to read the article to find out what two experts predict for the future.

- Divide students into three groups. The article discusses predictions about health, technology, and lifestyles. Assign one set of predictions to each group to paraphrase and present to the class.
- Have the other students agree or disagree with the predictions, and explain why.

A3: After You Read

- Have students do this exercise individually and mark the places in the text where they found the answers. Explain any new vocabulary.
- Ask students to compare answers with a partner.
- Circulate and note any difficult or problematic items. Then go over these with the whole class.
- Call on students to tell you which products and trends they chose.
- As a follow-up activity have each student write down one unique prediction about the future on a piece of paper.
- Then have students exchange papers with the person sitting next to them and write a response to the prediction. Tell them to explain if they agree or disagree with it.
- When they finish, have students get back their original papers and read their partner's opinions. Call on students to share their responses.

B FORM

The Future Continuous and Review of Future Forms

EXAMINING FORM

Method 1
(For students not familiar with the structure)

- **Question 1:** Write the three future forms from the article (*be going to*, *will*, and *future* *continuous*) at the head of three separate columns on the board. Elicit one example of each future form from the article (e.g., *are going to buy, will enable,* and *will be doing*) and write them in the appropriate columns.

- Elicit the form of *be going to* (*and/is/are going to* + verb), *will* (*will* + verb), and the future continuous (*will be* + verb + *-ing*).
- Have students work individually to find the other examples of each form, and then have them compare lists with a partner.
- Ask three students to complete the columns on the board, one student for each form.
- **Question 2:** Have students find one example of the present continuous used as future (*Cigarettes aren't going away either.*). Point out to students that this is not the future with *be going to*. The verb *aren't going* is used in the present continuous to indicate future.
- **Question 3:** Ask students which other tense can be used to express the future (the simple present, e.g., *The train leaves at 10:00 am.*).

Method 2
(For students familiar with the structure)

- Have students work in pairs to answer the questions.
- Give students a few minutes to refer to the charts to check their answers and review the structures.
- Call on students to go over the exercise. Discuss any disagreements and have students make any necessary corrections.

FORM CHARTS

- Tell students to read the affirmative and negative statements in the future continuous charts.
- Call students to the board to write two new future continuous sentences, one affirmative and one negative, using two different verbs.
- Have students look at the examples in the other future continuous charts. Then call on them to change the new sentences they created to *Yes/No* questions and information questions.
- Tell students to close their books for a review of future forms. Write the names of the five future forms (*future continuous, future with be going to, future with will, present continuous as future,* and *simple present as future*) on the board. Read an example sentence from the chart for each form and call on individual students to tell you which form was used.
- Alternatively, divide students into groups and give them one example sentence for each type of future form on separate slips of paper. Have one student in each group read the sentence to the other group members and ask them to identify the type of future form used. Then have them open their books to confirm their answers.

C MEANING AND USE 1

Contrasting *Will* and the Future Continuous

EXAMINING MEANING AND USE

- Tell students to underline the future forms in each sentence (*I'll pick up* and *I'll be picking up; he'll be eating* and *he'll eat*).
- Have students discuss Questions 1 and 2 with a partner, and then call on students to give their answers to the whole class (1. 1b describes a plan and 1a describes a promise; 2. 2a refers to an activity in progress and 2b refers to the beginning of an activity).

MEANING AND USE NOTES

- Help students understand that the essential difference between the future with *will* and the future continuous is that the future continuous indicates that the action will be in progress at a future time, whereas *will* indicates the start of an action in the future.
- To emphasize the difference between the forms, tell students to read the Notes. Have them pay careful attention to Note 2, which points out that *will* has a special meaning in the first person—to make a promise.
- Answer questions students have about any of the Notes. Then write new examples of paired sentences on the board—one with the future with *will* and one with the future continuous:

Kelly will drive to work at 8:00. Kelly will be driving to work at 8:00. Ask students to explain the difference in meaning. (In the first, Kelly will *start* driving at 8:00; in the second, she will already be on the road at that time.)

D MEANING AND USE 2

Contrasting *Be Going To*, the Present Continuous as Future, and the Simple Present as Future

EXAMINING MEANING AND USE

- Ask students to examine the three sentences and explain in what situation they might hear each of them.
- Have them answer the two questions in the exercise (1. a and c; 2. b).
- Give students a few minutes to refer to the Notes to check their answers.
- Go over the answers as a class. Discuss any disagreements and have students make any necessary corrections.

MEANING AND USE NOTES

- Explain that sometimes we can use different future verb forms to express the same meaning, but other times we have to use one specific form.
- Tell students to read the Notes. Then test their understanding by writing the following sentences on the board and asking which sentences are correct or incorrect and why.

    They're going to go camping soon. (Correct—future plan.)

    I begin my classes in two days. (Correct—set schedule.)

    *She's winning the race tomorrow. (Incorrect—this sentence describes a prediction, so the present continuous as future cannot be used.)

    He's having dinner at our house on Thursday. (Correct—future plan.)

- Tell students to work in pairs to create a two-line dialogue incorporating each of the correct sentences above (e.g., *Is Dave doing anything special this week? He's having dinner at our house on Thursday.*). Have each pair read these to the class and explain why the specific future form was used for each of the four dialogues.
- Next have the pairs write two new dialogues using any of the future forms. Refer them to the Notes as necessary.
- Then have the pairs share their dialogues on the board (or combine pairs, if the class is big) and let students comment on the correct use of the future in the sentences.

E MEANING AND USE 3

Contrasting *Will*, the Future Continuous, and *Be Going To*

EXAMINING MEANING AND USE

- Have students read each pair of sentences and underline the future verb forms.
- Have students discuss questions 2 and 3 with a partner. Then bring the class together and call on students for the answers (2. 2a and 2b; 3. 1a and 1b).
- Discuss any disagreements and have students make any necessary corrections.

MEANING AND USE NOTES

- Have students read the explanation in Note 1B and remind them that the choice between *will*, the future continuous, and *be going to* can depend on the level of formality of the context. To reinforce this, write the following sentences on the board and call on students to tell you a possible context for each sentence.

    Experts say that humans will walk on Mars by 2050. (newspaper article or news report)

    Mommy, we're going to go on a field trip tomorrow. (child talking to parent)

    Mr. Vice President, what will the President discuss in his speech tomorrow? (journalist to politician)

    Will you be joining us for dinner this evening? (one business acquaintance to another)

    Point out that in more formal contexts *will* or the future continuous are sometimes used.

- Divide the class into three groups and assign each group one of the remaining three Notes.

Chapter 3   13

- Ask each group to read the Note and prepare to teach the explanation to the class. Tell each group to paraphrase the explanation and write original sentences, based on the examples, that clearly illustrate the particular aspect of meaning and use.
- For the group presentations, have one student present the explanation and one write the new example sentences. Elicit and offer feedback as necessary.

Beyond the Sentence: Repeating Future Forms in Discourse (p. 71)

This section is intended to give students practice with the meaning and use of grammar as it functions naturally in paragraphs and conversations.

- Make sure that students understand the basic idea that *be going to* or the future continuous is used to introduce a topic, and *will* or present continuous as future are used in the following sentences to supply detail.

ADDITIONAL ACTIVITIES

Discussing and Writing a Story Ending

The purpose of this activity is to practice using *will* and *be going to* while predicting an ending to a story.

- Type up the two unfinished stories below and distribute them to the students.
- Have students work in small groups or pairs to discuss possible one-sentence endings to these unfinished stories. Remind them to choose between *will* and *be going to* in their predictions: If they are more certain of the outcome because there is some evidence for it, they should use *be going to*; if they are less certain, they should use *will*. To model the activity, you might want to go over some possible endings for Story 1.

    1. *This is the most important basketball game of the high school season. Kevin is a senior and he has never made an important play. This is his last chance to be a high school hero. The score is tied. Jenny is watching. Kevin has adored her for four years, but she doesn't even know he's alive. Oh, no! The ball is coming toward him. "Grab it and score!" he screams to himself.*

    Possible endings to the story: *He is going to make the winning basket. He is going to trip and fall on his face.*

    2. *Henri Berger and Elisabeth Roux came to the United States ten years ago. Since coming here, they have worked very hard and have saved some money. But they still do not have enough money to fulfill their dream: to open their own fine French restaurant. One day they are sitting on a park bench talking about their dream when someone behind them says, "Excuse me, but I couldn't help overhearing you." Henri and Elisabeth turn to see a man in a white suit. "Who are you?" they ask. The man replies, "My name doesn't matter. I heard you discussing your plans, and I would like to help you."*

- For homework, tell students to choose one of the stories they discussed and write a one-paragraph ending for it, using appropriate tenses.
- In class, group or pair students according to the story they worked on. Tell them to read their endings out loud to the other group members and see if they are similar.
- Then review students' paragraphs to correct any errors in form, meaning, or use.

Speaking About Predictions

The purpose of this activity is for students to use various future forms in a discussion on predictions.

- Divide students into small groups or pairs and tell them to make a list of at least five predictions (about topics such as technology or lifestyle) that they haven't yet discussed in class.
- Once students have a list of predictions, tell them to discuss which events could happen and which ones they think are less likely to happen in the next ten to fifteen years. Remind them to use appropriate future forms.
- Finally, ask students to choose one prediction that seems possible and one that seems unlikely. Tell them that they will present their ideas to the class. The other students will listen and state whether they agree or disagree with these ideas.

CHAPTER 4

The Present Perfect

Overview

Unlike the present and past tenses, which focus on one particular time period (e.g., *I live in Spain. I lived in Spain last year.*), the present perfect focuses on the link between the past and the present. The present perfect is used for a situation that started in the past and continues until now (e.g., *I have lived in Spain for ten years.*), or for a situation with no definite time specification that could have occurred any time up to the present (e.g., *I have lived in Spain.*).

Form: Mastery of the present perfect involves learning and remembering the spelling of many irregular past participles. Refer students to Appendix 6 of the Student Book. Give quizzes on the most common irregular past participles to help students learn them.

A GRAMMAR IN DISCOURSE

The Questions That Stump the Scientists

A1: Before You Read

- Explain that the article is about scientific discoveries and areas scientists still want to explore. Give students an example of something that scientists haven't figured out, such as how to cure the common cold, or why dinosaurs became extinct.
- Divide students into small groups to discuss the questions in their books. Remind them that there are no right or wrong answers.
- Have students share their ideas together as a class.

A2: Read

- Before students read, elicit or explain the meaning of the verb *to stump* (to make someone unable to answer). Look at the word in context of the title of the article. Elicit what the title means (the questions that scientists are not able to answer).
- Tell students to read the first paragraph and explain what they think the main idea of the article is. (Although there have been many important scientific discoveries, there are still many more to be made.) Then point out that the article will explore three areas of science: memory, matter, and life on other planets.
- Organize a jigsaw reading. First, divide students into three groups and assign one of the three areas to each group. Ask students to read and discuss their section and then write a one- or two-sentence summary.
- When students finish, send one member of each group to another group so that there is at least one member representing each of the three areas. Each student will explain to the new group the section that he or she read.

A3: After You Read

- Have students do this exercise individually and mark the places in the text where they found the answers
- Ask them to compare answers with a partner.
- Then bring the class together and ask students which statements are false (1, 3, 4, and 5). Call on individual students to turn them into true statements.
- As a follow-up activity put students into pairs and have them brainstorm some additional questions that have not yet been answered by scientists.
- Combine pairs into groups of four and let them share their ideas and discuss if they think the different questions will ever be answered (or if the questions maybe already have been answered).

B FORM

The Present Perfect

EXAMINING FORM

Method 1
(For students not familiar with the structure)

- As an introductory activity, write this sentence on the board: *I have visited New York.*
- Underline *have visited* and elicit how many parts the verb has (two). Explain that this form is the present perfect and the parts of the verb are *have* (or *has*) and the past participle, in this case verb + *-ed*. If students don't know the term *past participle*, explain that it is a past verb form, like the past tense, but is used with *have* in the present perfect (e.g., *I walked.* vs. *I have walked.*). Explain that when the verb ends in *-ed*, this is a regular past participle. Elicit some more examples of regular verbs in the present perfect (e.g., *I have looked. She has lived. We have started.*).
- Now write this sentence on the board: *I have seen the Statue of Liberty.*
- Underline *have seen* and explain that this form is also the present perfect, but the past participle does not end in *-ed*. Explain that this is called an irregular past participle and that these come in many forms. Elicit some additional examples of irregular verbs in the present perfect (e.g., *I have eaten the banana. This door has broken three times. I have told him the bad news.*). Tell students that the only way to learn irregular past participles is to memorize them. Refer students to Appendix 6 for lists of irregular verbs.
- **Question 1:** Direct students to the reading and have them call out the two underlined present perfect forms (*'ve come* and *have made*). Ask if the forms are regular or irregular. (Both verbs are irregular.) Then have students find seven more examples of the present perfect in the text. You may need to point out some of the irregular verbs.
- **Question 2:** Elicit that *have* has two possible forms (*have* and *has*), and see if the students can find and explain them. (*Has* is only used for third-person singular.)
- **Question 3:** On the board, draw two columns and label them *Regular Verbs* and *Irregular Verbs*. Elicit the difference between regular and irregular verbs. (Regular verbs have past participles that end in *-ed*. Irregular verbs have past participles that vary in form.) Then call students to come up to the board and write the examples of the present perfect they found in Question 1 in the appropriate columns. Elicit or offer corrections as necessary.

Method 2
(For students familiar with the structure)

- Have students work in pairs to answer the questions.
- Give students a few minutes to refer to the charts to check their answers and review the structures.
- Call on students to go over the exercise. Discuss any disagreements and have students make any necessary corrections.

FORM CHARTS

- Read the three example sentences in the first chart out loud as the students look at them in their books. Call on one student to identify the auxiliary (*have* or *has*), and on another student to identify the main verb (the past participle) in each sentence. Tell students to continue doing this in pairs until they have read all the examples in the charts.
- Ask students to write several new present perfect sentences: one affirmative, one negative, one *Yes/No* question with a short answer, and one information question.
- Call on several students to read their sentences. Make any necessary corrections.

Informally Speaking: Omitting *Have* and *You* (p. 84)

- Choose two students to read the text in the speech bubbles. Then tell the class you will play the recording and that they should listen to how the underlined form in the cartoon is different from what they hear. If needed, play the recording more than once.

- Have students point out the differences. (The cartoon reads *Have you seen any good movies lately?* On the recording the form is shortened to *Seen any good movies lately?*) Explain that the form on the recording is considered more informal English. Point out that the form in the cartoon is standard English and students should use this form when writing and speaking, although they may hear native speakers using the informal form.

C MEANING AND USE 1

Indefinite Past Time

EXAMINING MEANING AND USE

- Have students work in pairs to answer the questions (1. b; 2. a).
- Give students a few minutes to refer to the Notes to check their answers.
- Call on students to go over the answers. Discuss any disagreements and have students make any necessary corrections.

MEANING AND USE NOTES

- Ask students to read the Notes.
- Write other paired example sentences on the board to highlight the contrast in meaning between the present perfect and the simple past (e.g., *I've ridden on a motorcycle.* vs. *I rode on a motorcycle one time with my brother.*). Call on individual students to explain the difference. (The first sentence uses the present perfect because it refers to an indefinite time in the past. The second sentence uses the simple past because it refers to a specific time that is now completed.)
- Follow up this activity by having students write one present perfect sentence in their notebooks about foods they have eaten and one about places they have been to (e.g., *I've eaten Mexican food. I've visited Thailand.*).
- Have several students write their sentences on the board. Then, next to each sentence, have students write the same sentence in the simple past. Remind students to specify a time, e.g., *last year, in 1980, in September.* Call on students to explain the difference in meaning between each pair of sentences.

D MEANING AND USE 2

Recent Past Time and Continuing Time up to Now

EXAMINING MEANING AND USE

- Have students read the example sentences and answer the questions with a partner.
- Call on students for answers to the questions (1. c; 2. a and b; 3. b). Have other students agree or disagree with the answers.

MEANING AND USE NOTES

- Tell students to read the Notes.
- Ask students how they know that the events in the example sentences in Note 1 are recent. (In some sentences there are clues such as *lately, recently,* and *just*; in other examples the context helps show that the event is recent—airport announcements mention recent arrivals; telephone recordings indicate that a call was just made; a ringing doorbell means that somebody has just arrived.)
- For the information in Note 2A, draw a horizontal time line like this:

After you read each sentence in the Note out loud, ask students to tell you how to draw the events on the time line. The finished time line should look like this:

- Elicit from students that each of the sentences suggests the same thing: I still live here.

Trouble Spots

Many students have learned the meaning and use of *since* and *for* as part of the present perfect and may believe these words can be used only this way. Although *since* is used mostly with the present perfect, *for* is often used with other tenses (e.g., Simple past: *I lived in Japan for two years.* Future: *I'm going to study for an hour.*).

Vocabulary Notes: Adverbs That Express Recent Past Time (p. 91)

- Ask students to close their books.
- On the board, write three sentences from the Notes, one with *just*, one with *recently*, and one with *lately*. Ask students to explain the meaning of each adverb.
- Tell students to open their books and look at all six sentences. Have them note where the different adverbs can be positioned in a sentence, and how their meanings do not change. For example, these two sentences have the same meaning, but the adverb is placed differently in each one: *She's recently been away. She's been away recently.*
- Put students into groups and have them make up two sentences each with *recently* and *lately* in different positions. Circulate as the groups work and make sure they use the present perfect in the sentences.

E) MEANING AND USE 3

Contrasting the Present Perfect and the Simple Past

EXAMINING MEANING AND USE

- Have students read the two sets of sentences and note the verbs and other words that refer to time in the sentences. Do the first one with them (*I've worked; for three years; I love*). Then have them answer the questions.
- Call on individual students for the answers and to explain the meaning of the simple past and present perfect in the sentences. (In 1a the person still works in Los Angeles. This is indicated by the use of the present perfect *'ve worked* and the use of the simple present in *I love my job.* In 1b the person no longer works here. This is indicated by the use of the simple past *worked* and *loved*. In 2a the speaker asks for an exact time of a past event, such as *last night* or *on March 5*, whereas in 2b the speaker wants to know only *if* the person has seen the movie, not when.)
- Discuss any disagreements and have students make any necessary corrections.

MEANING AND USE NOTES

Draw a horizontal time line on the board like this:

- Ask several students to come to the board to illustrate the verbs in the first few example sentences in Note 1. For the first pair of sentences (*She's been lucky all her life. She was lucky all her life.*), their time lines should look like this:

- Elicit feedback from the class to help the students at the board, and make corrections where necessary.
- Then have students read through the remaining two Notes in pairs and think up additional example sentences.
- Go over any questions regarding the explanations in the Notes. Then have students write their example sentences on the board. Elicit or offer feedback as necessary.

Beyond the Sentence: Introducing Topics with the Present Perfect (p. 97)

This section is intended to give your students practice with the meaning and use of grammar as it functions naturally in extended discourse such as paragraphs and conversations.

- Make sure that students understand the basic idea—that the present perfect introduces the general idea, and that the simple past is used in the sentences that follow to supply details about specific past events.
- To supplement this activity, bring in a short newspaper article in which the present perfect and simple past are used together. Try to find a short article of high interest, such as a story about a local hero, that does not have complex vocabulary.
- Give students copies of the article to read individually.
- Divide students into small groups or pairs and have them discuss the main idea of the article.
- Tell students to underline the verbs in the article and explain why the simple past or present perfect was used. For example, *John Doe has always been a hero in his neighborhood. Last year, the town named him their bravest resident.* The second sentence offers specific details by using the simple past to indicate definite past time.
- If possible, show the article on an overhead projector and go over the answers. Otherwise, ask students to look at their handouts. Call on students to read the verbs they underlined, identify the simple past or present perfect, and explain why each one was used.

ADDITIONAL ACTIVITIES

Speaking About Job Candidates

The purpose of this activity is for students to practice using the present perfect and simple past while looking at résumés and matching job candidates to specific professions.

- Find or make up four sample résumés, and bring four to five copies of each to class. Make sure the vocabulary is level-appropriate.
- Divide the class into groups and give each group a set résumés. Have students read them to get an idea of the background of each candidate.
- Then write the names of four professions on the board, loosely tied to the experience described in the résumés, and tell students to match each person to a profession. Tell students to support their choices using the present perfect (e.g., *Jana has worked as an office assistant.*) and the simple past (e.g., *Tom studied Accounting in college.*) as necessary.
- Circulate as the students work and listen for correct use of the simple past and present perfect.
- Then bring the class together and allow the groups to compare their matches. Elicit or offer corrections as necessary.

Returning to Grammar in Discourse

The purpose of this activity is to check students' understanding of key meanings and uses of the target structures in the chapter, by returning to the article at the beginning of the chapter and applying what they have learned.

- Write the following extracts from the article on the board (or type them up and photocopy them before class) and have students work in pairs to find them in the article. Make sure they read the complete sentences these extracts come from.
  1. *We've come to "the end of science" . . .*
  2. *Physicists have estimated the total quantity of material in the universe . . .*
  3. *. . . life has evolved elsewhere in the universe.*
  4. *. . . we've only just begun to make important discoveries.*
- Now write the following on the board:
  a. *indefinite past time*
  b. *recent past time*
- Have students think about the type of past time in each extract, and match each one to the letter above that best describes it (1. b; 2. a; 3. a; 4. b).
- Bring the class together. Call on pairs for the answers and have them offer explanations. If students still have problems, revisit the Meaning and Use Notes.

Chapter 4   19

CHAPTER 5: The Present Perfect Continuous

Overview

Like the present perfect, the present perfect continuous can be used to describe an activity that began in the past and continues up to now (e.g., *I have lived here since May. I have been living here since May.*). The focus on the ongoing activity, however, is often stronger in the present perfect continuous than in the present perfect (e.g., *I've been thinking about you.* vs. *I've thought about you.*). The present perfect continuous is also used to describe an activity that has recently ended (e.g., *I need a drink of water because I've been running.*). Students may need help identifying the subtle differences between the present perfect continuous and present perfect.

Form: Remind students that verbs with stative meanings are not usually used with continuous forms.

A GRAMMAR IN DISCOURSE

Aging—New Answers to Old Questions

A1: Before You Read

- Before students discuss the questions, ask them if they personally know any people in their 70s, 80s, or even 90s. These could be grandparents, neighbors, etc.
- If students do know older people, ask them to think about the kinds of lives they lead. Write the following questions on the board for students to discuss in small groups: *Do they live alone? How is their health? Are they active? How are their lives different from when they were younger?*
- Ask students to discuss the Before You Read questions in small groups. Remind them to think about the lives of the older people they have just discussed.

- As an additional question, ask students *Why do some people live longer than others?*
- Have a student from each group summarize the answers for the class.

A2: Read

- Before students read the article, have them preview it by reading the title, the first sentence of every paragraph, and the conclusion.
- Call on a variety of students to predict what researchers are learning about the process of growing old.
- Have students read the article.

Cultural Notes

There is an increasing focus on the elderly in the United States as the percentage of older people in the population increases—a change brought about largely by improved health care, higher standards of living, and a lower birthrate. It is common to see seniors who are physically active and continuing to work. Seniors are often given discounts on public transportation and at movies, restaurants, and museums. Recently, there have been a number of famous movies featuring elderly characters, and the issues concerning seniors are often topics of political debate.

A3: After You Read

- Have students do this exercise individually and mark the places where they found the answers.
- Ask them to compare answers with a partner.
- Circulate and note any difficult or problematic items. Then go over these with the whole class.
- As a follow-up, write these questions on the board for the students to discuss in pairs: *Has this article changed the way you feel about getting older? Does getting older seem more positive or negative now than it did before you read the article?* Bring the class together and have students share their ideas.

B) FORM

The Present Perfect Continuous

EXAMINING FORM

Method 1
(For students not familiar with the structure)

- **Question 1:** Write the underlined verb from the article *(has been enjoying)* on the board. Do not underline the separate parts yet. Ask students to find five more examples of the present perfect continuous in the article. Then ask students to write them on the board.

- **Question 2:** Refer students back to the original example on the board. Elicit and underline the auxiliaries (there are two: *has* and *been*) and point out the ending of the main verb *(-ing)*. Then ask several students to come up and underline the auxiliaries and the *-ing* in the examples they wrote on the board for question 1.

- **Question 3:** Ask students to identify the two forms of *have* in the examples written on the board *(have* and *has)*. Elicit when each form is used *(has* for third-person singular, *have* for all other forms).

Method 2
(For students familiar with the structure)

- Have students work in pairs to answer the questions.
- Give students a few minutes to refer to the charts to check their answers and review the structures.
- Call on students to go over the exercise. Discuss any disagreements and have students make any necessary corrections.

FORM CHARTS

- Ask individual students *What have you been doing since our class started? What have you* not *been doing since our class started?* This should elicit responses such as *I've been learning grammar. I haven't been watching TV.*
- Write the students' responses on the board, even if the form is incorrect. Then have students look at the charts and correct any incorrect forms.

- Ask students to silently read the *Yes/No* questions, short answers, and information questions in the charts.
- Put students into pairs and have them ask and answer a new *Yes/No* question using a time expression and the verb *exercise* (e.g., *Have you been exercising these days? Yes, I have.*) and a new information question using a time expression and the verb *eat* (e.g., *What have you been eating lately?*). If necessary, elicit appropriate time expressions.
- Call on a few students to share their answers.

Informally Speaking: Omitting *Have* (p. 108)

- Choose two students to read the text in the speech bubbles. Then tell the class you will play the recording and that they should listen to how the underlined form in the cartoon is different from what they hear. If needed, play the recording more than once.
- Have students point out the differences. (On the recording, you don't hear the auxiliary *have*. *Have you been going* in the cartoon is read *You been going* and *I've been writing* is read *I been writing*.) Explain that the form on the recording is considered more informal English. Point out that the form in the cartoon is standard English and students should use this form when writing and speaking, although they may hear native speakers using the informal form.

C) MEANING AND USE 1

Focus on Continuing or Recent Past Activities

EXAMINING MEANING AND USE

- Have students read the example sentences and answer the questions in pairs. Remind them to look for words in the sentences that indicate whether the action is continuing *(still, for months)* or has been recently completed.
- Bring the class together to go over the answers (1. b, she is still searching; 2. a, the person is reaching a conclusion; 3. c, the person has finished knitting).

MEANING AND USE NOTES

- Show students how to illustrate the first example sentence in the Notes on a time line on the board.

- Ask several students to come to the board to draw a time line for the other two sentences in Note 1. (The time sequence, showing the past continuing toward the future, should be similar to the time line for the first sentence.)
- Tell students to compare the time lines on the board with the explanation in the Note.
- Then have students read the other two Notes.
- To check their understanding of all the Notes, write the following sentences on the board. Tell students to indicate which Note the example refers to.

   I'm tired. I've been driving for three hours. (continuing activity)

   I'm glad we reached you. We've been trying to call you for two hours. (recent past activity)

   I've been planning to see you, but I haven't had time. (excuse)

   You look great. I can see that you've been exercising. (conclusion)

D MEANING AND USE 2

Contrasting the Present Perfect Continuous and the Present Perfect

EXAMINING MEANING AND USE

- Give students a few minutes to analyze the two pairs of sentences.
- Ask which pair of sentences expresses the same meaning and which pair expresses different meanings (2a and 2b indicate that the action is still happening; 1a suggests that the action is still happening, whereas 1b indicates that it is finished).
- Ask students to look at 1a and 1b and decide who has probably finished the book (Vera), and who is probably still reading the book (Kathy).

Trouble Spots

Students may not fully understand the distinction between the present perfect and the present perfect continuous. Remind them that they both indicate a connection between the past and the present but with this difference: The continuous is more likely to refer to an action still in progress, whereas the present perfect can indicate that the action is finished (e.g., *I've been working for ten hours today, and I need to stop now.* vs. *I've worked a lot of hours this week, and I'm glad it's the weekend.*).

If the level of your class allows it, point out that sometimes the nature of the verb itself gives rise to the difference in meaning between the present perfect continuous and the present perfect, as in sentence pair 1 in Examining Meaning and Use. Verbs such as *read* and *build* are processes that result in an accomplishment, e.g., a book is read or a building is built. As a result, use of the present perfect continuous shows that the process or action is still in progress, whereas use of the present perfect indicates completion or accomplishment.

MEANING AND USE NOTES

- Have students read Note 1A and examine the sentence pairs. Ask *Is there a difference in meaning between these two sentences?* (No, there is no real difference.)
- Do the same with the sentence pairs in Notes 1B and 2, where the sentences do indicate a difference in meaning. After the students read each Note and examine the sentence pairs, ask *What is the difference in meaning between these two sentences?* (In Note 1B, the continuous indicates stronger emotion. In Note 2, the present perfect suggests that the activity was completed sometime in the past, whereas the present perfect continuous suggests that the activity is still happening or was very recently completed.)
- To check students' comprehension of the material after the caution note, write the following sentences on the board and ask students to tell you which one is correct, which one is incorrect, and why.

We've taken the bus to school three times this week. (Correct.)

*I've been eating pizza twice since I came here. (Incorrect—the present perfect continuous usually does not indicate how many times an action is repeated.)

Beyond the Sentence: Connecting the Past and the Present in Discourse (p. 116)

This section is intended to give your students practice with the meaning and use of grammar as it functions naturally in extended discourse such as in paragraphs and conversations.

- Tell students that the example conversation shows much of what they have learned about connecting past events to the present.
- Ask students to read the conversation and decide why each verb form in bold is used. (*I've been working* and *I've known* are situations that started in the past and that are continuing into the present; *did you know* has an end point and *got married* is a completed action in the past; *you've been married* started in the past and continues in the present; *celebrated* and *spent* are completed actions.)
- Go over any difficult or problematic items with the whole class.

ADDITIONAL ACTIVITIES

Writing a Letter

The purpose of this activity is for students to practice using the present perfect continuous and present perfect, while writing a letter to a friend of family member.

- Give students some time to brainstorm things they have been doing lately (e.g., *I have been exercising a lot lately.*) and activities they have recently completed (e.g., *I have just finished writing a research paper.*). Then have them brainstorm questions they may ask someone in a letter (e.g., *Have you finished your classes yet?*).
- Put students into pairs and have them read each other's notes and share ideas.
- For homework, have students write a page-long letter to a friend or family member. Tell them to organize their brainstorm notes and offer more details where possible. Specify that the letter does not need to be true. The main point is to use the language correctly.
- Have students exchange letters with a partner and give each other feedback on the use of the present perfect and present perfect continuous.
- Collect students' letters and provide any necessary feedback on form, meaning, and use.

Returning to Grammar in Discourse

The purpose of this activity is to check students' understanding of key meanings and uses of the target structures in the chapter, by returning to the article at the beginning of the chapter and applying what they have learned.

- Write the following extracts from the article on the board (or type them up and photocopy them before class) and have students work in pairs to find them in the article. Make sure they read the complete sentences these extracts come from.

  1. *For the past several years, her active fingers have been knitting a pair of mittens every day for charity.*
  2. *Researchers have chosen the convent as a perfect place to study aging . . .*
  3. *. . . researchers at Tufts University have shown that exercise . . . has a dramatic effect on 72- to 98-year-olds.*
  4. *They have all avoided cigarettes . . .*
  5. *. . . but they have been getting closer to understanding aging.*

- Now write the following on the board:

  a. *a continuing activity or situation*
  b. *a completed action*

- Have students think about the use of the present perfect and the present perfect continuous in the extracts, and match each one to the letter above that best describes it (1. a; 2. b; 3. b; 4. a; 5. a).
- Bring the class together. Call on pairs for the answers and have them offer explanations. If students still have problems, revisit the Meaning and Use Notes.

CHAPTER 6

The Past Perfect and the Past Perfect Continuous

Overview

The past perfect is used to show events in the past that happened before a specified past time or event (e.g., *I had eaten my lunch when she called me.*). The past perfect continuous is used to emphasize that an activity was in progress before a specified past time or event (e.g., *I had been eating my lunch when she called me.*). Sometimes students mistakenly think that the past perfect and past perfect continuous express events that were in the very distant past, when in fact, they simply show the relationship between past events, regardless of how long ago they occurred.

Form: Point out to students that the past perfect form of *have* is *had had* (e.g., *I had had a very busy day and was happy to finally be in bed.*).

A GRAMMAR IN DISCOURSE

Wild Thing

A1: Before You Read

- Tell students they will read about a woman's attempt to challenge herself. Ask what the expression *to challenge oneself* means (to attempt something very difficult in the hope of achieving it). Point out that the word *challenge* is used as both a verb and a noun (*to challenge oneself* and *to face a challenge*).
- Ask a few volunteers to give examples of challenges (e.g., *running a marathon, climbing a mountain, getting a degree*).
- Divide students into small groups and give them ten minutes to discuss the questions.
- Ask a member of each group to give one reason some people like to face great challenges. Write these on the board and leave them there for the After You Read discussion.

Cultural Notes

Outward Bound is a worldwide not-for-profit organization that creates opportunities for young people to experience outdoor adventures such as rock climbing, hiking, camping, and mountain climbing. The philosophy behind the organization is that young people are capable of realizing their potential only by facing challenges.

A2: Read

- Ask students to guess what an outdoor educational program might be. Don't confirm or correct their answers just yet, as they will check their guesses when they read the excerpt.
- Tell students to read the excerpt and mark all the reasons the writer gives for participating in Outward Bound.
- Put students into pairs to compare answers.
- Call on each pair to name one item from their list and write it on the board. Leave these answers on the board for the After You Read discussion.

A3: After You Read

- Ask students if they guessed correctly what an outdoor educational program is. Ask why the woman wanted to challenge herself by joining Outward Bound. (She wanted to break away from the "I-could-never-do-that category.")
- Ask if her reasons for challenging herself were similar to any of the reasons listed on the board from the Before You Read discussion.
- Ask students to answer the true/false questions individually and then compare answers with a partner. Remind them to note the places in the excerpt where they found their answers.
- Call on individual students to give their answers and have them support their answers with information from the article.

24   Chapter 6

- As a follow-up activity, ask students *Has anyone participated in a program like Outward Bound?* If yes, ask them to share their experience. Otherwise, ask *If given the opportunity, would you like to participate in a program like Outward Bound. Why? Why not?*

B FORM

The Past Perfect and the Past Perfect Continuous

EXAMINING FORM

Method 1
(For students not familiar with the structure)

- **Question 1:** Ask students to look at the underlined example of the past perfect in the excerpt. Point out that this is the negative form, and elicit the affirmative form *(had eaten)*. Write this on the board.
- Elicit the form of the past perfect *(had + past participle)*.
- Have students work in pairs to find four more past perfect verbs in the excerpt, and call on a volunteer to write the verbs on the board in their full forms *(had + past partiple)*.
- Ask students for the contracted form of *had* in the past perfect *('d)*. Locate an example in the text *(I'd admired)* and elicit the full form *(I had admired)*.
- **Question 2:** Write the past perfect continuous example sentence on the board *(She had been searching for a way to challenge herself.)* next to the list of the past perfect verbs. Underline the two auxiliaries *(had been)* and circle the main verb *(searching)*.
- Elicit the differences in form between the past perfect and the past perfect continuous. Point out *been* and the *-ing* ending on the main verb in the past perfect continuous.

Method 2
(For students familiar with the structure)

- Have students do the exercise in pairs.
- Give students a few minutes to refer to the charts to check their answers and review the structures.

- Call on students to go over the exercise. Discuss any disagreements and have students make any necessary corrections.

FORM CHARTS

- Put students into pairs and assign them roles of Students A and B. Explain that they will quiz each other on the forms in the charts: Student B will close his or her book and listen to Student A read a sentence from the charts in the past perfect. Student B will change the sentence to the past perfect continuous. Student A will then confirm that the answer was correct or tell Student B to try again:

    Student A: *We had hiked for hours by then.*
    Student B: *We had been hiking for hours by then.*
    Student A: *Correct.*

- Students should quiz each other for a few minutes on sentences from each chart (affirmative, negative, *Yes/No* questions, short answers, and information questions). When they finish, Student B will quiz Student A by reading the sentences in the past perfect continuous and eliciting the past perfect.

- As a final check, write the following sentences on the board and ask students if they are correct or incorrect and why.

    We had had a very big test when we saw you. (Correct.)

    They had been liking baseball before they came to America. (Incorrect—*like* is a stative verb and isn't usually used in the continuous.)

    My instructor had already wrote a letter to my advisor by the time I turned in my late assignments. (Incorrect—*written*, not *wrote*, is the past particle of *write*.)

Informally Speaking: Reduced Forms of *Had* (p. 129)

- Choose two students to read the text in the speech bubbles. Then tell the class you will play the recording and that they should listen to how the underlined form in the cartoon is different from what they hear. If needed, play the recording more than once.

Chapter 6   25

- Have students point out the differences. (The cartoon reads *Dan had* whereas on the recording this is pronounced "*Dan'd*"). Explain that the form on the recording is considered more informal English. Point out that the form in the cartoon is standard English and students should use that form when writing and speaking, although they may hear native speakers using the informal form.

C MEANING AND USE 1

The Past Perfect

EXAMINING MEANING AND USE

- Have students work in pairs to answer the questions (1. a, *because a tree had fallen across my driveway*; b, *after she had enrolled*; c, *He'd been on a mountain climbing expedition*; d, *Although I'd been terrified*; 2. past perfect; 3. simple past).
- Give students a few minutes to refer to the Notes to check their answers.
- Discuss any disagreements and have students make any necessary corrections.

Trouble Spots

Students may expect the past perfect to always appear in a sentence with the simple past, which shows the later past event or time. Emphasize that the past perfect sometimes occurs without the simple past. Show students examples in which the second event or time is not indicated by the simple past but is nevertheless understood to be the later of the two events or times. For example: *At 11:00 A.M., I had already eaten a big breakfast and part of my lunch.* The action expressed by *had eaten* happened before 11:00 A.M. *By 1995, I had already studied two languages.* Studying the two languages happened before 1995.

MEANING AND USE NOTES

- Draw this time line on the board:

- Write the example sentences from Note 1A above the time line.

- Mark the time line to show the order of events in the sentence like this:

- Divide the class into groups and assign each group one Note.
- Ask each group to read the Note and prepare to teach the explanation to the class. Tell each group to paraphrase the explanation and write original sentences, based on the examples, that clearly illustrate the particular aspect of meaning and use. Tell students to use time lines in their explanations where helpful.
- For the group presentations, have one student present the explanation and another one write the new examples sentences and draw time lines. Elicit and offer feedback as necessary.

D MEANING AND USE 2

The Past Perfect Continuous

EXAMINING MEANING AND USE

- Have students work in pairs to answer the questions (1. a; 2. b).
- Give students a few minutes to refer to the Notes to check their answers
- Discuss any disagreements and have students make any necessary corrections.

MEANING AND USE NOTES

- Divide students into three groups and assign one of the Notes to each group.
- Tell each group to read their Note and prepare to teach the explanation to the class. Each group should paraphrase the information and write an original sentence that clearly illustrates the meaning and use.
- Circulate as the groups work, helping with vocabulary for the paraphrase and pointing out any problems in the example sentences.

- As the groups present, ask the rest of the class if the example sentences are correct. If not, work together to improve them.

Beyond the Sentence: Adding Background Information in Longer Discourse (p. 139)

This section is intended to give students practice with the meaning and use of grammar as it functions naturally in extended discourse such as paragraphs and conversations.

- Ask students to read the example paragraph and guess what it is describing (a long and difficult plane trip).
- Elicit the mood-setting details that are expressed using the past perfect continuous and the past perfect (e.g., *We had been traveling for thirteen hours . . . ; The seat had been uncomfortable . . . ; I hadn't slept . . .*).
- As a follow-up to Exercise D5, Part B, have students underline the past perfect and past perfect continuous verbs they used in their paragraph. Ask them to explain why they used those forms when they did (to set the tone for the background of the event).

ADDITIONAL ACTIVITIES

Writing About an Unbelievable Experience

The purpose of this activity is for students to practice using the past perfect and past perfect continuous to describe an unbelievable past experience.

- For homework, tell students to write a one-page essay in which they describe an unbelievable experience from the past. Explain that *unbelievable* means that something is true but hard to believe because it is so unusual. In describing the experience, tell students to set the scene with background information that helps explain the story.

- Write the following model on the board to help students start their essays: *I had been living in Miami for five months when an unbelievable thing happened to me. I had just gone to the supermarket when all of a sudden . . .* Remind students to use the past perfect and the past perfect continuous for the background information and wherever else appropriate.
- Review students' essays to correct any errors in form, meaning, or use.

Returning to Grammar in Discourse

The purpose of this activity is to check students' understanding of key meanings and uses of the target structures in the chapter, by returning to the excerpt at the beginning of the chapter and applying what they have learned.

- Write the following extracts from the excerpt on the board (or type them up and photocopy them before class) and have students work in pairs to find them in the excerpt. Make sure they read the complete sentences these extracts come from.
  1. *I watched a puddle form at the foot of my sleeping bag . . .*
  2. *. . . I had plenty of time to think about that question.*
  3. *. . . I'd always lumped myself in the I-could-never-do-that category.*
  4. *. . . I became increasingly terrified.*
  5. *I begged my mother to cancel for me.*
- Now write the following on the board:
  a. *during the specific day in July*
  b. *before the specific day in July*
- Have students match each extract to the letter above that best describes the time frame (1. a; 2. a; 3. b; 4. b; 5. b).
- Bring the class together. Call on pairs for the answers and have them offer explanations. If students still have problems, revisit the Meaning and Use Notes.

CHAPTER 7
Modals of Possibility

Overview

This chapter introduces modals of present possibility, which are used to express guesses about present situations (e.g., *Jan must be sick again.*), and modals of future possibility, which are used for predictions about the future (e.g., *She should be here later.*). Note that some modals have more than one meaning. As in the examples above, *must* and *should* can function as modals of possibility. However, *must* can also function as a modal of obligation (e.g., *You must arrive on time.*), and the modal *should* can also function as a modal of advisability (e.g., *You should eat less junk food.*). Students are likely to be less familiar with the meaning and use of modals of possibility than these other forms. They may need help recognizing the subtle differences.

Form: Modals are followed by the base form of a verb. They never take the third-person *-s*, the *-ing* for continuous, or the *-ed* past tense endings. They do not require *do* for negation or questions.

A GRAMMAR IN DISCOURSE

Going to the Dogs

A1: Before You Read

- Ask students to work in pairs to discuss the questions in their books. If they have never owned a pet, ask them to think about a person they know who does and make a list in their notebooks of the advantages and disadvantages of owning a pet.
- After they have made their lists, take a vote to find out if there are more advantages to owning one type of pet over another. For example, do some students think it is better to own a cat or a dog? a goldfish or a parrot?
- Make two columns on the board, one labeled *Advantages* and one labeled *Disadvantages*. Elicit from students the advantages and disadvantages of pet ownership and write them on the board.

Cultural Notes

The article refers to two American dogs—Lassie and Spot. Before students read the article, explain that Lassie was the name of a dog that starred in a famous long-running TV show from the 1950s to the 1960s. In every episode, she rescued or helped someone in danger. Spot was once a very popular name for dogs.

A2: Read

- Tell students to read the whole article once to find out what researchers have learned about the benefits of owning a dog.
- Have students note unfamiliar vocabulary.
- After they have read, clarify the meanings of unfamiliar words.

A3: After You Read

- Have students do this exercise individually and mark the places in the text where they found their answers.
- Ask them to compare answers with a partner.
- Circulate and note any problematic items. Then go over these with the whole class.
- Call on several students to tell you the advantages of pet ownership discussed in the article (longer life, companionship, etc.). Write these on the board.
- As a follow-up activity, divide students into small groups and ask each group to think of things in life that can provide similar advantages to those that pets provide, e.g., a healthy diet, loving relationships, exercise, relaxation techniques, etc.

- Have one member of each group share the group's ideas and write them on the board.

B FORM

Modals of Present and Future Possibility

EXAMINING FORM

Method 1
(For students not familiar with the structure)

- **Question 1:** Tell students to look at the underlined modal form in the article *(must be)*. Ask them to find six more modals in the article. Call on students for examples and list these on the board. If they don't remember the form of other modals, remind them that these are words like *may, could,* and *might*.
- **Question 2:** Make two columns, one labeled *Be* and one labeled *Other Verbs*. Locate the first modal followed by *be* in the article and write this in the *Be* column *(must be)*. Do the same with the first modal followed by a different main verb, putting it in the *Other Verbs* column *(might do)*.
- Have students work in pairs to find more modals and verbs that follow them, writing them in their notebooks in two columns like those on the board.
- Ask two volunteers to come up to the board to complete the two lists.
- Point to each item in the list *Other Verbs*. Ask students to identify each modal. Elicit that the verb that follows the modal is always in the base form (e.g., *might do, might have*).

Method 2
(For students familiar with the structure)

- Have students work in pairs to answer the questions.
- Give students a few minutes to refer to the charts to check their answers and review the structures.
- Call on students to go over the exercise. Discuss any disagreements and have students make any necessary corrections.

FORM CHARTS

- Give students some time to study the charts. Then write the following sentences on the board and call on students to tell you which form is used:

    That can't be a Labrador. Look at his tail. (negative present modal)

    The Thompsons won't be walking their dog this evening. (negative future modal)

    That has to be a Siamese cat. (present modal)

    I might be buying a house for my dog next month. (future modal)

- Ask students how the negative statements are formed (the word *not* is put between the modal and the verb).
- Write these sample affirmative sentences on the board and have individual students come up to change them to the negative:

    She might be having a birthday party for her goldfish. (She might not be having a birthday party for her goldfish.)

    Steven could be taking a vacation with his cat. (Steven couldn't be taking a vacation with his cat.)

    Those pets must need a lot of attention. (Those pets must not need a lot of attention.)

- To check students' comprehension of the charts, ask whether the following sentences are correct:

    *There aren't any lights on. They mustn't be home. (Incorrect—*must not* has no contracted form as a modal of possibility.)

    *The dog isn't barking. It maybe sleeping. (Incorrect—the sentence requires modal + verb [*may be*], not the adverb *maybe*.)

- Ask students to compare the forms of *have to* and *have got to* with *ought to*. Elicit that *have to* and *have got to* change form for the third-person singular but *ought to* does not.
- Check students' comprehension of the Form Notes by asking whether the following sentences are correct:

    *It have got to be right. (Incorrect—*have* becomes *has* in third-person singular.)

    *She oughts to go with you. (Incorrect—*ought* never changes form.)

Trouble Spots

Students often confuse the phrasal modal *have got to,* which voices necessity (e.g., *I have got to finish my homework.*) with the verb *have got,* which means *have* (e.g., *I have got a lot of homework.*). On the board, write the sentence *I have a car.* Then write *I've got a car.* Explain that these sentences mean the same thing. Write the sentence *She has a motorcycle.* Then ask students to change this to the *have got* version (*She's got a motorcycle.*). Ask them to tell you what follows *has got* (a noun). Next, write the sentences *You've got to be hungry. She's got to know the answer.* Ask students to identify the phrasal modals (*you've got to* and *she's got to*). Underline them and ask students to tell you what follows the phrasal modals (the verbs in the base form, *be* and *know*).

C) MEANING AND USE 1

Modals of Present Possibility

EXAMINING MEANING AND USE

- Put students in pairs to examine the sentences and answer the questions (1. In a, c, and f the speaker is more certain; 2. In b, d, and e the speaker is less certain).
- Discuss the differences between the modals with the whole class. The meanings of modals vary from less certain to more certain, although the difference in meaning between each modal is not precise.
- Ask students to close their books.
- Draw a vertical line on the board and label it according to the model.
- Ask students where to put the six modals from the sample sentences as well as *ought to, have to,* and *have got to.*
- Ask students to open their books and examine the vertical line showing modals in Meaning and Use Note 1 to see if they accurately guessed their meanings.

MEANING AND USE NOTES

- Have students silently read the information in the Notes. Then call on students to form new sentences using modals. For example, for Note 2, if a student is absent and the reason is not known or obvious, call on students to guess where she or he is, using *could, might,* or *may.*
- For Note 3, ask students *When do you plan to finish your assignment?* (Make sure they answer using *should* or *ought to*).
- For Notes 4A and 4B, make statements such as *I didn't have breakfast this morning. I won a hundred dollars.* Ask students to make conclusions, such as *You must be hungry. You've got to be excited.*

Trouble Spots

In this chapter, students are learning only about modals of possibility. Students may occasionally be confused with other meanings of the same modals, for example, *must* for necessity and obligation (e.g., *I must take the final exam. You must not touch that.*). In the same way, the modal *should* could be confusing, since it also is used for advisability (e.g., *You should study more. You should call the doctor tomorrow.*).

D) MEANING AND USE 2

Modals of Future Possibility

EXAMINING MEANING AND USE

- Put students into pairs to examine the sentences and discuss the questions.
- Go over the questions with the whole class (1. In a and c the speaker is less certain; 2. In b and d the speaker is more certain; 3. a and c have about the same meaning).
- Ask students to close their books. Draw a vertical line on the board like the one in Note 1 of Meaning and Use 2. Ask students to tell you where to put the four modals from the sample sentences as well as *ought to* and *may.*
- Have students check the vertical line against Note 1.

MEANING AND USE NOTES

- Divide students into small groups and assign each group one of the modals from Note 1.

- Have them write one sentence predicting a future class activity (a field trip, a test, a visitor, a project) using their modal (e.g., *We may have a test on modals. I might pass it.*). Refer students to Notes 2–4 to help them.
- Have the groups write their sentences on the board, and ask the class if the modals are in the correct form. Then ask students to write the sentences in their notebooks and number them in order of future probability from less certain to more certain, the number 1 indicating the least certain.
- Have students number the sentences on the board. Point out that some sentences, such as those with *might* and *could*, will have an equal amount of certainty.

ADDITIONAL ACTIVITIES

Writing About Weather Reports

The purpose of this activity is to listen to the authentic use of modals of possibility in a weather report.

- Record a brief video or audio clip of a weather report that particularly uses modals of possibility and bring it to class. If the speaking speed is very quick, transcribe the script to be able to use in class for a dictation
- Have students watch or listen to the clip once for general comprehension, and then once (or more times if necessary) to write down the information verbatim. If the speaking speed proves too quick for the students, dictate the transcription to the students slowly.
- Put students into pairs to compare their transcriptions. Then have them underline all the modals and analyze their uses.
- Bring the class together to go over the answers and discuss the meanings and uses.

Returning to Grammar in Discourse

The purpose of this activity is to check students' understanding of key meanings and uses of the target structures in the chapter, by returning to the article at the beginning of the chapter and applying what they have learned.

- Write the following extracts from the article on the board (or type them up and photocopy them before class) and have students work in pairs to find them in the article. Make sure they read the complete sentences these extracts come from.
    1. . . . there must be a positive connection between health and pet ownership.
    2. . . . it could be due to their function as man's best friend.
    3. . . . and dogs might strengthen those feelings of support.
    4. It may be a hassle for some people who are not used to it . . .
- Now write the following on the board:
    a. more certain
    b. less certain
- Have students think about the modal of possibility used in each extract and match each one to the letter that best describes the level of certainty (1. a; 2. b; 3. b; 4. b).
- Bring the class together. Call on pairs for the answers and have them offer explanations. If students still have problems, revisit the Meaning and Use Notes.

CHAPTER 8 Past Modals

Overview

Past modals have a variety of meanings and uses. Similarly to modals of present and future possibility, modals of past possibility are used to make guesses about past situations (e.g., *You must have been tired after the long trip.*). The chapter also covers other uses of past modals, such as to express past ability (e.g., *I could have helped you.*), advice (e.g., *Thomas should have gone to bed early.*), obligation (e.g., *You shouldn't have lied to me.*), and regrets (e.g., *I shouldn't have spent so much money.*).

Form: Potential errors with past modals include leaving out the *have* auxiliary (e.g., **I could gone home.* Incorrect) or not using the past participle of the main verb (e.g., **She would have be happy.* Incorrect). Students may also be confused because the form resembles the present perfect, however, the meanings and uses of the two are unrelated.

A GRAMMAR IN DISCOURSE

The Really Early Birds

A1: Before You Read
- Bring in pictures of birds in flight to help explain the words *flap*, *lift*, and *glide*.
- Ask students to guess how birds are able to fly. Write their guesses on the board. Students will refer to them after they read.

A2: Read
- Tell the class to read the first paragraph of the article, and then ask students to predict what the article will talk about (how prehistoric birds first learned to fly).
- Organize a jigsaw reading of the rest of the article. Divide students into small groups and have each group read one of the remaining paragraphs and write a one- or two-sentence summary.
- As the groups work, circulate and answer questions about unfamiliar vocabulary or concepts.
- When students finish their summary, assign them to new groups so that there is at least one member representing each of the paragraphs. Make sure the students discuss the paragraphs in chronological order.

A3: After You Read
- Ask students to do this exercise individually (students may need to reread the entire article first). Remind them to note the places in the article where they found their answers.
- Go over any difficult or problematic items with the whole class.
- As a follow-up activity, divide the students into small groups and ask them to choose a reporter, who will present the group's ideas to the class. Write this question on the board for the groups to discuss: *What are some of the ways that scientists might use their knowledge about prehistoric birds?*
- Call on the reporters to share with the class the most interesting or important ideas from their groups.

B FORM

Past Modals

EXAMINING FORM

Method 1
(For students not familiar with the structure)
- **Question 1:** Read the underlined past modal in the article to the students *(may have gotten)*,

and ask them to identify the main verb *(gotten)*, the modal *(may)*, and the auxiliary *(have)*.

- Write the form of past modals on the board (modal + *have* + past participle).
- Have students work in pairs to find six more past modals. Then ask students to tell you what they are. Have one student write these on the board.
- **Question 2:** Ask one student to identify two past modals with singular subjects and two with plural subjects in the article; then ask if there is a form difference (no). To confirm, ask students to find another singular past modal and another plural past modal and analyze the forms.
- **Question 3:** If students can't answer this question, refer them to one of the examples on the list on the board. Point out the auxiliary *have* and the past participle form of the main verb.

Method 2
(For students familiar with the structure)

- Have students work in pairs to answer the questions.
- Give students a few minutes to refer to the charts to check their answers and review the structures.
- Call on students to go over the exercise. Discuss any disagreements and have students make any necessary corrections.

FORM CHARTS

- Tell students to close their books. On the board, write the sentence *I could pass the test.* Ask students to tell you how to change this to past time *(I could have passed the test.)*. Write this sentence on the board and write *may have, might have, should have,* and *must have* in a list as it appears in the chart so students see the sentence with a variety of modals.
- Ask students to tell you the form of past modals and write this on the board (modal + *have* + past participle).
- Tell students to transform the example sentence to a negative statement *(I could not have passed the test.)* and a *Yes/No* question *(Could you have passed the test?)* using all the modals on the board.
- Tell students to open their books to confirm their answers. Ask them to read the charts and bulleted notes.
- Tell students to close their books again. On the board, write the sentence *He ought to have come.* Ask students to identify the phrasal modal *(ought to)*, the auxiliary *(have)*, and the main verb *(come)*. Then write the sentence *She has to have known.* Ask students to identify the phrasal modal *(have to)*, the auxiliary *(have)*, and the main verb *(known)*. Tell students to open their books to check their answers.
- To check students' comprehension of the Form Notes, write the following sentences on the board and ask students if the form is correct. If it is incorrect, have students tell you how to correct it.

  *She mights have gone to the store. (Incorrect—*might* doesn't change form.)
  Could you have asked for some help? (Correct.)
  *Should have he taken the bus? (Incorrect—the subject should be before *have* in a question.)
  *They've got to been aware of the danger. (Incorrect—the auxiliary *have* should come before *been*.)

Trouble Spots

Past phrasal modals are more complex in form than other past modals. Point out that with the phrasal modal *have to*, we use *did* in questions, negatives, and short answers instead of changing the word order of the modal (e.g., *Did you have to leave?* rather than **Had you to leave?* Incorrect). For this particular phrasal modal, the form rules are an exception to modal rules.

Informally Speaking: Reducing Past Modals (p. 175)

- Choose two students to read the text in the speech bubbles. Then tell the class you will play the recording and that they should listen to how the underlined form in the cartoon is different from what they hear. If needed, play the recording more than once.

- Have students point out the differences. (The cartoon reads *should have*, whereas on the recording this is pronounced *"should-uv"*; and the cartoon reads *could have*, whereas on the recording this is pronounced *"could-uv"*.) Explain that the form on the recording is considered more informal English. Point out that the form in the cartoon is standard English and students should use this form when writing and speaking, although they may hear native speakers using the informal form.

C) MEANING AND USE 1

Modals of Past Possibility

EXAMINING MEANING AND USE

- Divide students into small groups to discuss the sentences in their books and answer the questions.
- Call on one group to explain in which sentences the speaker is more certain (a and d) and in which sentences the speaker is less certain (b and c).
- Write the modals from the sentences on the board and have students close their books. Draw a vertical line on the board like the one in Meaning and Use Note 1. Ask students to tell you how to order the modals from the sentences on the vertical line according to degree of certainty.
- Ask students to open their books and examine the vertical line showing modals in Meaning and Use Note 1 to see if they accurately guessed the degrees of certainty.

MEANING AND USE NOTES

- Divide students into three groups and assign one of the remaining Notes to each group.
- Tell each group to read the Note and prepare to teach the information to the class. The groups should write two new sentences that clearly illustrate the meaning and use of the modals in their assigned Note.
- Circulate as the groups work, pointing out any problems in their example sentences.

- Ask each group to present their Note, and have the rest of the class check if the example sentences are correct. If not, work together to improve them.

D) MEANING AND USE 2

Other Functions of Past Modals

EXAMINING MEANING AND USE

- Have students work in pairs to answer the questions (1. b, c; 2. a; 3. c).
- Give students a few minutes to refer to the Notes to check their answers.
- Call on students to read the questions and answers aloud. Discuss any disagreements and have students make any necessary corrections.

MEANING AND USE NOTES

- Emphasize that *could have*, *should have*, and *ought to have* are used to talk about things that never happened but that had the possibility of happening or were supposed to happen. (Conversely, *shouldn't have* and *ought not to have* indicate that something *did* happen and that the speaker believes it was not supposed to or was not a good idea.)
- Call on different students to read each of the Notes 1, 2A, and 2B out loud. Then ask students to create original sentences following the examples.
- Call on individual students to read their sentences out loud. After each sentence, ask, *Did the person do it? Did the event actually happen?*
- Finally call on a student to read Note 3. Elicit more example sentences from the class and answer any questions.

ADDITIONAL ACTIVITIES

Speaking About a Person in the News

The purpose of this activity is for students to use past modals to express their opinions about what someone should have, should not have, or could have done.

- Bring in recent newspapers and magazines covering a variety of news items. Divide students into pairs and have them find an article about a person in the news who has done something that they both disagree with. It can be a political figure, president of a company, a musician, actress, etc.
- Tell students to read their articles and underline the things they disagree with. Encourage them to write down things they may know about the person from other sources.
- Then have students use modals of past ability and opportunity, and advice and obligations to list their opinions about what the figure should have, should not have, or could have done.
- Combine the pairs into groups of four and have each pair present their findings to the other pair. Specify that each pair should first introduce their figure and explain what they disagree with. Then they should share their opinions using past modals. Instruct the groups to listen to each other for the correct use of past modals.
- When each pair has finished presenting, the other pair should say if they agree or disagree with them. If they agree, they can offer additional thoughts on what the person should have, should not have, or could have done. If they disagree, they should explain why.
- Circulate as the groups work and take notes on recurring problems with past modals. Once the groups have completed the assignment, bring the class together. Write the errors you noted on the board and elicit corrections.

Returning to Grammar in Discourse

The purpose of this activity is to check students' understanding of key meanings and uses of the target structures in the chapter, by returning to the article at the beginning of the chapter and applying what they have learned.

- Write the following extracts from the article on the board (or type them up and photocopy them before class) and have students work in pairs to find them in the article. Make sure they read the complete sentences these extracts come from.
    1. *That has to have been enough to enable the crow-sized bird to fly, or at least glide, through the Jurassic skies.*
    2. *This could have helped a bird like archaeopteryx into the air . . .*
    3. *. . . archaeopteryx's wings must have acted more like an airplane's engines, providing extra speed.*
    4. *Flying might have developed as the archaeopteryx ran faster and faster.*
- Now write the following on the board:
    a. *more certain*
    b. *less certain*
- Have students think about the past modal used in each extract and match each one to the letter above that best describes the level of certainty (1. a; 2. b; 3. a; 4. b).
- Bring the class together. Call on pairs for the answers and have them offer explanations. If students still have problems, revisit the Meaning and Use Notes

CHAPTER 9
Passive Sentences (Part 1)

Overview

Students usually know how to mechanically transform sentences from active to passive and vice versa; however, they often are not sure when to use the passive. The active voice is used when the focus in on the doer of the action, or the agent (e.g., *Maria completed the project on Monday.*). The passive voice is used when the focus is on the receiver of the action (e.g., *The project was completed by Maria on Monday.*). It is also possible for the passive to be used with no agent, when the doer of the action is unknown, unimportant, or obvious in the sentence (e.g., *The project was completed on Monday.*).

Form: Only transitive verbs (verbs that can be followed by a direct object) can be put in the passive voice. Intransitive verbs such as *come*, *sleep*, and *stay* do not take a direct object and cannot be made passive.

A GRAMMAR IN DISCOURSE

The Expression of Emotions

A1: Before You Read

- Ask students to look at the four pictures in the text and write the emotion they think each one portrays.
- Divide the students into groups to compare their responses. They will probably agree on what the expressions represent, laying the foundation for the idea in the excerpt that the expression of emotions is universal.

A2: Read

- Ask students to read the excerpt to find out if the expression of emotions is universal.
- Tell students to note the places in the reading that answer this question.

A3: After You Read

- Ask students to do this exercise individually and mark the places in the text where they found their answers.
- Ask them to compare answers with a partner.
- Circulate and note any problematic items. Then go over these with the whole class.
- As a follow-up activity, divide students into groups and ask them to choose a reporter.
- Write these questions on the board for the groups to discuss: *How could you use the information from the article in your daily life?* (e.g., to be aware when someone else is happy or angry; to cheer up another person, etc.); *Who else might find this information useful?* (psychologists, sociologists, and people who deal with cross-cultural communication); *Why?* (because it will allow them to see the similarities between people's behavior patterns throughout the world).
- Call on the reporters to share their group's answers with the class.

B FORM

The Present and Past Passive

EXAMINING FORM

Method 1
(For students not familiar with the structure)

- **Question 1:** Write the underlined example from the excerpt on the board (*are found*) and ask students how the passive is formed (*be* + past participle) and what tense the verb *be* is in (present). Ask them if the subject is singular or plural (plural).

- Tell students to find three more passives in the simple present. Students may need help limiting their search to the simple present form of the passive since other passive forms appear in the reading as well.
- Ask two students to make two lists on the board, one labeled *Singular* and the other *Plural*. Ask one student to write the singular present passive verbs and another to write the plural present passive verbs in the appropriate columns. Ask other students if they agree.
- **Question 2:** Follow the same procedure for the past passive. Write the example on the board *(was noted)*. Elicit the form. (The tense is formed with *was* or *were* + past participle.)
- Have students find three more examples of singular or plural past passives and sort them into columns labeled *Singular* and *Plural*.
- **Question 3:** Ask students to look at the two sample sentences in Question 3 and note the forms used. Then have them find one example of each form in the text. Go over these with the class, providing any necessary clarification.

Method 2
(For students familiar with the structure)
- Have students work in pairs to answer the questions.
- Give students a few minutes to refer to the charts to check their answers and review the structures.
- Call on students to go over the exercise. Discuss any disagreements and have students make any necessary corrections.

FORM CHARTS
- Ask students to read the charts to themselves. Then ask one student to explain the form in each chart and another to read the example sentences out loud.
- Check students' comprehension of each form by asking *What is the auxiliary verb? (be)* and *What is the past participle?*
- Introduce the concept of agent and receiver: First ask a student to drop his or her book on the floor. Ask *What did he/she do?* Elicit the sentence *He/She dropped the book*. Write the sentence on the board and underline *He/She*. Explain that the student is the doer of the action, also called the agent.
- Circle *the book*. Explain that the book received the action, so it is the receiver.
- Ask students to put the sentence into the passive *(The book was dropped.)*.
- Point out that it is possible to include the agent in the sentence by adding the phrase *by him/her*.
- Once students understand the meaning of *agent* and *receiver*, call on individuals to add a different *by* + noun phrase to the end of some of the sentences in the charts (e.g., *The directions were explained* by the police officer. *Was the study published* by the academic journal?).

C MEANING AND USE 1

Changing Focus from Active to Passive

EXAMINING MEANING AND USE
- Have students read the sentences. Then ask if each pair of sentences has about the same meaning or different meanings (about the same).
- Have students determine the focus in the active and passive sentences. Students should notice that 1a and 2a focus more on the noun that is performing the action or causing something to happen, and 1b and 2b focus more on the noun that is receiving the action.
- Tell students to read the explanations in Notes 1A and 1B to check their answers.

MEANING AND USE NOTES
- Have students close their books and write the two sets of sentences from Note 2 on the board.
- Call on individual students to explain the focus of each set of sentences. (In the first one, the focus is on the word *we* and what *we* did. In the second set, the focus is on the results of the storm and the things that were affected by it.) Have students open their books to Note 2 to confirm their answers.

Vocabulary Notes: Verbs with No Passive Form (p. 201)

If you think it is necessary, remind your students how to determine whether a verb is transitive or intransitive.

- On the board, write these partial phrases using transitive verbs with write-on lines in place of the nouns:

    Mark eats _____.
    We like _____.
    They are watching _____.

- Read each partial phrase out loud and ask students to suggest a noun to make a complete sentence. Then call on students to identify the subject and object of each sentence.
- Then do the same with phrases using intransitive verbs:

    We arrived _____.
    He died _____.
    She slept _____.

- Students will discover that these verbs can not be followed by an object. These verbs are called intransitive verbs and they cannot be made passive.
- Refer students to Appendix 7 in the Student Book for a list of common intransitive verbs.
- Introduce transitive stative verbs. These are verbs that take noun objects but are not usually put into the passive. Remind students that they learned about stative verbs, such as *become* and *have*, in Chapter 1.
- Write the following sentence on the board, and ask students if it is correct:

    *The car is had by Mary. (Incorrect—transitive stative verbs are not usually used in the passive.)

D) MEANING AND USE 2

Reasons for Using the Passive

EXAMINING MEANING AND USE

- Have students work in pairs to answer the questions (1. In 1b the agent is unknown; In 1a the agent is *a former employee*; 2. In 2a the agent is inferable [Dr. Lewis or the management]; In 2b the agent is Dr. Lewis).
- Give students a few minutes to refer to the Notes to check their answers.
- Call on students to read the questions and answers out loud. Discuss any disagreements and have students make any necessary corrections.

MEANING AND USE NOTES

- Divide students into small groups and assign one of the Notes to each group.
- Tell each group to read the Note and prepare to teach the information to the class. Each group should paraphrase the information and write two original sentences that clearly illustrate the meaning and use.
- Circulate as the groups work, helping as necessary.
- As the groups present, ask the rest of the class if the example sentences are correct. If not, work together to improve them.

Beyond the Sentence: Keeping the Focus (p. 206)

This section is intended to give your students practice with the meaning and use of grammar as it functions naturally in extended discourse such as paragraphs and conversations.

- Ask students to read the example sentences.
- Have them draw an arrow from the subject pronoun in the second sentence (in both sentence pairs, *it*) to the noun it refers to in the first sentence (in both sentence pairs, *his wallet*). This will underscore how the focus is maintained across the two sentences.

ADDITIONAL ACTIVITIES

Writing About Food

The purpose of this activity is to practice using the passive voice by describing a strange food (how it is eaten, where is is found) and having classmates guess what it is.

- Tell students they will write a paragraph about the strangest food they have ever eaten.

- Give them a few minutes to work individually to make a list of some strange foods they have eaten in their lives.
- Then tell students to mark a check next to the food they remember the most and could best describe.
- Tell students to brainstorm quickly about the food. Write these questions on the board to help them: *What does the food look like? What does it taste like? How is the food eaten? How is the food prepared and served? Where is the food eaten? Where is the food grown or found? When and where was the food discovered?* Leave these questions on the board for students to refer to later.
- Have students use their notes to write a one-paragraph description of the food. The paragraph must include a definition of the food and examples of how and where it is eaten. Instruct students to use the passive where appropriate. Tell students *not* to use the name of the food in their paragraphs because the class will have to guess it.
- As students write their paragraphs, write the following example on the board: *It is an animal that is found in the sea. It is common in New England, in the United States. Some people say it was discovered by the Native Americans who lived there before the Europeans arrived. The outside is red when it is boiled, and the inside is white. It is usually served with melted butter. It is expensive, but it is delicious.*
- Read the example to the class and have the students guess what you are describing. (It is a lobster.)
- Then have students share their paragraphs and guess answers either in small groups or as an entire class. If students cannot guess the food, encourage them to ask each other questions, using the passive, to help them guess the food (e.g., *Is this food eaten with a knife and fork?*).

Returning to Grammar in Discourse

The purpose of this activity is to check students' understanding of key meanings and uses of the target structures in the chapter, by returning to the excerpt at the beginning of the chapter and applying what they have learned.

- Write the following extracts from the excerpt on the board (or type them up and photocopy them before class) and have students work in pairs to find them in the excerpt. Make sure they read the complete sentences these extracts come from.
  1. *Joy and sadness are found in diverse cultures around the world . . .*
  2. *. . . the expression of several basic emotions . . . is universally recognized.*
  3. *. . . the participants were permitted to report whether they thought that . . .*
  4. *Emotions are also being studied from other perspectives.*
- Now write the following on the board:
  a. *the agent is unimportant or unknown*
  b. *the agent is obvious from the context*
- Have students think about the use of the agentless passive in each extract and match each one to the letter that best explains the reason for its use (1. a; 2. a; 3. b; 4. b).
- Bring the class together. Call on pairs for the answers and have them offer explanations. If students still have problems, revisit the Meaning and Use Notes.

CHAPTER 10

Passive Sentences (Part 2)

Overview

This chapter covers complex passive forms: future passive (e.g., *A cure will be/is going to be found.*), present perfect passive (e.g., *A cure has been found.*), modal passive (e.g., *A cure must be found.*), phrasal modal passive (e.g., *A cure has got to be found.*). The passive voice is commonly used in academia to convey an objective and authoritative tone.

Form: The key challenge with these more complex passives is remembering the multiple parts of the various forms of passive verbs with modals and other auxiliaries:

- affirmative verb forms have three parts, including two auxiliaries (e.g. *will* + *be*; *have/has* + *been*; *modal* + *be*; *phrasal modal* + *be*) + past participle
- questions and negatives with the phrasal modals *have to* and *need to* have four parts, since the additional auxiliary *do* must also be used (e.g., *Do you need to be paid today? I don't need to be paid today.*)

A GRAMMAR IN DISCOURSE

Should Parents Be Punished for Their Children's Crimes?

A1: Before You Read

- Point out that juvenile crime is a serious problem in the United States, in particular, shootings by teenagers.
- Have students answer the questions in pairs. Then bring the class together and call on students from different countries to discuss juvenile crime and punishment in their society.
- After the discussion, ask *Should parents be punished for the crimes committed by their children?* Tell students to support their reasons. Write these on the board.

A2: Read

- Ask students to read the article to find out what lawmakers in the U.S. are doing about children's crimes.
- Have students make a list on a separate piece of paper of the types of punishment mentioned for parents whose children commit crimes.

Cultural Notes

Many students may be unfamiliar with the related issue of gun control in the United States. If so, briefly outline the debate between those who believe it is a fundamental right of Americans to own a firearm and those who believe the government should control the process by which Americans acquire guns.

A3: After You Read

- Have students do this exercise individually and mark the places in the text where they found the answers.
- Ask them to compare answers with a partner.
- Circulate and note any problematic items. Then go over these with the whole class.
- As a follow-up activity, refer students to the list of types of punishment for parents they wrote up while reading the article. Ask students to rank these in terms of how effective they think they are. A rank of "1" indicates the punishment is the most effective and "5" least effective. Ask if they could think of any other types of punishment to add to the list. If students do not believe parental punishment is effective, ask them to write one or two alternative ideas for reducing juvenile crime.
- Call on students to share their rankings and ideas.

B FORM

The Future, Present Perfect, and Modal Passive

EXAMINING FORM

Method 1
(For students not familiar with the structure)

- **Question 1:** Write *must hold* on the board. Elicit that this is a modal + verb. Ask students how they might form the passive of this modal. Write the correct passive form on the board *(must be held)*, and direct students' attention to the underlined verb in the article. Point out the parts of the form: modal + *be* + past participle.
- Ask students to find five more modal passives in the article.
- Call on students to list them. Write them on the board in the column labeled *Modal Passives.*
- **Question 2:** Repeat the procedure for the circled verb in the article, *will be introduced,* by writing *will introduce* on the board and eliciting that this is a modal + verb. Explain that *will be introduced* is the future passive and that the parts of the form are *will* + *be* + past participle.
- Ask students to find and call out two more future passive verbs. Write them on the board in the column labeled *Future Passive.*
- Elicit the three parts of the *be going to* passive (*be going to* + *be* + past participle).
- **Question 3:** Ask students to tell you the three parts of the verb form *have been made* in the example sentence. Explain that this is the present perfect passive and that the parts of the form are *has/have* + *been* + past participle.

Method 2
(For students familiar with the structure)

- First, divide the board into three columns labeled *Modal Passive, Future Passive,* and *Present Perfect Passive.*
- **Question 1:** Ask the class to quickly call out all the modals they can think of before they answer Question 1 *(could, can, should, may, might,* and *must).* If they mention *will,* explain that this modal forms the future passive, not a modal passive. Then tell students to work individually to find five more modal passives in the article.
- Call on students to tell you the modal passives they found, and write them in the appropriate columns on the board. Now ask students to tell you the three parts of the modal passive (modal + *be* + past participle). Write the form under the column head.
- **Question 2:** Have students find two future passives, and call on one student to write these on the board. Elicit the three parts of future passives (*will* + *be* + past participle) and write this form under the column heading.
- Elicit the three parts of the *be going to* passive (*be going to* + *be* + past participle).
- **Question 3:** Have students find two present perfect passives. Call on two students to write them on the board. Then have them write the three parts of the present perfect passive next to their sentences (*has/have* + *been* + past participle).

FORM CHARTS

- Ask students to close their books.
- On the board write the sentence *TV violence is limited.* Tell students to work in pairs to change this sentence to the future passive with *will* (*TV violence will be limited.*), the present perfect passive (*TV violence has been limited.*), and the modal passive with *must* (*TV violence must be limited.*).
- Tell students to open their books to check their sentences against the charts.
- Then ask them to close their books as you follow the same procedure for questions and short answers. On the board, write *Are the parents blamed? Yes, they are.* Ask students to change the example to a modal passive question and a short answer with the modal *should* (*Should the parents be blamed? Yes, they should.*), the future passive with *will* (*Will the parents be blamed? No, they won't.*), and the present perfect passive (*Have the parents been blamed? Yes, they have.*).
- Erase the board.

- Have students read the explanations of the future passive with *be going to* and phrasal modal passives.
- To check their comprehension, write this sentence on the board: *Children will be taught to stay away from guns.*
- Then write the following list of forms on the board. Tell students to change the above sentence to these forms:

  future passive with *be going to*
  (*Children are going to be taught to stay away from guns.*)

  passive *Yes/No* question with *be going to*
  (*Are children going to be taught to stay away from guns?*)

  negative phrasal modal passive with *have to*:
  (*Children don't have to be taught to stay away from guns.*)

  passive *Yes/No* question with *have to*:
  (*Do children have to be taught to stay away from guns?*)

- Bring the class together and call on students to write the answers on the board. Answer any remaining questions. Make sure that students use *do* with the negative and question forms of the phrasal modal *have to*.

C) MEANING AND USE 1

The Role of the Agent

EXAMINING MEANING AND USE

- Put students into pairs. Have them underline the agent in each sentence and then discuss Question 2.
- Ask which agents give important or unexpected information (1b and 2a).
- Ask students which agents seem unnecessary (In 1a and 2b, the agent is unnecessary because including it does not provide any new or important information).

MEANING AND USE NOTES

- Ask students to close their books. Write the sentences from Note 1A on the board. Read them out loud and ask why the agent is mentioned in two sentences (in the first one, the agent is surprising; in the second one, the agent is unexpected), and why it isn't mentioned in the other two sentences (in both, the agent is obvious).
- Ask students to open their books to read Note 1A and 1B. Have them check their answers by reading the explanations.
- For Note 1C, read the two sentences and ask students which one is vague or incomplete (*Washington, D.C. was designed.*) and which one is specific and complete (*Washington, D.C. was designed by Pierre L'Enfant.*).

D) MEANING AND USE 2

The Passive in Academic and Public Discourse

EXAMINING MEANING AND USE

- Give students a few minutes to change the example sentences from passive to active. Call on several students to read their answers out loud (a, *We use sulfur dioxide to produce sulfuric acid.* b, *As a special benefit to on-line customers, we will ship orders free of charge.* c, *You must insure your vehicle. You must present proof of insurance.*).
- Students should notice that in all cases, the passive sentences sound more formal and objective and express more authority.
- The following are possible contexts for the passive sentences: a, a chemistry book; b, an Internet retailer; c, information from the Department of Motor Vehicles.

MEANING AND USE NOTES

- Ask students to close their books.
- Remind them that the passive is commonly used in less personal, more formal, or authoritative situations.
- Divide students into small groups. Give them a few minutes to list as many contexts as they can in which the passive might be used and write an example for each one.
- Elicit contexts and examples from all the groups and list the contexts on the board.

- Ask students to open their books and read the Notes, comparing the list on the board with the contexts in the book.

Informally Speaking: Using Passives with *Get* (p. 224)

- Choose two students to read the text in the speech bubbles. Then tell the class you will play the recording and that they should listen to how the underlined form in the cartoon is different from what they hear. If needed, play the recording more than once.
- Have students point out the differences. (The cartoon reads *I'm going to be promoted*. The form on the recording is *I'm going to get promoted*.) Explain that the form on the recording is considered more informal English. Point out that the form in the cartoon is standard English and students should use this form when writing and speaking, although they may hear native speakers using the informal form.

ADDITIONAL ACTIVITIES

Performing a Live News Show

The purpose of this activity is for students to practice using the passive voice in a role-play of a live news show. Students will first write their news segments in groups and then play the roles of anchors and reporters on the scene. The news show will be similar to a television news show, but the content will come from the students' own lives and activities.

- First, explain that each group will write and then present two news stories. If you have access to a video camera, explain that you will videotape the stories for the class to watch later. As in television news, the stories should be delivered by the anchor and the reporter on the scene. Bring in a short segment of a real news program and ask students to pay attention to the format (as well as the use of the passive).
- As a class, brainstorm a list of possibilities for stories: these might include current events in students' lives, a feature on an interesting personality in the class, or a custom from the country of one of the students.
- Write the list on the board. Explain that the stories should be around two paragraphs long.
- Divide the students into groups of four. Each group will choose two stories to cover. Each story will be presented by one anchor and one reporter, so ask students to pair off within their groups as anchor and reporter and then prepare their story. Give students time in class to plan their stories, organize their roles, or interview other students as necessary.
- Have each member of the group write one paragraph of his or her story for homework. Tell students to use the passive voice to describe processes and results and to give the news story an objective tone. Remind student that they can omit the agents in passive sentences when the agent is not important, unknown, or obvious.
- In class have students form their stories with their partner, and then have the other two group members read them for correct use of the passive. Have them check whether agents are necessary or unimportant.
- Give the groups time to put their stories together into a complete news show. Have them practice delivering their stories in their groups so they will be more comfortable presenting in front of the class.
- Circulate as the groups practice, reminding students to speak loudly and clearly. Also remind them that it is important to maintain eye contact with their audience.
- Have groups present their news shows to the class. If possible, videotape them so that the class can watch them later.
- Show the clips to the class twice. Ask students to listen first for the main idea of each story, and then to listen again, noting the use of the passive. Discuss the use of the passive as a class, focusing on form as well as the use of agents.

CHAPTER 11
Contrasting Gerunds and Infinitives

> **Overview**
> One of the difficulties students face with gerunds and infinitives is that there are few set rules to follow and a lot of memorization. Students may need help finding ways to remember which verbs can be followed only by gerunds (e.g., *finish, enjoy*) and which only by infinitives (e.g., *agree, plan*), and which by both (e.g., *like, stop*). Point out that for the latter category, a sentence with a gerund and the same sentence with an infinitive may not have the same meaning (e.g., *I stopped smoking.* vs. *I stopped to smoke.*).
>
> **Form:** Make sure students understand that a gerund is not a verb. It is the *-ing* form of the verb which is used as a noun—as a subject or an object of a sentence (e.g., *Skating is fun. I like skating.*).

A GRAMMAR IN DISCOURSE

Become a Less Aggressive Driver

A1: Before You Read

- Tell students that traffic congestion is a terrible problem in many cities in the United States. Ask if traffic congestion is a problem in their countries. Have students share their experiences driving in their countries and compare it with driving in the United States.
- Ask students to think of the last time they were delayed while driving in heavy traffic, and to visualize the experience.
- Write these questions on the board and tell students to think about them for a few minutes: *How are you feeling? Do you feel relaxed or tense? What are you saying to yourself? How do you feel about the other drivers around you? Are you driving differently than you do usually?* Focus students' attention on the stressful nature of driving in heavy traffic. Then, in pairs, have students discuss the questions.
- Bring the class together and call on students for comments about the stressful nature of driving in heavy traffic.
- Tell the class they are going to read an excerpt about stress, written by a psychologist. Ask students to predict what a psychologist might say about the dangers of driving in stressful situations (e.g., people become careless and can cause accidents, it is bad for one's health, etc.). Write these on the board to refer to during the After You Read activity.

A2: Read

- Tell students they will read the excerpt to find out what psychologist Richard Carlson has suggested for aggressive drivers.
- Divide students into small groups. Explain that half the groups will read and make a list of the characteristics of an aggressive driver, while the other half will read and make a list of the characteristics of a calm driver. Explain that the characteristics may not be stated directly, but can be inferred from the reading.
- Make two columns on the board, one labeled *Characteristics of Aggressive Drivers* and the other labeled *Characteristics of Calm Drivers.*
- Call on members from each group to write items from their list on the board.

Cultural Notes

There is much concern about the causes and effects of stress in the United States. As a result, stress is a popular topic of self-help books, magazine articles, and television shows. Many Americans think that stress is the result of social pressures on people to work hard, to achieve success, and particularly for women to combine families and careers.

A3: After You Read

- Have students to do this exercise individually and mark the places in the excerpt where they found their answers.
- Ask them to compare answers with a partner.
- Circulate and note any problematic items. Then go over these with the whole class.
- Direct students' attention to the predictions on the board that they made before reading the excerpt. As a class, check if these predictions were correct.
- As a follow-up activity, write these questions on the board: *What are the sources of stress in your life? Do you think stress really has a great impact on your ability to do things such as drive?* Encourage students to support their opinions with examples. Finally, ask *Do you think sources of stress are the same across cultures, or are they more specific to individuals, regardless of culture?*

Trouble Spots

Students sometimes confuse the *-ing* in the gerund form (e.g., *Swimming is fun.*) with the *-ing* in the continuous form (e.g., *She is swimming.*). This may cause problems when students see a stative verb (such as *know* or *have*) and, remembering that stative verbs do not typically occur in the continuous, hesitate to use a gerund. To avoid this confusion, point out that any verb can be used as a gerund, giving a few examples of stative verbs in the gerund form (e.g., *Knowing how to relax is important for your health. Having a job makes me very tired.*).

B) FORM 1

Gerunds and Infinitives

EXAMINING FORM

Method 1
(For students not familiar with the structure)

- **Question 1:** As a precursor, write the sentence *Driving is fun* on the board. Elicit the subject of the sentence (*Driving*). Elicit that *Driving* is a gerund that functions as the subject of the sentence.
- Direct students to the circled example in the excerpt (*driving in traffic*).
- Ask students to find another gerund in the text that is the subject of a sentence. Write it on the board in a column labeled *Gerunds*. Make sure students include the whole gerund phrase if appropriate.
- **Question 2:** As a precursor, write this sentence on the board: *I enjoy driving.* Elicit the verb of the sentence (*enjoy*). Point out that *driving* is not part of a verb here but that it is a gerund, the *-ing* form of the verb used as a noun. It is the object of *enjoy*.
- Direct students' attention to the underlined example in the article (*saving no time at all*). Elicit the form of the gerund (verb + *-ing*).
- Ask students to find and tell you one more example of a gerund following a verb in the article (*begin using your time*). Write this on the board in the column labeled *Gerunds*.
- **Question 3:** Ask students to tell you what the infinitive form of a verb is (*to* + base form of the verb). Elicit some examples. Direct their attention to the last paragraph of the excerpt to find the infinitive that directly follows a verb (*try to relax*). Write this on the board in a column labeled *Infinitives*.
- **Question 4:** Elicit the infinitive in the example sentence (*to speed*). Direct students' attention to the subject of the sentence (*It*).

Method 2
(For students familiar with the structure)

- Have students work in pairs to answer the questions.
- Give students a few minutes to refer to the charts to check their answers and review the structures.
- Call on students to go over the exercise. Discuss any disagreements and have students make any necessary corrections.

FORM CHARTS

- Have students read the charts and bulleted notes.
- Choose a few verbs from each of the categories in the charts and bulleted notes and write them on the board.

Chapter 11   45

- Ask students to write sentences using each verb and either a gerund or an infinitive.
- Put students into pairs to check their sentences. Refer them to the charts for assistance.
- Call on students to share their sentences and elicit or offer feedback as necessary.
- Then write the following sentences on the board:

    Learning a foreign language takes a lot of time.
    Doing homework regularly pays because you'll get higher grades.

- Have students rewrite these sentences beginning with the pronoun *It*. Ask three students to write their answers on the board.

    It takes a lot of time to learn a foreign language.
    It pays to do homework regularly because you'll get higher grades.

- Discuss any problems and answer any questions. Refer students to Appendices 8 and 9 for more information on gerunds and infinitives.

Vocabulary Notes: Short Answers to Questions with Infinitives (p. 236)

- Write the verbs *hope, expect, plan,* and *want* on the board.
- Put students into pairs. Ask each student to write one information question beginning with *What* and one *Yes/No* question for their partner. They should use two of the different verbs on the board + an infinitive (e.g., *Do you hope to get a degree from an American university? What do you want to do once you have finished this course?*).
- Have the pairs answer each other's questions using short answers *(Yes, I hope to. Enter my degree program.).*
- Circulate, checking that students are including or omitting *to* as appropriate.

C MEANING AND USE 1

Verbs Used with Infinitives and Gerunds

EXAMINING MEANING AND USE

- Ask the class to identify the infinitive and gerund in each pair of sentences.
- Ask the students to note the differences in meaning between each pair of sentences. They should see that in the first pair of sentences, there is a clear difference in meaning. With the infinitive, the verb indicates that a purpose or future action will follow, whereas with the gerund, the verb indicates that the action is completed. In the second pair, however, the meaning is the same with both the gerund and the infinitive.
- For additional clarification of the difference in meaning of sentence pair 1, direct students' attention to the sentences that provide a context (*It's so inexpensive.* vs. *It's so expensive.*).

MEANING AND USE NOTES

- Divide students into groups and assign one of the Notes to each group.
- Tell each group to read the Note and prepare to teach the information to the class. Each group should paraphrase the information and write a few original example sentences that clearly illustrate the meaning and use. Encourage the groups presenting Notes 3 and 4 to add information about their context to make the meanings clearer.
- Circulate as the groups work, helping as necessary.
- As the groups present, ask the rest of the class if the example sentences are correct. If not, work together to improve them.

D FORM 2

More About Gerunds and Infinitives

EXAMINING FORM

Before you begin the exercise, write the following terms on the board and elicit examples:

   verb phrase (e.g., *am tired, waste time*)
   phrasal verb (e.g., *run away, look out*)
   preposition (e.g., *under, in*)
   adjective (e.g., *tired, old*)

- **Question 1:** Make sure that students understand that the gerund can be more than just verb + *ing*. It can be a gerund phrase as shown in examples a, b, and c. Have them do the task individually and then check their answers in pairs.

- Go over the answers as a group. Make sure that students correctly identify the verb phrase, phrasal verb, and preposition. In b, the gerund follows a verb phrase ending in a noun (*probably spend a lot of time*); in c, the gerund follows a phrasal verb (*end up*); in a, the gerund follows a preposition (*of*).
- **Question 2:** Have students find the underlined phrase containing an infinitive and then identify what part of speech it follows (an adjective, *anxious*).

FORM CHARTS

- Give students time to read the Notes and ask questions.
- To check their comprehension, write the following sentences on the board and ask if they are correct:

    *I'm not accustomed to listen to different accents of English. (Incorrect—*accustomed to* is a *be* + adjective + preposition combination followed by a gerund.)

    Kim is afraid of walking home alone at night, and Rika is also afraid to walk home alone. (Correct—Point out the difference between *be* + adjective + preposition followed by a gerund vs. an adjective followed by an infinitive.)

- Refer students to Appendices 8 and 9 in the Student Book for more examples. Help students memorize different infinitive and gerund forms by giving quizzes and holding competitions in class.

E MEANING AND USE 2

Interpreting Gerunds and Infinitives

EXAMINING MEANING AND USE

- Have students work in pairs to answer the questions (1. In 1a, Jane is driving and in 1b Tom is driving; 2. In 2a, Sam might come early and in 2b, Susan might come early).

- Give students a few minutes to refer to the Notes to check their answers
- Call on students to read the questions and answers aloud. Discuss any disagreements and have students make any necessary corrections.

MEANING AND USE NOTES

- Divide students into small groups and assign one of the Notes to each group.
- Tell each group to read the Note and prepare to teach the information to the class. Each group should paraphrase the information and write two example sentences that clearly illustrate the meaning and use.
- Circulate as the groups work, helping as necessary.
- As the groups present, ask the rest of the class if the example sentences are correct. If not, work together to improve them.

ADDITIONAL ACTIVITIES

Writing About Language Learning

The purpose of this activity is to practice using gerunds and infinitives by writing an essay about the difficulties of learning a foreign language.

- Tell students they will write an essay titled "Difficulties Learning a Foreign Language."
- As a class, brainstorm a list of difficulties learning a foreign language. Encourage students to phrase their ideas in gerund form. Write the suggestions on the board. (Ideas might include: learning new vocabulary, understanding idioms, remembering grammar rules, pronouncing difficult words, following what the teacher is saying in class, writing clearly, etc.).
- Divide student into small groups and ask each group to choose two or three of the items on the board and to take notes on possible ways to overcome the various difficulties. (Examples might include keeping a vocabulary notebook and studying new words every night; practicing idioms and pronunciation with a native speaker; asking the teacher to speak more slowly, keeping a writing journal, etc.)

- Once the groups finish taking notes, they can start organizing their essays. Allow students to plan their essays as a group, but insist that each student then write his or her own essay. Tell students they must include at least three sentences with gerunds or infinitives.
- Allow time in class to write the essay, or assign it for homework.
- When the essays are completed, ask students to exchange them with a partner. Have the students tell each other what they like about the essay and what ideas they would like to know more about. Each partner will also identify the sentences with gerunds or infinitives and check to see if they are formed and used correctly.
- As students discuss their essays in pairs, circulate, answering questions and checking that the sentences with gerunds and infinitives are correct.
- Finally, ask students to revise their essays, incorporating ideas from their classmates and correcting any errors in form, meaning, or use.
- Collect the essays and give students more detailed feedback.

Returning to Grammar in Discourse

The purpose of this activity is to check students' understanding of key meanings and uses of the target structures in the chapter, by returning to the excerpt at the beginning of the chapter and applying what they have learned.

- Write the following extracts from the excerpt on the board (or type them up and photocopy them before class) and have students work in pairs to find them in the excerpt. Make sure they read the complete sentences these extracts come from.
    1. . . . <u>driving</u> gives me a chance to be alone.
    2. Finally, you end up <u>saving</u> no time at all.
    3. It simply doesn't pay <u>to speed</u>.
    4. Instead of tensing your muscles, try <u>to relax</u> them.
- Now write the following on the board:
    a. *to drive*
    b. *to save*
    c. *speeding*
    d. *relaxing*
- Have students decide whether the gerunds and infinitives listed above can meaningfully and grammatically replace the underlined gerund or infinitive in the corresponding extract (1. no; 2. no; 3. no; 4. yes).
- Bring the class together. Call on pairs for the answers and have them offer explanations. If students still have problems, revisit the Meaning and Use Notes.

CHAPTER 12
Indefinite and Definite Articles; Review of Nouns

Overview

The English article system has numerous rules and exceptions, making it one of the most difficult grammar areas for students to master. This chapter reviews count and noncount nouns and presents the various rules for definite and indefinite articles. Help students understand that articles must be used for singular count nouns: indefinite if the noun is not specific and definite if it is specific (e.g., *I read a book.* vs. *I read the book you recommended.*).

Form: Students may be only familiar with the articles *a/an,* and *the*. Point out that for plural count nouns the Ø article (no article) or *some* can be used (e.g., *I had cherries/some cherries for lunch.*) and for noncount nouns *the, some,* or Ø article can be used (e.g., *I drank the milk/some milk. Milk is good for you.*).

A GRAMMAR IN DISCOURSE

Chicken Soup, Always Chicken Soup

A1: Before You Read

- Before students start reading, check their comprehension of the key word *remedy*. On the board, write: *My remedy for a cold is tea.* Have them guess the meaning of the word (something that helps treat an illness).
- Divide students into groups. Tell them to discuss the questions and encourage them to share any remedies they have discovered on their own.

A2: Read

- Before students read, ask if any of them are familiar with the basic principles of scientific research. If no one is, explain that in order to prove (or disprove) a theory or idea, researchers often conduct experiments by testing their theory on subjects (participants in an experiment) under different conditions.
- Ask students to read the excerpt and note how a medical doctor was able to prove that old-fashioned chicken soup has medicinal properties.
- Put students into pairs to discuss their answers.
- Call on several students to state the main points of the study (see lines 42–50). Write them on the board.

Cultural Notes

Natural remedies have only recently become popular in the United States, compared with their long-established use in many other countries.

A3: After You Read

- Ask students to do this exercise individually and note the places in the article where they found their answers.
- Ask them to compare answers with a partner.
- Circulate and note any problematic items. Then go over these with the whole class.
- As a follow-up activity, ask students to make a list of the natural or herbal medicines that are popular in their countries. The list should also include the conditions treated by the medicines.
- Divide students into small groups to compare their lists.
- Call on several students to share items from their list. Write these on the board.

B FORM

Indefinite and Definite Articles; Review of Nouns

EXAMINING FORM

Method 1
(For students not familiar with the structure)

- **Question 1:** Give students a few minutes to find the nouns.
- **Question 2:** Have students tell you the nouns that only have adjectives before them (*early medical literature*).
- Have students tell you the nouns that only have articles before them (*the drugs, the soup*).
- Finally elicit the nouns that have both adjectives and articles before them (*a certain chemical, a common drug*).
- **Question 3:** Have students name the nouns that do not have adjectives before them (*centuries, Chicken*).
- **Question 4:** Make two columns on the board labeled *Singular* and *Plural*. Elicit and list the singular nouns (*literature, Chicken, chemical, soup, drug*) and plural nouns (*centuries, drugs*).

Method 2
(For students familiar with the structure)

- Have students work in pairs to answer the questions.
- Give students a few minutes to refer to the charts to check their answers and review the structures.
- Call on students to go over the exercise. Discuss any disagreements and have students make any necessary corrections.

FORM CHARTS

- Give students a few minutes to read the charts and ask questions if necessary.
- Divide the class into four groups and assign each group one of the four sections of the bulleted notes. Have each group read over the information and prepare to present it to the class with examples.
- Circulate as the students work and offer assistance as necessary.

- To review, elicit the answers to these questions: *What article can we put in front of a singular count noun?* (*a, an,* and *the*); *What article can we put in front of a plural count noun?* (*the, Ø,* or *some/any*); and *What article can we put in front of a noncount noun?* (*the, Ø,* or *some/any*).
- Check students' comprehension of *some* vs. *any* by writing the following sentences on the board and asking if they are correct or incorrect and why.

  Sally doesn't want any rice with her meal. (Correct.)

  *We're going to do any homework this weekend. (Incorrect—use *any* for negative statements with noncount nouns; use *some* in affirmative statements.)

C MEANING AND USE 1

The Indefinite Article

EXAMINING MEANING AND USE

- Put students into pairs to study the sentences and discuss the questions.
- Call on several pairs to share their answers (1. 1a; 2. 2b refers to a small quantity of the underlined noun, 2a classifies the underlined noun). Ask students to explain how they arrived at their answers.
- Ask the pairs to create a context or situation in which each sentence might be heard.

MEANING AND USE NOTES

- Help students understand that the choice of article is determined by the extent to which the speaker and listener share the same information. If they do not share the information, the noun is not specific and an indefinite article is used. If they do share information, the noun is specific and the definite article is used.
- Ask students to silently read the Notes.
- For Note 1A, reinforce students' understanding of the indefinite article by having them create additional sentences. Give each student a verb/noun pair, such as *read/book, went/restaurant, visited/friend,* and ask them, *What did you do*

last night? (*I read a book. I went to a restaurant, I visited a friend.*).

- For Note 2, put students into pairs and have them interview each other about the occupations of their family and friends. For example, *What does your mother/father/sister/brother do? My mother is an artist. My father is a truck driver.*
- Then have the pairs write down a general statement about each occupation they mentioned above (e.g., *Doctors have to be on call all the time. Students don't have a lot of free time. Real estate agents have flexible hours.*).

D MEANING AND USE 2

The Definite Article

EXAMINING MEANING AND USE

- Put students into pairs to read and discuss the sentences and questions.
- Go over the activity as a class. For each question, call on a different pair to answer the question and explain what information in the sentence helped them to arrive at the answer (1. b, because the word *sweater* is mentioned twice; 2. a, because the sentence says *the mayor* and *the news*, so it is clear that the speaker and the listener live in the same city; 3. c, because the listener can obviously see the salt being referred to).

MEANING AND USE NOTES

- Read the introduction to the first Note out loud.
- Divide the class into small groups and assign one of the Notes to each group.
- Tell each group to read their Note and prepare to teach the explanation to the class. Each group should paraphrase the explanation and write two new example sentences that clearly illustrate the meaning and use.
- Circulate as the groups work, helping as necessary.
- As the groups present, ask the rest of the class if the example sentences are correct. If not, work together to improve them.

Vocabulary Notes: *Another* vs. *The Other* (p. 268)

- Have students read the Notes.
- Point out that a way to remember that *another* is indefinite is to look at the beginning of the word; it begins with *an*, which is an indefinite article.
- Check students' comprehension of the Notes by writing these sentences on the board and asking students to complete them using *another* or *the other*.

    I speak two languages. One is English, and . . . (*the other . . .*)

    Two students have read this book; one liked it, but . . . (*the other . . .*)

    Someone stole my book, so I had to buy . . . (*another . . .*)

    There are so many countries I'd like to visit. One is Australia and . . . (*another is . . .*)

Beyond the Sentence: Connecting Information (p. 269)

This section is intended to give students practice with the meaning and use of grammar as it functions naturally in extended discourse such as paragraphs and conversations.

- Ask students to read the explanation and the paragraph once for general meaning.
- Elicit the main idea of the paragraph. (A family got a puppy, and the boy loved it so much that, at first, he slept in the kitchen with it.)
- Ask students to circle the indefinite articles and underline the definite articles in the paragraph. There is one indefinite article and five definite articles.
- Tell students to think about why these articles were used in these sentences.
- Call on students to share their answers.
- Then point out to students the bolded pronouns in the paragraph. Remind them that pronouns also help make sentences clear and connect ideas in a paragraph or conversation.

E MEANING AND USE 3

Article Use with Generic Nouns

EXAMINING MEANING AND USE

Before you start the exercise, you may want to do the following task to review the concept of a class of nouns.

- Write the following lists of nouns on the board and have students name the class for each list. Write the class above each list.

Chinese	apple	penguin
Spanish	peach	eagle
Farsi	plum	parrot
French	banana	ostrich
Greek	orange	hawk

  (The classification for column 1 is *languages*, column 2 is *fruit*, and column 3 is *birds*.)

- Once students understand the concept of a class of nouns, put them into pairs and ask them to examine the sentences in their books and answer the questions.

- Call on individual students to tell you which underlined nouns refer to a whole class or group of nouns (1b, 2a, 3b, and 4a). Then ask other students to identify the underlined nouns that refer to a specific noun or nouns (1a, 2b, 3a, and 4b).

MEANING AND USE NOTES

- Read Note 1 out loud. Explain that this Note introduces the other Notes in the section.
- Give students time to read Notes 2, 3, and 4. Answer any questions or clarify meaning as needed.
- Divide students into small groups. Give each group a different singular count noun. Ask them to write three sentences that use the noun generically: one with no article, one with an indefinite article, and one with the definite article. Tell students to provide a context if necessary to clarify the use of the articles. Possible singular count nouns:

  <u>cell phone</u> (e.g., *Cell phones are popular with teenagers. A cell phone is not as reliable as a standard phone. The cell phone is a useful invention for business people.*)

  <u>family</u> (e.g., *Families like to spend the holidays together. A family consists of a person's closest relatives. The family is important to a well-functioning society.*)

  <u>airplane</u>

  <u>computer</u>

  <u>microwave</u>

- As the groups work, circulate and help as necessary.
- Call one student from each group to write the group's sentences on the board. Ask the class to comment on accuracy of form and on correct meaning and use.

Beyond the Sentence: Indefinite Generic Nouns in Discourse (p. 274)

This section is intended to give students practice with the meaning and use of grammar as it functions naturally in extended discourse such as paragraphs and conversations.

- Ask students to read the explanation and the paragraph for the main idea.
- Elicit the generic noun that the paragraph is about *(an onion/onions)*. Reinforce the idea that despite repeated use, *onion* does not become definite because it is generic.
- Ask students where they would expect to see a paragraph like this one (in a magazine or book). Point out that this style of writing or speaking is considered more formal.

F ADDITIONAL ACTIVITIES

Conducting and Presenting a Survey

The purpose of this activity is to give students exposure to writing, conducting, and presenting a survey, while applying the varied rules for using articles discussed in this chapter.

- Divide students into small groups.
- Explain that each group will survey people outside the class, asking them how they feel about using natural remedies for a particular health problem, e.g., headaches, stress, insomnia, backaches. Explain that when they finish the survey, they will compile and present their findings to the class.

- Give each group time in class to decide which type of health problem they want to investigate, or assign specific health problems if time is limited. Then have the students write questions for their interview (e.g., *What do you do when you have a headache? Have you ever taken herbs for this?*). Each group should have three to five questions in the survey. Make sure each group member has a copy of the survey.
- Review polite ways to approach people to survey (e.g., *Excuse me. Could you answer a few questions for me?* or *Excuse me. Would you mind answering a few questions?*).
- Encourage students to practice asking their survey questions in their groups before they talk to people outside the class.
- For homework, have individual students survey people on their campus or in their community. Tell them to take notes on people's responses.
- Back in class, have the groups compile their results. They should write a general summary of the different responses for each question. Ask the groups to also discuss the implications or significance of their answers. Give them an example, such as *Do you think that more people are using natural cures for their health problems?*
- Explain that during the presentation, one student will introduce the topic and read the questions from the group survey; another will present the results; and the others will present the implications of the results. Each presentation should contain at least one definition (e.g., *Acupuncture is a type of medicine from China in which the doctor puts needles in special places on the patient's body.*). This definition will familiarize the class with the topic while practicing the indefinite article.
- Ask the class to take notes on the use of articles as the groups present.
- Note article use as well and give the groups written or oral feedback at the end of the presentation.

Returning to Grammar in Discourse

The purpose of this activity is to check students' understanding of key meanings and uses of the target structures in the chapter, by returning to the excerpt at the beginning of the chapter and applying what they have learned.

- Write the following extracts from the excerpt on the board (or type them up and photocopy them before class) and have students work in pairs to find them in the excerpt. Make sure they read the complete sentences these extracts come from.
    1. *The prescription was probably effective because . . .*
    2. *This substance is remarkably similar to a common drug for bronchitis . . .*
    3. *Dr. Sackner is the author of the famous chicken soup study . . .*
    4. *In fact, the drug was originally made from chicken feathers and skin.*
- Now write the following on the board:
    a. The noun is mentioned for the first time in the context.
    b. The noun is mentioned previously in the context.
    c. The noun is considered to be unique.
- Have students think about the use of articles in the underlined noun phrase in each extract, and match each one to the letter above that best explain the reason for its use (1. b; 2. a; 3. c; 4. b).
- Bring the class together. Call on pairs for the answers and have them offer explanations. If students still have problems, revisit the Meaning and Use Notes.

CHAPTER 13
Relative Clauses with Subject Relative Pronouns

Overview
Relative clauses are dependent clauses that modify nouns. This chapter focuses exclusively on relative clauses with subject relative pronouns. There are two types of relative clauses: restrictive and nonrestrictive. A restrictive relative clause is used to distinguish one noun from another (e.g., *The company that produces women's hair products is going bankrupt.*). A nonrestrictive relative clause is used to provide extra information about a noun (e.g., *The company's products, which are made from 100 percent organic materials, are very expensive.*).

Form: Typical errors students make with relative clauses are incorrectly placing the clause in the sentence (e.g., **Mr. Berry lives in San Francisco, who is my English teacher.* Incorrect) and not knowing which relative pronoun to use (e.g., **Mr. Berry, that is my English teacher, lives in San Francisco.* Incorrect).

A GRAMMAR IN DISCOURSE

Formal Wear Gives Company New Attitude

A1: Before You Read
- Give students some time to discuss the questions in their books in pairs. Call on several students to share their answers.
- Ask the class if they know the meaning of *Casual Friday* and *dressing down*. If they don't, explain that *Casual Friday* refers to the common practice in American workplaces of wearing casual clothes (or dressing down) on Friday, the last day of the American workweek.

Cultural Notes
One generalization often made about Americans is that they are very casual dressers, especially at work.

A2: Read
- Before students start reading, write the title of the article on the board and explain any unknown vocabulary. Ask students to guess what the article is about. Write their predictions on the board.
- Have students read the article to find out why one business decided that its employees should dress formally.

A3: After You Read
- Before they begin the exercise, have students compare the predictions on the board with the information in the article to see if they guessed correctly.
- Have students do the exercise individually and mark the places in the text where they found the answers.
- Ask them to compare answers with a partner.
- Circulate and note any difficult or problematic items. Then go over these with the whole class.
- As a follow-up activity, write these questions on the board: *Would you prefer to dress casually or formally for work? All the time or some of the time? What are the advantages and disadvantages of each? Is formal dress more important for certain professions?*
- Divide students into small groups to discuss the questions.
- Call on a member of each group to summarize the group's position for the class.
- Take a quick poll to find out how students prefer to dress for work.

B FORM

Relative Clauses with Subject Relative Pronouns

EXAMINING FORM

Method 1
(For students not familiar with the structure)

- **Question 1:** Have students look at the three underlined relative clauses in the article. Then have them underline six more.
- Call on several students to write each sentence on the board and underline the relative clause. Check that the commas have been copied correctly.
- **Question 2:** Have a new group of students come to the board to circle the subject relative pronoun (*who, which,* or *that*) in each relative clause and the noun or noun phrase it refers to.
- **Question 3:** Ask two students to come to the board and label the sentences as having restrictive or nonrestrictive relative clauses. They should write *R* next to those with restrictive relative clauses and *NR* next to those with nonrestrictive relative clauses. Remind students that nonrestrictive relative clauses are surrounded by commas, and restrictive relative clauses are not.

Method 2
(For students familiar with the structure)

- Have students work in pairs to answer the questions.
- Give students a few minutes to refer to the charts to check their answers and review the structures.
- Call on students to go over the exercise. Discuss any disagreements and have students make any necessary corrections.

FORM CHARTS

- Give students time to read the charts and the bulleted notes and ask questions.
- Write the following sentences on the board and have students copy them in their notebooks:

    Belinda knows a man . . .
    I have a friend . . .
    He likes eating food . . .
    We saw a movie . . .

- Tell students to add a relative clause to each sentence.
- When they are finished, call on a few students to write their completed sentences on the board.
- Check students' comprehension of the bulleted notes by having them look at the sentences on the board and identify the subject of each relative clause. Make sure students understand that the verb in the relative clause agrees with the noun in the main clause.
- Ask students if they added restrictive or nonrestrictive relative clauses. If necessary, refer students to the bulleted notes to go over the difference between the two.
- For more practice, write the following sentences on the board. Explain that each sentence has a relative clause error. Give students time to read the sentences and discuss them in pairs. Call on individual students to explain the errors.

    *I like movies that they are romantic. (Incorrect—the pronoun *they* should not be used after the subject relative pronoun *that.*)
    *I saw three students who is in my class. (Incorrect—the verb in the relative clause, *is*, should be plural to agree with the noun in the main clause, *three students.*)
    *San Francisco, that is in California, is my favorite city. (Incorrect—*that* is used only in restrictive relative clauses. *Which* is the relative pronoun that must be used here.)

C MEANING AND USE 1

Identifying Nouns with Restrictive Relative Clauses

EXAMINING MEANING AND USE

- Have students work in pairs to answer the questions (1. 1b; 2. 2b).
- Give students a few minutes to read the Notes to check their answers.
- Then call on students to read the questions and answers out loud. Elicit corrections.

Chapter 13   55

MEANING AND USE NOTES

- First, ask students to explain the meaning of *restrict*. Students might use gestures to illustrate the definition (limiting or making something smaller).
- For Note 1A, read the information out loud and ask students to explain the difference in meaning between the two pairs of sentences. (In the sentence without a relative clause, it is not clear which girl and boy are B's children. The sentence with the relative clause provides clear information identifying B's boy and girl.)
- Divide students into small groups and assign them Notes 1B or 1C. Tell each group to read and discuss the Note and example sentences. Then have them write two original example sentences, one with and one without a relative clause.
- Circulate as the groups work, helping as necessary.
- Ask a student from each group to write the group's sentences on the board. The class should decide which sentences are more descriptive: those with or without relative clauses. Leave the sentences on the board.
- Give students time to read Note 2. Check for comprehension and discuss as necessary.
- If any of the student sentences on the board have a subject relative pronoun + *be*, ask students to come to the board and reduce the restrictive clauses. If none of the clauses can be reduced, write the following examples on the board for students to reduce:

  The man who is standing on the corner is my brother. (The man standing on the corner is my brother.)

  The movie that is at the Lido this week is great. (The movie at the Lido this week is great.)

Beyond the Sentence: Combining Sentences with Relative Clauses (p. 293)

This section is intended to give your students practice with the meaning and use of grammar as it functions naturally in extended discourse such as paragraphs and conversations.

- Tell students to close their books. Read the two paragraphs out loud and have students tell you which one is smoother and less repetitious (paragraph 2). Then ask them why. (It uses relative clauses.)
- Tell students to open their books and read the two paragraphs silently. Ask them to note the number of sentences in each paragraph. Elicit which has fewer (paragraph 2). Ask students to circle each noun in paragraph 1 that is replaced with a relative clause in paragraph 2.

D) MEANING AND USE 2

Adding Extra Information with Nonrestrictive Relative Clauses

EXAMINING MEANING AND USE

- Have students work in pairs to answer the questions (1. a, necessary information; b, not essential information; 2. b).
- Give students a few minutes to read the Notes to check their answers.
- Then call on students to read the questions and answers out loud. Discuss any disagreements and have students make any necessary corrections.

MEANING AND USE NOTES

- Have students read the information in Note 1A to check if they understand the difference between the two types of relative clauses in the Examining Meaning and Use exercise above.
- Tell students to read Note 1B silently. Then write this sentence on the board to elicit if it is possible to use a restrictive relative clause with a proper noun or a unique noun: *My father who lives in Germany called me last week.* (No, it is not possible. This sentence is incorrect because proper nouns and unique nouns are already restricted. An exception is the case where there is more than one proper or unique noun, e.g., *I went to the Manhattan that is in Kansas, not the one that is in New York.*)
- Have students practice writing nonrestrictive relative clauses with proper nouns by writing sentences about the cities they live in, come from, and would like to visit.
- Give a few models on the board first:

I come from New York, which is the city that never sleeps.

I would like to visit Venice, Italy, which has river canals.

- Have students share their answers in small groups. Then ask a few volunteers to write their sentences on the board. Elicit and offer feedback as necessary.

- Have students read Note 2. It reminds students that restrictive relative clauses allow us to distinguish one noun from another, while nonrestrictive relative clauses simply add extra information about a noun. Write this sentence on the board and ask if it is restrictive or nonrestrictive: *My mother, who is a teacher, lives in Kansas.* (nonrestrictive). Then ask why it cannot be rewritten as a restrictive relative clause. (We have only one mother, so we do not need to distinguish which mother we are referring to.)

- For Note 3, write the first example sentence (*I spoke to Pedro, who is the boss.*) on the board, and explain that this form can be reduced by omitting the relative pronoun + *be*. Cross out these words in the example sentence.

- To check students' understanding, write these sentences on the board and elicit the reduced forms from the class.

    I phoned Alex, who is my friend. (I phoned Alex, my friend.)
    Teresa, who was lying in the sun, felt sleepy. (Teresa, lying in the sun, felt sleepy).

ADDITIONAL ACTIVITIES

Writing About One's Closest Friend

The purpose of this activity is for students to practice using relative clauses with subject relative pronouns in a writing assignment about one's closest friend.

- Have students freewrite (write without stopping and worrying about grammar or spelling) about their closest friend. Tell them they can write about anything that comes to mind connected to this friend: the friend's background, education, appearance, personality, habits, hobbies, etc. Once most students have written about a page, tell the class to stop writing.

- Have students share their freewrite with a partner. Then tell them to reread what they wrote and see if there are any short or disconnected sentences that could be combined with relative clauses. Circulate and offer assistance as students work.

- For homework, have students use the freewrite from class to write an essay about their closest friend.

- Back in class, have students exchange essays and note the use of relative pronouns. Encourage students to suggest to each other additional areas where relative pronouns can be used to connect ideas.

- Collect student essays and give feedback on form, meaning, and use.

Returning to Grammar in Discourse

The purpose of this activity is to check students' understanding of key meanings and uses of the target structures in the chapter, by returning to the article at the beginning of the chapter and applying what they have learned.

- Write the following extracts from the article on the board (or type them up and photocopy them before class) and have students work in pairs to find them in the article. Make sure they read the complete sentences these extracts come from.
    1. *. . . which is a marketing and public relations firm.*
    2. *. . . that is also good for business.*
    3. *. . . that had read about Formal Fridays.*
    4. *. . . who wears gowns and tuxedos . . .*
    5. *. . . who was dressed in a tuxedo.*

- Now write the following on the board:
    a. *adds information that identifies the noun*
    b. *adds information that is not essential for identifying the noun*

- Have students match the letter that best describes the relative clause in the numbered example (1. b; 2. a; 3. a; 4. a; 5. b).

- Bring the class together. Call on pairs for the answers and have them offer explanations. If students still have problems, revisit the Meaning and Use Notes.

CHAPTER 14
Relative Clauses with Object Relative Pronouns

Overview
Whereas relative clauses with subject relative pronouns differ in form from those with object relative pronouns, their meanings and uses are similar. Relative clauses with object relative pronouns can be restrictive, used to distinguish one noun from another (e.g., *I helped the kind man who I met at the bus stop.*), and nonrestrictive, used to provide extra information about a noun (e.g., *The blue house on our block, which I pass every day, has been robbed.*).

Form: One key difference in form between subject and object relative pronouns is that object relative pronouns are followed by a subject + verb (e.g., *I read the essay that Roberta wrote.*), and subject relative pronouns are followed by a verb (e.g., *Roberta, who is a good writer, won a scholarship.*).

A GRAMMAR IN DISCOURSE
The New Face of a Role Model

A1: Before You Read
- Ask students if they enjoy playing or watching soccer. Ask if they saw or remember the 1999 Women's World Cup. Then ask if anyone remembers who won the championship and who some of the stars were. Ask if anyone recognizes the name Mia Hamm and explain that the class is going to read an article about her.
- Before students look at the article, elicit the meaning of *role model* by giving students a few example sentences and asking them to guess the meaning of the term. (*A lot of kids want to grow up and be like Michael Jordan; he is a role model to them. My daughter's role model is our doctor. She wants to be just like her when she grows up.*)
- Put students into pairs to discuss the questions in the book.
- Call on several students to share their opinions about the qualities of a good role model. Write these on the board to refer to during the After You Read activity.

A2: Read
- Tell students they will read about soccer star Mia Hamm to find out what she thinks about being a role model.
- Do the reading in two parts. First ask students to silently read the section before the interview and prepare a one-minute oral summary. Tell them to jot down notes as they read.
- Put students into pairs to present their summaries to each other.
- Have students read the interview section of the article silently to themselves. Then have them read the interview out loud in pairs, with one partner reading the interviewer's part and the other reading Mia Hamm's part.

Cultural Notes
This article introduces students to an important element of America's battle with discrimination: the relatively recent enactment of laws providing girls with equal access to school sports. This issue may come as a surprise to many students, who may come from countries where women never engage in sports, or conversely, countries where no law has ever been necessary because women and men have always been treated equally in sports.

A3: After You Read
- Have students do this exercise individually and mark the places in the text where they found the answers.
- Ask them to compare answers with a partner.

- Circulate and note any problematic items. Then go over these with the whole class.
- As a follow-up activity, put students into pairs and have them compare the information on the board from the Before You Read about good role-model qualities with the information in the article about Mia Hamm. On the board write: *Do you think Mia Hamm is a good role model? Why or why not?*
- Call on students to share their answers.

B FORM 1

Relative Clauses with Object Relative Pronouns

EXAMINING FORM

Method 1
(For students not familiar with the structure)

- **Question 1:** Elicit the relative pronouns that students have been working with (*who, that,* and *which*).
- Write the first sentence from the first paragraph of the article on the board (*The Women's World Cup, which the media called the biggest female sporting event in history, arrived for the first time in the United States in 1999.*). Underline the relative clause as in the book.
- Elicit the object relative pronoun of the clause (*which*). Circle it on the board.
- Elicit the noun or noun phrase it modifies (*The Women's World Cup*). Circle it on the board.
- Ask students to examine each relative clause with an object relative pronoun and mark it in the same way in their books.
- **Question 2:** Direct students' attention to the subtitle of the article. Write it on the board (*In women's soccer, girls finally get the role model they deserve: Mia Hamm.*).
- Elicit the relative clause (*they deserve*). Elicit the noun it modifies (*role model*).
- Ask students what the object relative pronoun is. (There is none.) Explain that the relative pronoun is implied. Insert the pronoun *that* or *who* into the sentence on the board. Remind students that one of these pronouns must be used because *role model* refers to a person. The pronoun *which* cannot be used, because it refers to things.
- Give students time to insert a pronoun into the other relative clauses that are missing one in the rest of the article.
- Circulate, helping students to choose a pronoun based on the noun it modifies. Several answers are possible.

Method 2
(For students familiar with the structure)

- Have students work in pairs to answer the questions.
- Give students a few minutes to refer to the charts to check their answers.
- Call on students to go over the exercise. Discuss any disagreements and have students make any necessary corrections.

FORM CHARTS

- Tell students to read the example sentences in the charts and then the bulleted notes. Ask them to tell you which relative pronouns can be used with each kind of relative clause, restrictive and nonrestrictive. (In restrictive clauses, *who, whom,* and *that* are used for people; *which* and *that* are used for things. In nonrestrictive clauses, *who* and *whom* are used for people; *which* is used for things.)
- Students may need more practice identifying object relative pronouns. Write the following sentences on the board. Have students identify the relative clause and the relative pronoun and tell you whether the relative pronoun is the subject or object of the clause.

    The movie that you told me about was terrible. (The relative pronoun, *that*, is the object of the relative clause.)

    My friend who works at the university is coming for dinner. (The relative pronoun, *who*, is the subject of the relative clause.)

    The fish that we had last night was delicious. (The relative pronoun, *that*, is the object of the relative clause.)

    New York, which we visited last year, is my favorite city. (The relative pronoun, *which*, is the object of the relative clause.)

- If necessary, tell students that the easiest way to determine whether a relative pronoun is an object relative pronoun is to see if a noun or pronoun directly follows the relative pronoun. If so, that noun or pronoun is the subject of the relative clause and the relative pronoun is the object of the clause. (For example, *We looked at the photos that we had bought*. In the relative clause *that we had bought*, the subject is *we* and the object is the relative pronoun *that*.)
- Follow up by asking students in which sentences on the board we can omit the relative pronoun (Sentences 1 and 3). To explain Sentence 2, point out that we cannot delete the subject relative pronoun because the verb in the clause is *work* (and not *be* + participle or *be* + prepositional phrase). For Sentence 4, point out that object relative pronouns cannot be omitted when the relative clause is nonrestrictive.

Vocabulary Notes: Object Relative Pronouns (p. 307)

- Give students time to read the Notes.
- Divide students into small groups and ask them to write two sentences using an object relative clause with *who*. Tell them to think of a situation in which these sentences would be appropriate (talking to a friend, writing a personal letter, etc.).
- Ask students to write the same sentences again using *whom*. Tell them to think of a situation in which these sentences would be appropriate (talking to a professor, writing a business letter, etc.).
- Call on several students to share their answers. Write them on the board.
- Ask another student to come to the board to delete the relative pronouns where possible.

C) MEANING AND USE 1

Identifying Nouns and Adding Extra Information

EXAMINING MEANING AND USE

- Read each sentence in the Student Book out loud. Ask students to identify the relative clause in each one. (In 1a, the relative clause is *that costs $200*. In 1b, the relative clause is *you wanted*—there is an omitted object relative pronoun. In 2a, the relative clause is *who was only 16*. In 2b, the relative clause is *who I know*.)
- Elicit a possible relative pronoun for the one omitted in sentence 1b (*that* or *which*).
- Have students answer the questions in pairs. Then call on individual students to explain their answers. (The noun referred to in both 1a and 1b is *coat*; the noun referred to in 2a and 2b is *Megan Quann*.)
- Elicit that sentences 1a and 1b contain restrictive relative clauses, which help to identify the noun, and that sentences 2a and 2b contain nonrestrictive relative clauses, which provide extra information about the noun but are not needed to identify it.

MEANING AND USE NOTES

- Have students close their books. Write several example sentences from the Notes on the board and ask students to explain the purpose of each relative clause (to identify the noun in restrictive clauses; to add extra information in nonrestrictive clauses).
- Ask students to open their books and read Note 1B silently. Then have them work in pairs to write two new sentences using a relative clause with an object relative pronoun. One sentence should introduce a person using an indefinite article. The second sentence should talk about a definite noun (e.g., *A man I know sells cars. That's the student who I met on the bus.*).
- Call on several students to read their sentences to the class. Offer feedback as necessary.

D) FORM 2

Object Relative Pronouns with Prepositions

EXAMINING FORM

Method 1
(For students not familiar with the structure)

- Do a quick review of prepositions. Write this sentence on the board: *I put the apple on the table.* Underline the word *on*, and ask students to name the part of speech (preposition). Tell students to name other prepositions. Write them on the board.

- Have students read the sentences in the exercise and ask if they have the same meaning (yes).
- **Question 1:** Then have students work individually to identify the object relative pronouns and prepositions. (In sentence a, the object relative pronoun is *that* and the preposition is *about*. In sentence b, *about* is the preposition and *which* is the object relative pronoun.)
- **Question 2:** Write the sentences on the board. Give students a minute to examine the prepositions. Then ask a student to come to the board to label the words in the relative clauses (object relative pronoun + subject + verb + preposition for sentence a; preposition + object relative pronoun + subject + verb for sentence b). Offer feedback as necessary.
- Elicit from students that the relative pronoun *that* in sentence a can be replaced by *which* or omitted altogether. In sentence b, only the relative pronoun *which* can be used.

Method 2
(For students familiar with the structure)

- Have students work in pairs to answer the questions.
- Give students a few minutes to refer to the charts to check their answers and review the structures.
- Call on students to go over the exercise. Discuss any disagreements and have students make any necessary corrections.

FORM CHARTS

- Ask students to read the charts and bulleted notes silently.
- Put students into pairs and have them write four new sentences with relative clauses, two ending in prepositions and two beginning with prepositions.
- Circulate as students work and offer feedback.
- Call on pairs to write their sentences on the board. Elicit corrections from the class.

E MEANING AND USE 2

Reducing Relative Clauses

EXAMINING MEANING AND USE

- Ask students if the three sentences in their book express the same idea (yes).
- Then give them a few minutes to think about and answer the question. (Sentence b sounds the most formal.)
- Give students a few minutes to refer to the Notes to check their answers.
- Discuss any problems as a class and have students make any necessary corrections.

MEANING AND USE NOTES

- By this point, students should know that it is possible to omit the relative pronoun as well as write a relative clause with the preposition at the end (e.g., *Give the names of two professors you have taken courses with.*). However, they may not know which of these options to choose when speaking or writing. Have students read the Notes.
- Then write the following sentences on the board:
  1. a. *Have you finished the work about which you were talking?*
     b. *Have you finished the work you were talking about?*
  2. a. *He attended the lecture in which he was interested.*
     b. *He attended the lecture he was interested in.*
  3. a. *The least expensive thing I saw that you would like is a silver ring.*
     b. *The least expensive thing that I saw that you would like is a silver ring.*
- For the first pair of sentences, ask *Where does the preposition move to when we omit the relative pronoun?* (To the end of the sentence as in 1b.)
- For the second pair of sentences, ask *Which sentence is more formal?* (2a) *Why?* (The preposition is before the relative pronoun.)
- For the third pair of sentences, ask *What is the difference between these sentences?* (In sentence a the first object relative pronoun is omitted.)

Vocabulary Notes: *When* and *Where* in Relative Clauses (p. 320)

- Give students time to read the Notes.
- Divide them into small groups and ask them to write two sentences using *when* and *where* as replacements for prepositions and object relative pronouns. Tell them they can write about a school where they studied English before (e.g., *The school where I studied English in my country was . . .*) and a time when they did something interesting (e.g., *The summer when I traveled through Europe was . . .*).
- Call on several groups to share their sentences. Write them on the board and elicit corrections as necessary.

ADDITIONAL ACTIVITIES

Writing About a Role Model

The purpose of this activity is for students to write an essay about a role model they had when they were growing up, using relative clauses with object relative pronouns.

- Have students list in their notebooks all the good role models they had when they were growing up. Stress that role models don't have to be rich or famous and that their list can include parents, older friends, and other people they have known. Remind students that good role models are people with important qualities they admire, such as generosity, intelligence, discipline, or great talent.
- Then tell students to look over their list, choose their most important and influential role model, and briefly write down all the characteristics of that person.
- Tell students that they will write a one-page essay describing their role model and explaining why this person was important to them and how he or she influenced them. Remind students to use at least three relative clauses with object relative pronouns.
- When students finish, put them into pairs and have them exchange essays. The reader must tell the writer one thing he or she liked about the essay and two things he or she would like to know more about.
- Ask students to revise their essays, incorporating the feedback from their partner.
- After they write the second draft, have students underline each relative clause, double-underline the relative pronoun in each relative clause, and examine the clause for form, meaning, and use. (This includes determining that the appropriate level of formality was used.)
- Review students' essays to correct any errors in form, meaning, or use.

Returning to Grammar in Discourse

The purpose of this activity is to check students' understanding of key meanings and uses of the target structures in the chapter, by returning to the article at the beginning of the chapter and applying what they have learned.

- Write the following extracts from the article on the board (or type them up and photocopy them before class) and have students work in pairs to find them in the article. Make sure they read the complete sentences these extracts come from.
    1. *. . . girls finally get the role model they deserve . . .*
    2. *. . . it was her father's soccer passion that she followed*
    3. *Here are some things that she says about life . . .*
    4. *What's the most important thing your mother taught you?*
- *Now write the following on the board:*
    a. *who*
    b. *which*
    c. *that*
    d. *no relative pronoun*
- Have students think about the use of object relative pronouns in each extract and match all other possible relative pronouns from the list above that could replace them (1. a, b, c; 2. b, d; 3. b, d; 4. b, c).
- Bring the class together. Call on pairs for the answers and have them offer explanations. If students still have problems, revisit the Meaning and Use Notes.

62   Chapter 14

CHAPTER 15

Real Conditionals, Unreal Conditionals, and Wishes

Overview

This chapter introduces real and unreal conditionals, and wishes. The real conditional is used for events that could potentially happen (e.g., *If I study for this test, I will pass it.*), or to express a fact (e.g., *If you heat ice, it melts.*). The unreal conditional is used for imaginary situations (e.g., *If I had a million dollars, I would quit my job.*). Similar to the unreal conditional, the verb *wish* is used to express a desire for an unreal situation (e.g., *I wish I had a million dollars.*).

Form: Students are often confused by the past tense form in unreal conditionals (e.g., *If she knew how to sew, she would save a lot of money.*), which does not indicate past time, but indicates that the situation is not real at the present time (in the above example, she does not know how to sew).

A) GRAMMAR IN DISCOURSE

Reflections on Life

A1: Before You Read

- Ask students to make a list of three to five wishes they have. Give them some examples to encourage diverse responses (e.g., *live in a different time period, be president, be rich*). Tell them they do not need to write in complete sentences.
- Put students in pairs to compare their lists and discuss the questions.

A2: Read

- For students who have not heard of the various writers, explain that Sir Walter Alexander Raleigh (not to be confused with the explorer Sir Walter Raleigh) was a British essayist and critic who lived in the late 1800s/early 1900s. Jane Seymour is a British actress who has appeared in American films and television. Nadine Stair was an American woman who was eighty-five years old when she wrote this poem (which is often incorrectly attributed to Jorge Luis Borges, the Latin American poet). Elicit the meaning of *anonymous*. Ask *Is it a name?* (*Anonymous* means *not named or identified*. This word is used when the name of a writer is unknown.)
- Ask students to follow along in their books as you read the Chinese proverb.
- Elicit the main idea and write it on the board. (Peace in the world depends on the interrelation between the individual, the family, and the nation.)
- Divide students into three groups and assign one of the three remaining passages to each group. Ask the groups to read their passage and summarize the writer's outlook. Have a member of each group write the summary on the board.
- Tell students to silently read the summaries on the board and decide which is closest to his or her personal outlook on life and why.
- Have students discuss their opinions in groups.
- Call on several students to report the opinions from their group.

A3: After You Read

- Ask students to do this exercise individually and mark the places in the text where they found their answers.
- Have them compare answers with a partner.
- Circulate and note any difficult or problematic items. Then go over these with the whole class.
- As a follow-up, write these questions on the board for the students to discuss in groups: *Is there anything in your life that you regret doing or not doing? Do you know anyone who regrets doing or not doing something?*

- Some students may be reluctant to speak about themselves or those close to them in this way. If so, do not pressure them. Tell them to simply invent someone to speak about.
- Put students into pairs to discuss their answers.
- Then call on a few students to share their answers.

B) FORM

Real Conditionals, Unreal Conditionals, and Wishes

EXAMINING FORM

Method 1:
(For students not familiar with the structure)
Before you start the Examining Form, you may want to do the following exercise with your students to review the terms *clause* (*dependent* and *independent*) and the verb *wish*.

- Write this sentence on the board: *If I had a kitten, I would be very happy.*
- Ask students if they can identify which part of the sentence is a clause (there are two clauses: *If I had a kitten* and *I would be very happy*). If necessary, confirm that students know what exactly a clause is (a group of words that has a subject and verb). Note the subject and verb in each of the above clauses (*I had* and *I would be*).
- Ask the students these questions to test their knowledge: *Which of the two clauses in the above sentence can stand alone and make sense?* (*I would be very happy*); *What is the name of this type of clause?* (independent, not dependent on another clause); *Can the other clause stand alone and make sense?* (No, it leaves you waiting for more information.); *What is the name of this type of clause?* (dependent, it depends on another clause). Explain that a clause starting with *if* is a dependent clause and needs a main clause to accompany it.
- Finally write the sentence *I wish I had a kitten*. Ask students what the sentence means (I would like a kitten very much, but I don't have one.).

- **Questions 1 and 2:** Have a student read out the underlined example of an *if* clause in the Chinese Proverb, and write the complete sentence on the board (*If there is light in the soul, there will be beauty in the person.*).
- Have students give you another example of the real conditional with the simple present in the *if* clause (*If there is beauty in the person . . .*). Write the complete sentence under the other one on the board and label this column *Real Conditionals*.
- Ask students to call out the other two examples (*If there is harmony. . .* and *If there is order. . .*) and ask two students to write these in the same column.
- Have students find the sentences with the simple past in the *if* clause in selections 2 and 3 (selection 2: *if I had it to do over again* and *if I had my life to live over*; selection 3: *if it were over tomorrow*). Call on two students to write the complete sentences on the board in another column. Label this column *Unreal Conditionals*.
- Ask one student to come to the board and underline the verbs in the *if* clauses of both types of conditional sentences and explain to the class which tense is used in each type (present in real conditionals, past in unreal conditionals).
- Have another student come to the board to underline and describe to the class the verb forms in the main clause for both real and unreal conditional sentences (*will* + verb in real, *would* + verb in unreal).
- **Question 3:** Tell students to underline all the verbs that follow *wish* in the Sir Walter Alexander Raleigh passage. Explain that in sentences with *wish*, the simple past is used in the *that* clause. If necessary, clarify that *that* is left out of the sentences, but it is implied.
- Leave the sentences from Examining Form on the board to refer to when introducing the Form Notes.

Method 2
(For students familiar with the structure)
- Have students work in pairs to answer the questions.

- Give students a few minutes to refer to the charts to check their answers and review the structures.
- Call on students to go over the exercise. Discuss any disagreements and have students make any necessary corrections.

FORM CHARTS

- Divide students into groups. Tell them to read the charts and mark any new verb forms in the main clauses that are not in the sentences on the board. (*Be going to, could, might,* and *may* can be used in addition to *will* in the real conditional main clause. *Could* and *might* can be used in addition to *would* in the unreal conditional main clause.)
- Tell students to skim the bulleted notes and write three examples each of the real and unreal conditional using the new verb forms. Circulate and offer feedback as necessary.
- Have the students read the chart *Wishes About the Present and Future*. Tell them to note the verb forms in sentences with *wish* that are not on the board (negative, past continuous, would, could).
- As students mark the new forms for unreal conditionals and wish sentences, point out that in these types of sentences, *be* changes to *were* with all subjects.

Informally Speaking: Using *Was* (p. 334)

- Choose two students to read the text in the speech bubbles. Then tell the class you will play the recording and that they should listen to how the underlined form in the cartoon is different from what they hear. If needed, play the recording more than once.
- Have students point out the differences. (The cartoon reads *I wish I were taller*. On the recording the form is *I wish I was taller*. The cartoon reads *If it were earlier*, whereas on the recording the form is *If it was earlier*.) Explain that the form on the cassette is considered more informal English. Point out that the form in the cartoon is standard English and students should use this form when writing and speaking, although they may hear native speakers using the informal form.

C) MEANING AND USE 1

Real Conditionals

EXAMINING MEANING AND USE

- Have students work in pairs to answer the questions (b, a promise; a, a statement of fact; d, a warning; and c, an instruction).
- Give students a few minutes to refer to the Notes to check their answers.
- Call on students to read and label the sentences. Discuss any disagreements and have students make any necessary corrections.

MEANING AND USE NOTES

- Read the explanation in Note 1 and ask students to identify first the *if* clause and then the main clause in the example. Then ask them what meaning is expressed in the main clause (a possible result), and what meaning is expressed in the *if* clause (a possible condition).
- Divide students into groups of three and assign one of the remaining Notes to each group. Have each group read the Note and prepare to present it to the class with a couple new example sentences.
- Circulate among the groups and check that they are on the right track. Make any necessary corrections.
- Have each group present their Note and share the new example sentences on the board.
- Check the form and meaning of each sentence as a class and answer any questions.

Vocabulary Notes: *If* and *Unless* (p. 339)

- Write the following sentence on the board: *Unless you study, you will fail the test.* Tell students to identify the dependent and independent clause (dependent: *unless you study*; independent: *you will fail the test*).
- Then ask students to think of another way to say the same thing. If they don't know, hint to start the sentence with *If* (*If you don't study, you will fail the test.*). If students forget to change the affirmative verb to negative in the dependent clause, point out that the sentence does not make sense: *If you study, you will fail*

Chapter 15   65

the test. Explain that *unless* has the same meaning as the negative *if* clause.

- Give students time to read the Notes and ask questions.

- To check students' comprehension, write the following sentences on the board and ask students to rewrite them using *unless*.

    You won't pass the exam if you don't study. (You won't pass the exam unless you study.)

    If she doesn't get a scholarship, she won't be able to go to college. (Unless she gets a scholarship, she won't be able to go to college.)

    The airlines won't sell you a ticket if you don't have a visa. (The airlines won't sell you a ticket unless you have a visa.)

- Have a student come to the board to write the answers. Answer any outstanding questions.

D) MEANING AND USE 2

Unreal Conditionals

EXAMINING MEANING AND USE

- Have students work in pairs to answer the questions (1. 1a is more likely to happen and 1b is probably imaginary; 2. 2b is more direct and 2a is more indirect).

- Give students a few minutes to refer to the Notes to check their answer.

- Call on students to read the questions and answers out loud. Discuss any disagreements and have students make necessary corrections.

MEANING AND USE NOTES

- Give students time to read Notes 1A, 1B, and 1C and ask questions. Write a few *if* clauses on the board that you are certain are not true (e.g., *If I were a native speaker of English . . .*; *If I were an Olympic gold medalist . . .*).

- Ask students to complete the sentences with their own ideas and write them in their notebooks.

- Call on several students to share their answers.

- Tell students to close their books and listen carefully as you read the two sample sentences from Note 2. Ask students to tell you which sentence seems more direct (the sentence with a modal) and which seems more indirect (the sentence with an unreal conditional). Have students open their books to check their responses.

- Finally, tell students to read the conversations in Note 3 in pairs, switching parts after each one. When they finish, ask them to write their own dialogue in which they practice using conditionals to ask permission. Write some interesting topics on the board to make the activity more lively, e.g., asking permission to use the family car, to go to the movies, to stay out late.

Beyond the Sentence: Omitting *If* Clauses (p. 343)

This section is intended to give your students practice with the meaning and use of grammar as it functions naturally in extended discourse such as paragraphs and conversations.

- Give students a minute to read the explanation and the example paragraph.

- Elicit the omitted *if* clause for each sentence (*If I were the boss, . . .*).

- Refer students to the passage "If I Had My Life to Live Over" on page 328 in their books. Explain that this is another example of omitting *if* clauses. Elicit that each sentence is a result of the condition *If I Had My Life to Live Over.*

E) MEANING AND USE 3

Wishes

EXAMINING MEANING AND USE

- As a precursor, explain that we can make wishes for different time frames (present, future, and past) and for different purposes (to express desire, disappointment, complaints, regret).

- Have students work in groups to answer the questions (1. 1b is present and 1a is future; 2. 2a is a complaint and 2b is a regret).

- Give students a few minutes to refer to the Notes to check their answers.

- Then call on students to read the questions and answers out loud. Discuss any disagreements.

MEANING AND USE NOTES

- Set up a jigsaw activity for the Notes. Divide students into three groups, and assign one Note to each group.
- Tell each group to read the Note and write a paraphrase of the explanation. Ask students to write a new example sentence that expresses the meaning and use of this grammar point. Give groups about ten minutes to prepare this information.
- Divide students into new groups so that there is at least one member from each of the four original groups. Each member of the new group will explain his or her information and example sentence to the others.
- Circulate as the groups work, helping them with any problems.

ADDITIONAL ACTIVITIES

Writing and Speaking About Nationality

The purpose of this activity is to give students an opportunity to use the unreal conditional while imagining what their lives would be like if they were born in a different country.

- Write these questions on the board: *What difference does nationality make in a person's life? Does it matter which country a person is from? Why?* Give students a few minutes to think about this. Have them list any ideas or examples to help them prepare for a discussion on this issue.
- Have students work in groups to share their opinions. Encourage them to defend their opinions with examples.
- Have students choose a country and imagine what their life would be like if they were from that country. Ask students to freewrite (write without stopping and without worrying about grammar or spelling) for 10 to 15 minutes on the question *What would my life be like if I were from _____?* Have them start their paragraphs with *If I were from _____, I would . . .*, and freewrite sentences with *would* to express further imaginary results. Remind them not to repeat the *if* clause in each sentence.
- When the students finish their freewrite, tell them to read it over silently. Explain that their freewrite will have many ideas, some of them more interesting and important than others. Give students a few minutes to underline the most important ideas.
- For homework have students write an essay in which they explain three ways their life would be different if they were from the country they freewrote about.
- Review students' essays to correct any errors in form, meaning, or use.

Returning to Grammar in Discourse

The purpose of this activity is to check students' understanding of key meanings and uses of the target structures in the chapter, by returning to the selections at the beginning of the chapter and applying what they have learned.

- Write the following extracts from the selections on the board (or type them up and photocopy them before class) and have students work in pairs to find them in the selections. Make sure they read the complete sentences these extracts come from.
  1. *. . . there will be peace in the world.*
  2. *. . . I've had my moments . . .*
  3. *. . . if it were over tomorrow . . .*
  4. *. . . I thought, what jolly fun!*
- Now write the following on the board
  a. a wish
  b. a prediction
  c. a factual statement
  d. an imaginary condition
- Have students think about the use of conditionals and wishes in the extracts and match each one to the letter above that best describes it (1. b; 2. c; 3. d; 4. a).
- Bring the class together. Call on pairs for the answers and have them offer explanations. If students still have problems, revisit the Meaning and Use Notes.

CHAPTER 16
Past Unreal Conditionals and Past Wishes

Overview

The past unreal conditional is used for imaginary situations that did not take place in the past (e.g., *If Li had studied hard, she would have passed the test*.). The reality is that Li did not study hard and as a result did not pass her test. The verb *wish* can be used similarly to express a desire for an unreal past situation (e.g., *Li wishes she had studied harder*.). Another way to express past wishes is with the construction *if only* (e.g., *If only Li had studied harder*.).

Form: In the *if* clause, the past perfect is used to indicate the situation was unreal in the past. In the result clause, *would have, could have,* or *might have* indicate the result was unreal in the past.

A GRAMMAR IN DISCOURSE

The Ifs of History

A1: Before You Read

This is a longer and more complex text than the previous ones, so allow plenty of time for students to read it.

- To introduce the concept of *what if?*, give students five minutes to answer the questions in the book.
- Put students in pairs and have them share what they wrote with a partner.
- Explain that the article discusses several important historical events, some of which they may not know.
- Write the names Adolf Hitler, Cleopatra, Franklin Delano Roosevelt, and Vincent van Gogh on the board. Point out that these are historical figures, and ask students if they know who any of them are. If so, call on these students to give some information about the historical figure. Describe the figures that the students are unfamiliar with. *(Adolf Hitler was the fascist leader of Nazi Germany during World War II. Cleopatra was an Egyptian queen famous for her beauty, who lived about 2000 years ago. Franklin Delano Roosevelt was President of the United States during World War II, and he is credited with pulling the United States out of its worst economic depression. Vincent van Gogh was a Dutch painter who is as famous for his insanity as he is for his artistry. He once cut off his ear.)*

A2: Read

- Before students read, give them some examples of ifs from your own life, perhaps describe what would have happened to you if you hadn't experienced whatever it was that inspired you to become a teacher. Explain that the article explores some possible alternatives to actual historical events.
- The first three paragraphs of the article introduce the main idea. Tell students to read them and write one sentence that expresses the main idea. (The article encourages us to imagine how history would have turned out if certain events had happened differently.)
- Call on several students to read their sentences out loud.
- Divide students into four groups, one for each historical personality described in the article. Each group will be responsible for reading, understanding, discussing, and summarizing the "if" described in the paragraph.
- When they are finished, one group member will present the information to the class. The other students will listen and ask questions. The four personalities are Franklin Roosevelt (paragraph 2), Adolf Hitler (paragraph 4),

Cleopatra (paragraph 5), and Vincent van Gogh (paragraph 6).
- After they finish, ask students if they agree with the writer's ideas. Make sure they explain why or why not.

A3: After You Read
- Have students to do this exercise individually and mark the places in the text where they found the answers.
- Ask them to compare answers with a partner.
- Circulate and note any difficult or problematic items. Then go over these with the whole class.
- As a follow-up activity, ask students to think of a major event in the history of their countries that affected the lives of many people (e.g., the election of a president, the birth or death of a member of a royal family, a currency crisis, etc.).
- Put students into pairs to discuss their answers. If possible, pair students from the same country so they both have knowledge of the event.

B) FORM

Past Unreal Conditionals and Past Wishes

EXAMINING FORM

Method 1
(For students not familiar with the structure)
- **Question 1:** Direct students' attention to the first underlined past unreal conditional sentence. Ask *How many clauses are in this sentence?* (two); *What are they?* (the *if* clause and the main clause).
- Ask students to find and note three more examples of past unreal conditional sentences. Call on several students to tell you the sentences. Write them on the board.
- **Question 2:** Elicit the verb form used in the *if* clause (past perfect) and the one used in the main clause (*would have* + past participle). Some students may say that the present perfect is used in the main clause, but point out that this is not true.

Method 2
(For students familiar with the structure)
- Have students work in pairs to answer the questions.
- Give students a few minutes to refer to the charts to check their answers.
- Call on students to go over the exercise. Discuss any disagreements and have students make any necessary corrections.

FORM CHARTS
- Tell students to read the *Past Unreal Conditionals* charts to see all the possible modals for the main clause (*would, could,* and *might*) Then ask them to compare these with the modals in the main clauses of the sentences from the Examining Form.
- Ask students to write three of the sentences from the exercise in their notebooks and change *would* in the main clause to *could* or *might* (*What might have happened if there had been no Franklin Delano Roosevelt?*).
- Have students read the bulleted notes. Then check their comprehension by writing the following sentences on the board and asking students to identify and explain the errors.

    *I would have come to the party, if you had invited me. (Incorrect—there should be no comma if main clause is first.)

    *If she called me, I'd have come to the meeting. (Incorrect—the past perfect must be used in the *if* clause.)

    *If he had been on time, he would have missed his train? (Incorrect—questions are formed with the main clause in question word order: *would he have missed his train?*)

- Tell students to read the *Past Wishes* chart, then elicit a few examples of things students wish they had done last year, e.g., studied harder, moved to a new apartment, saved money, etc. Write these prompts on the board.
- Call on various students to create complete sentences from the prompts on the board (e.g., *I wish (that) I had studied harder.*).

Chapter 16

Informally Speaking: Reduced Forms of Past Modals (p. 357)

- Choose two students to read the text in the speech bubbles. Then tell the class you will play the recording and that they should listen to how the underlined form in the cartoon is different from what they hear. If needed, play the recording more than once.

- Have students point out the differences. (The cartoon reads *Well, I would have shown him the mistake. I sure wouldn't have paid the extra money*. On the recording this is pronounced *Well, I "woulda" shown him the mistake. I sure "wouldn't-uv" paid the extra money*.) Explain that the form on the recording is considered more informal English. Point out that the form in the cartoon is standard English and students should use this form when writing and speaking, although they may hear native speakers using the informal form.

C MEANING AND USE 1

Past Unreal Conditionals

EXAMINING MEANING AND USE

- Have students work in pairs to answer the questions (1. a; 2. b).
- Give students a few minutes to refer to the Notes to check their answers.
- Call on students to read the questions and answers out loud. Discuss any disagreements and have students make any necessary corrections.

MEANING AND USE NOTES

- Have students read the information in Note 1A. Call on one student to create another sample sentence by asking *If you had been the boss, what would you have done?*
- Elicit the modals that can be used in the result clause of a past unreal conditional sentence *(would, could, might)*. Write these on the board. Ask *Which of these modals indicates the most certainty?* *(would)*.
- Give students time to read Note 1B and ask questions. Elicit the full form of the contraction *(had had)* and point out to students that although this may look unusual, this is the correct form.

- Direct students' attention to the example sentences in Note 2. Ask if the sentences have the same or a different meaning (the same). Elicit which is a more direct way of giving the advice (the sentence with *should*). Point out that giving advice with an unreal conditional is perceived as more polite or indirect. Give students time to read Note 2 and ask questions.

- Ask students to read Note 3 and answer any questions. Have them to write a pair of sentences with the same meaning: one past unreal conditional, and the other a true sentence with *but*. Write an example on the board for the class first (e.g., *I would have called you if I hadn't lost your number. I would have called you, but I lost your number.*).

- Call on several students to write their sentences on the board.

D MEANING AND USE 2

Past Wishes

EXAMINING MEANING AND USE

- Have students work in pairs to answer the questions (1. 1a and 2a are about present situations, 1b and 2b are about past situations; 2. 2a and 2b express stronger feelings).
- Give students a few minute to refer to the Notes to check their answers.
- Call on students to read the questions and answers out loud. Discuss any disagreements and have students make any necessary corrections.

MEANING AND USE NOTES

- Tell students to read Note 1, and elicit the form by asking *Was the weather nice yesterday? How was the weather yesterday?*
- Tell students to read the information in Note 2. Call on one or two students to read the examples out loud and try to show regret or dissatisfaction in their voices. Model such a tone for them if necessary.

- Follow the same procedure with tone for the *if only* sentences in Note 3.
- Have students read the Note and create two more sentences using *if only*. Call on students to share their sentences and go over them as a class. Encourage students to experiment with tone as they read the sentences.
- Point out that *if only* is used to express strong feelings of regret. Explain that this language is slightly more formal and common in written English.

ADDITIONAL ACTIVITIES

Speaking About History

The purpose of this activity is for students to practice using past conditionals by giving a panel presentation about the life of a famous person who changed the course of history.

- Tell the class to think of people who were so important that they changed the course of world history. These people could be political or military leaders, artists, scientists, or writers. Elicit the names of several such people and their accomplishments and write them on the board.
- Give students some time to think about the list, and then ask them to choose the person they want to speak about. Try to assign students to groups of three, according to their preference.
- Explain that each group will give a presentation that covers the following three points: 1) who was this person and what did he or she do to change the course of history; 2) what would have been different if this person had not lived; and 3) could someone else have accomplished the same things.
- Have students research the information they need for homework and bring it to class. In class give the groups time to organize their material and practice their presentation. Encourage students to prepare some notes to speak from. However, make it clear that they should not simply read their presentation. Remind students that in order to express this hypothetical information in points 2 and 3 above, they must use past conditionals. Tell them to practice that part of the presentation carefully.
- Give each group 15 to 20 minutes to present. As each group presents, encourage the others to raise their hands and disagree, agree, and ask questions.
- Take notes during the presentations so that you can give feedback on form, meaning, or use.

CHAPTER 17 Noun Clauses

Overview

Noun clauses are dependent clauses that can occur in the same place as a noun or noun phrase in a sentence. There are three types of noun clauses: *Wh- Clauses* (e.g., *I don't know where she is.*), *If/Whether Clauses* (e.g., *I wonder whether it stopped raining.*), and *That Clauses* (e.g., *I think that you are smart.*).

Form: Students may confuse the form of noun clauses with question forms, and this can explain word order error such as, *I don't know what time is it*. Remind students that just as nouns and noun phrases can function as objects in a sentence, so can noun clauses (e.g., *I don't understand the question* [noun]. *I don't understand what you just asked me* [noun clause].). Stress that nouns and noun clauses are used the same way.

A GRAMMAR IN DISCOURSE

Career Currents

A1: Before You Read

- Divide students into small groups to discuss the first question. Their answers may vary according to their background.
- Ask a volunteer from each group to come to the board and write one way to find a job that was discussed by their group.
- When all groups have contributed to the list, read it out loud. Elicit other ways to find a job. Add these to the list. Ask the class to rank the top three ways to find a job. Write the appropriate number (1–3) beside each of these.
- Tell students to discuss the other two questions in their groups.
- Take a class vote to find out how many students would quit their job before finding a better one. Ask students who have different opinions to share their reasons.

Cultural Notes

Many students may not know that it is not uncommon for Americans to hold several jobs in several kinds of careers before retiring. Point out that this is a fairly recent trend. In fact, in previous generations, people would rarely leave a good job and would often have the same job for their entire career. This may come as a surprise to students who come from more traditional backgrounds, such as Japan, where it is customary to keep one job for a very long time.

A2: Read

- Before students begin reading, elicit some of the benefits of looking for a job even if you have a job (make sure students understand that you mean *looking for* a job and not *changing* jobs). Make a list of these on the board.
- Tell students to read the article to find out some of the benefits of looking for a new job.
- As a class, check the list on the board. Add any new benefits mentioned in the article.

A3: After You Read

- Ask students to do this exercise individually and then compare their answers in pairs.
- Go over any difficult or problematic items.
- As a follow-up activity, ask students to consider their own job search experiences. Write these questions on the board for students to discuss in pairs: *How did you search for a job? prepare a résumé? prepare for an interview?* If students have never looked for a job, ask them to think about a friend's or family member's job search experience.
- Divide students into small groups to discuss their experiences.

- Ask the groups to devise the most effective job-search plan based on the group members' experiences.
- Call on several groups to share their plans.

B FORM

Noun Clauses

EXAMINING FORM

Method 1:
(For students not familiar with the structure)

- **Question 1:** Have students work individually to find three examples of each type of clause in the article and then compare their answers with a partner.
- Explain that *how* is grouped with *wh-* words (*who, what, why, where, when*) even though it does not begin with *wh*.
- **Question 2:** Call on several students to write the examples of the different types of clauses they found on the board. Make sure there is at least one example of each type of clause. Tell students to circle the subject and verb. Have them write *S* above the subject and *V* above the verb. *S* followed by *V* is statement word order. Point out to students that statement word order is used in all the clauses.

Method 2
(For students familiar with the structure)

- Have students work in pairs to answer the questions.
- Give students a few minutes to refer to the charts to check their answers and review the structures.
- Call on students to go over the exercise. Discuss any disagreements and have students make any necessary corrections.

FORM CHARTS

- Tell students to label the subjects and verbs of the noun clauses in the charts with an *S* and *V* and compare this with the labeling they did in Examining Form. (Again, this will reveal statement word order.)

- Ask students to read the bulleted notes. Tell them to underline the subjects and verbs in the examples of noun clauses in the Notes.
- Explain the concept of embedded questions. These are questions that appear within a statement (e.g., *He asked who she is.*) or a question (e.g., *Do you know if he is here?*).
- Check students' comprehension of embedded questions by writing these sentences with word order errors on the board and calling on students to correct them. Underline the embedded question in each example.

    *Do you know when did she leave? (Incorrect—Do you know when she left?)

    *I wonder where did the sun go? (Incorrect—I wonder where the sun went.)

    *I don't know if is she here today. (Incorrect—I don't know if she is here today.)

- For the second and third sentence, explain that these are not questions and should not be punctuated with question marks. Write the correct forms on the board and then analyze them together. Point out that the incorrect sentences use question word order instead of statement word order.

C MEANING AND USE 1

Wh- and *If/Whether Clauses*

EXAMINING MEANING AND USE

- Have students work in pairs to answer the questions.
- Give students a few minutes to refer to the Notes to check their answers (1. *Decide, know,* and *wonder* express mental activities; 2. 2b).
- Then call on students to read the questions and answers out loud. Discuss any disagreements and have students make any necessary corrections.

MEANING AND USE NOTES

- Put students into pairs. Tell them to read the Notes and examine the examples in Notes 1A, 1B, and 1C. Have them write new sentences using some of the verbs from 1B, the expressions from 1C, and a *wh-* word or *that* clause (e.g., *I decided where to go. She figured out that he was lying.*).

- Ask one person from each pair to read one of the sentences to the class. Offer feedback as necessary.
- Give students a few minutes to read Note 2 and ask questions. Ask the same pairs to choose two of the verbs and phrases, and write sentences with *wh-* or *if/whether* clauses.
- Have one person from each pair read one of these sentences. Offer feedback as necessary.
- Tell students to read the explanation and examples in Notes 3A and 3B. Then give them a new *wh-* question: *Where is the nearest pay phone?* to change into an indirect question (*I was wondering where the nearest pay phone is.*).
- Repeat the procedure with a new *Yes/No* question: *Is the subway on this block?* Have students change it into an indirect question (*Do you know if the subway is on this block?*).

Vocabulary Notes: *If* and *Whether* (p. 382)

- Give students a few minutes to read the Notes and example sentences.
- Point out that although *whether* is considered more formal, it is not actually informal or impolite to use *if*. *If* is used even more often than *whether*.

D MEANING AND USE 2

That Clauses

EXAMINING MEANING AND USE

- Ask students to silently read the two pairs of sentences and tell you which pair has the same meaning (2a and 2b).
- Write the sentences on the board and ask a student to come up and underline the noun clauses. Ask another student to come up and circle the verb in each noun clause and tell you the form of the verbs (2a, *was*, simple past; 2b, *is*, simple present).
- Repeat the procedure for the first pair of sentences. (The meaning is different. In 1a, the verb is *left*, simple past. In 1b the verb is *'s leaving*, present continuous.)
- Ask students to explain why the meaning is different in pair 1 but the same in pair 2. If necessary, direct students to the particular verbs. (In sentence 1a, the past tense means that the action in the noun clause is in the past and complete; in sentence 1b, the present continuous means that the action is in progress or will happen soon. In the second pair, the verbs in the noun clause express a fact that is always true. For example, after someone has visited another country, she might describe it two ways: *Italy was beautiful. Italy is beautiful.* She may have felt that way when she was there, but the information is still true now.)

MEANING AND USE NOTES

- Tell students to silently read the explanations and examples in Notes 1A, 1B, and 1C.
- Divide students into pairs and ask them to choose two of the mental activity verbs to use in new sentences with *that* clauses.
- Ask several groups to share their sentences. Offer feedback as necessary.
- For Note 2A, have students write three new sentences using the same verb and format: present + present; present + past; present + future.
- For Notes 2B, 2C, and 2D, read the explanations and examples in each box out loud. Tell students to work in their pairs again. For each Note, give the pair a few minutes to create a new sentence using the same main verb as in the example sentence (e.g., *thought, knew*).
- Ask a few students to write their sentences on the board for each Note. Tell the other students to check the verb use in each and correct any errors.

Trouble Spots

The use of both the present tense and the past tense to talk about generalizations is often confusing to students who have been taught only to use a past form to talk about something that happened in the past. The key here is to emphasize that the rule for generalizations applies only to events and actions that are factual or general truths. For example, we can say, *Columbus believed that the world* is *round*. We can also say, *Columbus believed that the world* was *round*.

ADDITIONAL ACTIVITIES

Speaking About Jobs

The purpose of this activity is for students to practice using noun clauses while writing up and conducting a job survey, and presenting a report about it to the class.

- First, as a class, brainstorm a list of possible topics related to working. This might include attitudes about employees, changing jobs, employee-employer relations, relationships between co-workers, and job satisfaction. Write the list on the board.
- Divide students into groups and assign one topic per group. Explain that each group will brainstorm a list of possible questions about the topic. Remind them to use noun clauses in some of their questions. (e.g., *Do you think that an employee should be friends with his or her boss?* or *Can you tell me if it is OK for people to have many jobs?*)
- Tell each group to agree on five questions, and have them proofread the questions for correct noun clause use.
- Explain that each group member will survey five people outside of class. Encourage students to survey their friends, family, or students on campus.
- Give students class time to practice asking their questions in their groups. Review phrases to use when asking people to respond to the survey. For example, *Excuse me. Would you mind answering a few questions?* or *Could I please ask you a few questions?* or *I was wondering if I could ask you a few questions.*
- When class meets again, have groups compile their results and prepare a report to present to the class.
- Each student should participate in the group's report. Again, remind students to use noun clauses (e.g., *Five people think that . . . ; Three people felt that . . .*).
- At the end of the report, one student should summarize the findings, using noun clauses where appropriate (e.g., *We learned that . . . ; This survey demonstrates that . . .*).

CHAPTER 18

Reported Speech

Overview

Reported speech is used to recount what someone has said or written, but from the point of view of the reporter rather than the original speaker or writer (e.g., *My mother said, "You can't go to the movies."* becomes *My mother said that I can't go to the movies.*).

Form: Reported speech has a reporting verb in the main clause (e.g., *say, tell, ask*) followed by a noun clause (e.g., *She said that I am early*.) or an infinitive (e.g., *Joseph asked us to help him.*). Reported speech often differs from quoted speech in tense, pronouns, and adverbs. Emphasize that tense choice plays an important role. Note this sentence: *I want to go home.* In reported speech it can change to these three forms: *He said that he wanted to home. He said that he wants to go home. He says that he wants to go home.*

A GRAMMAR IN DISCOURSE

Doctor-Patient Relationship in Critical Condition

A1: Before You Read

- This article focuses on the attitudes of doctors and patients in the United States. Involve students in the topic by asking if anyone has ever visited a doctor in the United States.

- Then put students into groups and write these questions on the board for them to discuss. (Encourage those students who have not visited a doctor in the United States to think of other questions to ask those who have.) *How long did you have to wait to get an appointment? How long did you wait in the waiting room before seeing the doctor? How well did the doctor communicate with you? Did you like him or her?* Some students may not feel comfortable talking about their experiences at the doctor's. Don't pressure them.

- Once students have answered these questions out loud, have them work individually to make a list of the qualities of a good doctor. Call on several students to share one of the qualities from their list. Write these on the board.

- Ask students to make a list of the bad qualities of some doctors they have seen or heard about. Call on several students to share one of the qualities from their list. Write these on the board as well.

Cultural Notes

The issue of doctor-patient communication may be unfamiliar to many students. They may come from countries where patients are assigned doctors and there are few choices for health care. Point out that in the United States, many people can choose their doctor and may change doctors if they become dissatisfied. Also, explain that the issue of doctor-patient communication and other issues related to patient care are widely discussed in the United States.

A2: Read

- Have students read the article to find out what happens when doctors and patients don't communicate well.

- Set up a jigsaw activity. Divide students into small groups and assign each group a paragraph from the article.

- Have each group write a one- or two-sentence summary of the information in the assigned paragraph.

- Form new groups, making sure that there is at least one member representing each paragraph. Each member will summarize his or her paragraph for the others.

A3: After You Read

- Have students to do this exercise individually and note the places in the article where they found their answers.
- Ask them to compare answers with a partner.
- Circulate and note any difficult or problematic items. Then go over these with the whole class.
- As a follow-up activity, ask students to compare their experiences seeing a doctor in their native country with seeing a doctor in the United States. Ask which experience was more positive and why. Tell them to focus on the cultural aspects of health care in their country and in the United States. If students have not yet visited a doctor in the United States, ask them what they expect the visit to be like.
- Call on several students to share their experiences.

B) FORM

Reported Speech

EXAMINING FORM

Method 1
(For students not familiar with the structure)

- For a quick review of reported speech, tell one student this sentence *You can go home early today.* Then elicit from the class what you just told the student *(You told him that he can go home early. You said that he can go home early.).* Write the responses on the board.
- **Question 1:** Have students look at the underlined examples of reported speech clauses and then circle the reporting verbs related to each example *(were asked, were asked, reported, ask).*
- **Question 2:** Have students identify which underlined clause is a *wh-* clause *(what health problem they had discussed with each patient)*, a that clause *(that they had such problems)*, an if/whether clause *(if they understand)*, and an infinitive clause *(to fill out a detailed questionnaire).* Have students check their answers with a partner.

- **Question 3:** Have students find other examples of reported speech in the third paragraph and circle the reporting verbs. Bring the class together to check the answers and go over any questions.

Method 2
(For students familiar with the structure)

- Have students work in pairs to answer the questions.
- Give students a few minutes to refer to the charts to check their answers and review the structures.
- Call on students to go over the exercise. Discuss any disagreements and have students make any necessary corrections.

FORM CHARTS

- Have students work individually to find the basic differences between quoted speech and reported speech in the charts.
- Tell students to read the bulleted notes to check their understanding of the basic differences in form. For example, *Yes/No* questions change to *if/whether* clauses (e.g., *Do you like Mexican food? She asked me if I like Mexican food.*), imperatives change to infinitives (e.g., *Don't go. He told me not to go.*).
- Ask students to silently read the information in the *Present Tense Reporting* chart.
- Ask a student to tell you the rule for present tense reporting in the bulleted note. (The tense in the *that* clause does not change if the reporting verb is in the present tense.)
- Have students read the examples in the *Past Tense Reporting* chart and the bulleted notes. Ask *What happens to present tense verbs?* (They change to past tense.); *What happens to present continuous verbs?* (They change to past continuous.); *What happens to future with* be going to *verbs?* (They change to *was going to.*); *What happens to the modals* can, may, *and* have to? (They change to *could, might,* and *had to.*).
- Ask students what they notice about the form of the modals *should, ought to,* and *could* in past reported speech. (There is no change.)
- Have students test each other in pairs. The first student should read the quoted speech in the

Chapter 18

book and the second student, with the book closed, should say the sentence in reported speech in the past tense, beginning with *I said*. When they finish, have students switch roles.

Trouble Spots

The verbs *say* and *tell* have a similar meaning and are widely used in reported speech. However, there is an important difference in form: *tell* is followed by a noun object and *say* is not (e.g., *Our teacher said that we would have a test on reporting verbs.* vs. *Our teacher told us that we would have a test on reporting verbs.*). Students often attempt to use these two verbs interchangeably, which explains why they produce such errors as **She said me to turn left at the corner.* (Incorrect.) Remind students that *say* isn't followed by a noun object and *tell* is. Ask students to write similar sentence pairs using *say* and *tell* so they can see the form difference (e.g., *She said that we should wait for her. She told us that we should wait for her.*).

Vocabulary Notes: *Tell, Say,* and *Ask* (p. 397)

- Give students a few minutes to read the Notes and example sentences.
- Check students' comprehension by asking *Which verbs are used to report statements?* (*tell* and *say*); *Which verb is used to report questions?* (*ask*); *Which verbs are used to report imperatives?* (*tell, say, ask*); *Which verb is not followed by a noun or a pronoun?* (*say*); *Which verb is followed by a noun or pronoun?* (*tell*).
- Point out that *ask* can be followed by a noun or pronoun, but it does not have to be.

C MEANING AND USE

Reported Speech

EXAMINING MEANING AND USE

- Have students work in pairs to answer the questions (1. a and c; 2. b).
- Give students a few minutes to refer to the Notes to check their answers.
- Then call on students to read the questions and answers out loud. Discuss any disagreements and have students make any necessary corrections.

MEANING AND USE NOTES

- Ask students to silently read the explanations in Notes 1 and 2. Explain that it is often necessary to change to the past tense in reported speech, but that this is not always true.
- Divide students into three groups and assign Notes 3A, 3B, 3C, to the groups. Explain that each group will teach the class about one of the reasons for not shifting the tense in a reported sentence. Have them read the explanations and the examples and then create a short dialogue, which two group members will perform for the class.
- Circulate as the groups work, helping with any difficulties.
- Begin each presentation by asking one student to explain in his or her own words the reason for not changing the tense (e.g., the event has just taken place or it is a generalization).
- Ask students to give the context of the conversation before performing the dialogue (e.g., *This is a telephone conversation between a store clerk and a customer at home. The customer on the phone is reporting the information to his wife.* Student A: *We close at 8:00 P.M.* Student B: *He said that they close at 8:00 P.M.*).
- Tell students to silently read the information and example sentences in Notes 4 and 5. Then write this sentence on the board: *I like my new job.* Ask students to change this to reported speech with *He stated that . . . (he likes his new job.).*
- To focus on adverb changes (e.g., *here, there*), write this sentence on the board: *I'll wait for you here until you come.* Ask students to change it to reported speech (*He said he'd wait for me there until I come.*).

Vocabulary Notes: More Reporting Verbs (p. 402)

- Give students time to read the Notes and examples.
- Clarify any unfamiliar verbs, though it may be difficult to clearly express all the nuances between them.

- Write this sentence on the board: *He took the wallet.*
- Ask students to use three of the verbs from the Notes to report the sentence. If they choose a verb such as *inform*, which requires an object pronoun, they can use *me* (e.g., *He informed me that he'd taken the wallet.*).
- Ask several students to read their sentences and give a context for each.

Vocabulary Notes: Reporting Verbs Used for Advising (p. 404)

This information is useful but rather complex, so cover it only after you feel your students have had enough practice using the easier reporting verbs and reported speech in this chapter.

- On the board, write sentences with some of the verbs from this Note:

    The teacher asked that we eat our lunch outside.

    The law requires that we drive slowly near a school.

    Many parents insist that their children behave well in public.

    The police officer demanded that we stop the car.

    Experts suggest that people get eight hours of sleep.

    My friend recommended that I talk to a doctor.

    Scientists advise that everyone stay out of the sun.

    We propose that we have homework only on the weekend.

- Read each sentence out loud, ask students to identify the reporting verb, and if necessary, elicit the meaning of the verb.
- Ask students to look at all the sentences and tell you what they notice about the form of the verb in the *that* clause. (It is always in the base form, even when the main verb is in the past tense [*They demanded that we* listen *to them.*] or third-person singular [*The woman insists that her daughter* visit *her more often.*].) This may be hard for students to understand or remember, so give them time and examples to practice it.

ADDITIONAL ACTIVITIES

Writing About a TV Program

The purpose of this activity is for students to practice reporting speech while recounting what happened on a TV program.

- Show students a short clip (about three minutes) of a TV sitcom. Be sure to choose a clip that is relatively easy to follow even if students have never seen the show. Tell students that they will watch the clip and write a paragraph that describes what happened.
- Tell students they will first note basic information about the scene: who the characters are, where the scene is, and generally what is happening.
- Play the clip once and then discuss the basic information as a class. Provide any necessary background information.
- Play the clip again. This time, students should take notes on the conversation.
- Play it a third time and tell students to add any information they missed to their notes.
- As a warm-up to the writing assignment, give students a few minutes to tell a partner what happened in the scene. Tell students to take more notes based on what their partner says.
- Assign the paragraph for homework. Tell students to describe the conversation in such a way that a person who did not see the clip would know what happened in the scene. Remind students to use a wide variety of reported speech forms, such as *He said that . . . , He told her to . . . , They asked him if . . . .*
- In class have students exchange assignments in pairs. Each student will underline the uses of reported speech and circle any errors. When students get their paragraphs back, they should correct the errors.
- Collect the assignments and note any errors.
- As a follow-up, ask students' permission to copy and distribute to the class several student paragraphs that use reported speech particularly effectively.

Returning to Grammar in Discourse

The purpose of this activity is to check students' understanding of key meanings and uses of the target structures in the chapter, by returning to the article at the beginning of the chapter and applying what they have learned.

- Write the following extracts from the article on the board (or type them up and photocopy them before class) and have students work in pairs to find them in the article. Make sure they read the complete sentences these extracts come from.
    1. *. . . only 45 percent of those patients reported that they had such problems.*
    2. *The survey concludes that patients often misunderstand their doctors.*
    3. *Experts suggest that doctors limit their use of medical jargon as much as possible.*
    4. *Doctors should also stop and periodically ask whether there are any questions . . .*
    5. *Experts tell patients to plan their visits to the doctor very carefully.*

- Now write the following on the board:
    a. *advise*
    b. *mention*
    c. *recommend*
    d. *inquire*
    e. *indicate*

- Have students decide which of the reporting verbs above can replace the verb in each extract without changing the form or the meaning (Answers: 1. b, e; 2. e; 3. a, c; 4. d; 5. a).

- Bring the class together. Call on pairs for the answers and have them offer explanations. If students still have problems, revisit the Meaning and Use Notes.

Student Book Tapescript

CHAPTER 1

A2 (p. 4)

Please refer to the magazine article in the Student Book.

B1: Listening for Form (p. 8)

1. Are you eating enough?
2. Are you getting enough sleep?
3. Do you have many new friends?
4. Are your friends studying English, too?
5. Do you have a lot of homework?
6. Do your classes meet every day?
7. Does your roommate speak Korean?
8. Is it raining there today?

Informally Speaking (p. 11)

F: You feeling OK?
M: No. I have a headache. You have any aspirin?

B5: Understanding Informal Speech (p. 11)

1. Feeling tired in the morning? Maybe you need a new mattress. Stop in at Sleep World for the answer to all your dreams.
2. Need a vacation? We have great deals at Star Travel. Call us today!
3. Having car problems again? Call Smith Auto Works. We're the best in town!
4. Doing it yourself? Let us help you at Stone Hardware. We have all the tools you need.
5. Have any old clothes in your closets? Donate them to the Youth Center Rummage Sale. Clean out your closets and help our kids at the same time.
6. Like to shop late? Then Norton's is for you. We're the only grocery store in town open twenty-four hours every day!
7. Working too hard? We have great weekend getaways. Call Travel Time for the best deals on many fares.
8. Need a house sitter? Well, look no further. We'll clean your house for you and watch it while you're away.

C1: Listening for Meaning and Use (p. 14)

1. What are you doing?
2. That story is unbelievable. Are you kidding?
3. What do you do?
4. What happens at the end of the movie?
5. Do you drink coffee at night?
6. What does "nap" mean?
7. Is Amir talking on the phone again?
8. Are you working hard these days?

D1: Listening for Meaning and Use (p. 19)

1. Jennifer feels sick today. Her throat itches and she has a fever.
2. Mr. Silva walks to work. He stops for coffee on the way. He carries his briefcase in one hand and his coffee in the other—and he tries not to spill it.
3. Dinner costs a lot at Joe's Restaurant, but it includes four courses. Lunch is cheaper. There are always at least two specials. Everything tastes fresh, and it smells so good.
4. A: Do you hear music?
   B: Yes, I think the radio is on.
5. Ms. Wilson's kindergarten class is behaving strangely today. Two children are running around the room, one boy is crying, and two others are yelling very loudly.
6. A: I can't see that sign. I'm nearsighted, and I don't have my glasses.
   B: Well, I don't see very well without my glasses either, but I'm farsighted. I need my glasses for things that are close.

Informally Speaking (p. 22)

F: Do you like the movie?
M: I'm loving it!
F: You're kidding! I'm just hating it!

D6: Understanding Informal Speech (p. 22)

1. I'm liking my apartment more and more each day!
2. I'm hating this new television show!
3. We're just loving the beautiful weather!
4. She's really disliking this trip!
5. I'm loving this movie!
6. I'm really liking my new job!

CHAPTER 2

A2 (p. 28)

Please refer to the book excerpt in the Student Book.

B1: Listening for Form (p. 32)

Where were you when the lights went out this morning? That's the question everyone is asking today. Early this morning, a construction crew was working on Thirty-third Street while people across the city were going to work. At 8:29 A.M., a simple mistake by the construction crew caused a blackout that cut off power to almost a million people.

The blackout forced airports to send incoming flights elsewhere. But according to one report, an Alaskan jet liner was landing just when the power in the control tower failed. After the jet lost contact with the tower, the pilot landed the plane himself with no problems.

The mayor declared a state of emergency. Fortunately, no major accidents or injuries occurred, and the power returned after six hours and twenty minutes, at 2:49 this afternoon.

C1: Listening for Meaning and Use (p. 36)

1. The professor was writing a book of poetry. He was looking for an editor to help him. When he met an experienced editor at a party, he hired her immediately.
2. Sam was eating dinner when he heard the terrible news on the radio. He finished his dinner quickly and left.
3. Vera was taking a bath, and the children were asleep. It was a peaceful evening.
4. I called Roger, but he couldn't talk to me. He was painting his kitchen. It took him all day, but it came out great.
5. Jill was baking a cake for her boyfriend's surprise party. When he suddenly walked into the kitchen, she didn't know what to say.
6. Jane was writing a letter in the library yesterday. She seemed so sad when she mailed it on her way out.

D1: Listening for Meaning and Use (p. 43)

1. When I went home, I opened the mail.
2. After I played tennis, I took a shower.

3. The phone rang while I was fixing the bathroom sink.
4. She came home before it started to rain.
5. While I was waiting for John, I saw Erica.
6. The water ran out when I opened the drain.
7. After I called the operator, she connected me with Bogotá.
8. When I shouted, she turned around.

CHAPTER 3

A2 (p. 50)

Please refer to the newspaper article in the Student Book.

B1: Listening for Form (p. 54)

1. Don't worry about me. I'll call you as soon as I get home.
2. It's not going to rain this afternoon. Look at the sky.
3. The movie starts in five minutes. You still have time to get a drink.
4. We'll be cruising at an altitude of thirty thousand feet. We expect a smooth flight, so sit back and relax.
5. We're leaving early tomorrow morning. Can you walk the dog when you get up?
6. They're going to send a lot of work to us tomorrow. Let's get ready for it.
7. I can't come on Saturday. John will be arriving at noon, and I have to pick him up.
8. Are you going skiing this weekend? I'd like to join you.

C1: Listening for Meaning and Use (p. 59)

1. I invited Jill to see our apartment.
2. The door is stuck!
3. Oh, no! The oven's broken.
4. I'm sorry I didn't finish the report today.
5. No one can come to the phone right now. Please leave your name and number.
6. The fax machine is out of paper.
7. Excuse me. My car just broke down.
8. Just imagine, next week at this time . . .

D1: Listening for Meaning and Use (p. 63)

1. Look. It's going to rain.
   Look. It's raining.
2. We're going to have a party for my aunt's fortieth birthday next week.
   We're having a party for my aunt's fortieth birthday next week.
3. I think our team is going to win the tournament.
   I think our team is winning the tournament.
4. I go to sleep early.
   I'm going to sleep early.
5. I'm going to take a trip this summer with the money I've saved.
   I'm taking a trip this summer with the money I've saved.
6. We're leaving before dawn. All the plans are made.
   We leave before dawn. All the plans are made.

E1: Listening for Meaning and Use (p. 67)

1. Nina, look out!
2. This recorded announcement will not be repeated. Please hold.
3. Bob, I can't answer the phone. My hands are covered with paint.

4. Why are you turning off the TV?
5. Would someone please help me with the dishes?
6. Let's hurry up. The sky is dark, and I hear some thunder.
7. Can I have a drink of water?
8. What are your summer plans?

CHAPTER 4

A2 (p. 78)

Please refer to the magazine article in the Student Book.

B1: Listening for Form (p. 81)

1. He's won the race.
2. They called their senator in Washington.
3. Who's read the book over there?
4. Where's the team playing this week?
5. She's worried about her father.
6. Who's gone fishing?
7. You've bought all of the equipment already.
8. We looked up his telephone number.

Informally Speaking (p. 84)

F1: Seen any good movies lately?
F2: Yes, as a matter of fact. Last night I saw that new Japanese movie.

B5: Understanding Informal Speech (p. 84)

1. Heard any good jokes lately?
2. You taken your vacation yet?
3. Been to the beach yet this summer?
4. Eaten at that new restaurant yet?
5. She left yet?
6. You seen my keys?
7. You done any programming?
8. He called you lately?

C1: Listening for Meaning and Use (p. 86)

1. How many times have you seen that movie?
2. Have you ever won a prize?
3. Has the number twenty-nine bus come yet?
4. Have you been to Tokyo?
5. Have you finished the assignment yet?
6. What have you done so far?

D1: Listening for Meaning and Use, A (p. 89)

1. Have you noticed a change in students' attitudes lately?
2. The captain has turned off the seat belt sign.
3. We've known each other for such a long time. We're almost like sisters.
4. People have studied the universe since ancient times.
5. We have a late-breaking news report. The governor has just declared a state of emergency.
6. I hear the mail carrier. I think the mail has arrived.

D1: Listening for Meaning and Use, B (p. 90)

1. Mary came to class at 10 A.M. She's been in class for one hour.
   What time is it?
2. It's 5 P.M. and the repairman still hasn't called. Our printer broke this morning.
   How long has the printer been broken?

3. Jennifer arrived exactly on time for her two o'clock appointment with the doctor. She's been in the waiting room for an hour and a half.
   What time is it now?
4. It's midnight. The baby has had a fever since 9 P.M. and her temperature still hasn't gone down at all. It's time to call the doctor.
   How long has the baby had the fever?

E1: Listening for Meaning and Use (p. 94)

1. I lived there for a year. I really miss that place.
2. We've worked with him for six months. We're getting along so well.
3. He's kept the secret all week. I know he'll never tell anyone.
4. She studied physics for two years. Then she changed her major.
5. I've had a dog for a long time. I love him.
6. I owned a car for years. I sold it when I moved.
7. They worked there for three years. Then they were laid off.
8. I've played the piano for years. It relaxes me.

CHAPTER 5

A2 (p. 102)

Please refer to the magazine article in the Student Book.

B1: Listening for Form (p. 105)

1. What's happening this week?
2. Jack has been visiting his grandparents.
3. It's been raining all day.
4. They're living in Florida.
5. He's been sleeping on the sofa.
6. She's been exercising at the gym.

Informally Speaking (p. 108)

M1: You been going to the study sessions?
M2: No. I been writing my English paper all week. It's due tomorrow.

B5: Understanding Informal Speech (p. 108)

1. What'cha been doing all day?
2. I been visiting my friend.
3. You been feeling OK?
4. No, I been having some problems with my back.
5. You been exercising at all?
6. I been walking a lot.

C1: Listening for Meaning and Use (p. 110)

1. A: I've been reading the latest John Grisham novel. I can't put it down.
   B: Really? I've been thinking about reading it.
2. A: I haven't been feeling well for a few months.
   B: Really? I was sick for a few months too.
3. A: So what have you been doing lately, Helen?
   B: I've been volunteering at the hospital. I enjoy it so much.
   A: I volunteered at the hospital for a while. I found it very rewarding.
4. A: How are your children, Max?
   B: They're good, thanks. What about yours?
   A: Terrific. I just visited them in Chicago.
   B: Really. I've been going to Chicago for medical treatments this year.
5. A: So, Helen, have you seen Eddie?
   B: No. I've been trying to call him for days, but his phone has been busy from morning until night.
   A: I know. He's always online. I was trying for a while, too, but I gave up.
6. A: So what else is new, Max?
   B: I've been learning to play chess. I love it.
   A: Oh, I love chess, but I haven't been playing at all since I moved here. Maybe I should start again.

D1: Listening for Meaning and Use (p. 114)

1. I've been painting my office all morning.
2. He's already taken a shower.
3. They've been giving free samples in the supermarket since yesterday.
4. We've known each other for only two months.
5. My sister has interviewed at that company.
6. The manager has been waiting for you. Hurry up!
7. I've lived here since last year.
8. We've just seen that movie.

CHAPTER 6

A2 (p. 122)

Please refer to the book excerpt in the Student Book.

B1: Listening for Form (p. 126)

In 1928, Amelia Earhart became the first woman to fly across the Atlantic. Ten years before, she'd been working as a nurse's aide when she visited an airfield near Toronto. She made up her mind that she wanted to fly an airplane right then. After her trans-Atlantic flight, Ms. Earhart became an instant heroine, although she really hadn't flown the plane. Her two male companions hadn't let her touch any of the controls. But the world didn't care. Charles Lindbergh had crossed the Atlantic a year earlier, and many aviators had been trying to repeat his successful flight since then. Sadly, fourteen pilots, including three women, had died since Lindbergh's triumph. Because Ms. Earhart had been embarrassed about her role in her first trans-Atlantic flight, she seemed more determined than ever to fly across the Atlantic alone. And that's exactly what happened in 1932 when she finally flew over the Atlantic by herself.

Informally Speaking (p. 129)

F1: Did you see Dan and Maria at the party last night?
F2: Dan'd already left by the time I got there, but I saw Maria.

B6: Understanding Informal Speech (p. 129)

1. She'd never been alone in the woods before.
2. Her family'd gone camping when she was young.
3. Her father'd taught her the skills she needed.
4. No one'd prepared her for this experience, though.
5. Why'd she signed up for this program?
6. Who'd she been trying to impress?

C1: Listening for Meaning and Use (p. 132)

1. The patient's condition had improved by the time the doctor came.
2. By the time the plane landed, we had gotten to the airport.
3. I entered the building before I took off my hat.
4. The emergency crew arrived after the building had collapsed.
5. I saw Betty before she heard the news.
6. He became vice president after he had worked hard.
7. After I called my mother, I spoke to my sister.
8. Even though she'd hurt her wrist, she went to work.

D1: Listening for Meaning and Use (p. 137)

1. I had just picked up the phone when the doorbell rang.
2. He was a good writer, but he'd written a boring book.
3. We'd been eating dinner before we heard the news.
4. I'd waited at home until she called.
5. I didn't want to read the book because I'd seen the movie.
6. I wasn't surprised by the traffic because I'd been listening to the traffic report.
7. We took the class because many people had recommended it.
8. She'd left town by the time I tried to contact her.

CHAPTER 7

A2 (p. 146)

Please refer to the magazine article in the Student Book.

B1: Listening for Form (p. 150)

The Abominable Snowman of the Himalayas and the Loch Ness Monster of Scotland are two creatures that may or may not be real—that depends on your beliefs. If you ask someone about them, they may respond, "That can't be true," or they might respond, "That must be true." Over the years, it has been difficult to separate fact from fiction as stories about these creatures continue.

Could it be true that an apelike creature with long hair lives high in the Himalayas? Could the large footprints found there belong to such a creature? While many scientists say this has to be a myth, others claim that there may be some kind of creature out there. But no one knows for sure.

In Scotland, could there really be a mysterious water monster with a long neck and a large body like a brontosaurus? Many claim that there's got to be some truth to this story that's been around since the fifteenth century. Just ask the two million tourists who visit the area each year, hoping to see the monster.

C1: Listening for Meaning and Use (p. 155)

1. The cat could be in the yard, or she might be under the porch.
2. It's 10:30. He must be on his way home.
3. The trip could take two days—maybe three.
4. He can't be getting an A. He failed two tests.
5. She must be so tired. She stayed up all night.
6. Your car should be ready. They said to pick it up at two.
7. The cake ought to be ready now. The oven timer just rang.
8. He might not be working right now, or maybe he is. Who knows?

D1: Listening for Meaning and Use (p. 162)

1. It might rain next week. Let's make a different plan, just in case.
2. The plane should arrive on time since it left on time.
3. The package will arrive tomorrow. I sent it by express mail.
4. There could be a storm tomorrow so let's be prepared.
5. The car shouldn't give us any more problems. It's been repaired.
6. In a few years, they won't be selling that type of computer.
7. In twenty years, we might be using robots to do housework. Who knows?
8. She ought to be here any minute. She left an hour ago.

CHAPTER 8

A2 (p. 168)

Please refer to the magazine article in the Student Book.

B1: Listening for Form (p. 172)

According to a recent poll, many people believe that aliens must have visited the earth at some time in the past. They believe that experts and government officials shouldn't have ignored the sightings of unusual flying objects and strange lights that people have reported over the years. In fact, a group of experts has conducted the first scholarly investigation of unidentified flying objects (UFOs) in thirty years. According to the experts, by ignoring reports of UFOs, we may have overlooked important information that could have led us to new discoveries. They point out how scientists in the past ignored reports of meteorites by saying that these objects couldn't have fallen from outer space. Looking back now, experts agree that it was inappropriate to assume that those reports were lies or dreams.

UFO believers are delighted with this news. According to one believer, "It's about time. The scientific community should have done this a long time ago. But it's also sad. They must have ignored hundreds, or maybe thousands, of good pieces of scientific data. They shouldn't have been so naïve."

Informally Speaking (p. 175)

F1: This traffic is terrible! We should-uv stayed in the office!
F2: Yeah. We could-uv left after rush hour.

B5: Understanding Informal Speech (p. 175)

F: I'm sorry I'm late. I should-uv called you. Then you could-uv met me downtown.
M: That might not-a worked anyway. I didn't get out of work until six. And then there must-a been fifty people waiting for the elevator. It took me ten minutes to get out of the building.
F: So where's Linda? She should-uv been here by now. She must-uv forgotten.
M: I doubt that. She could-a gotten stuck in traffic, or she might-a left work late, too. Let's sit down over there and wait for her.

C1: Listening for Meaning and Use (p. 177)

1. Neanderthals may have built shelters for safety.
2. They couldn't have sewn their clothing.

3. They can't have lived in Africa.
4. They have to have had a language.
5. They may not have had a complex language.
6. Cold weather might have driven them into Asia.
7. They could have died because of disease or change in climate.
8. They couldn't have been relatives of modern humans.

D1: Listening for Meaning and Use (p. 182)

1. All the students were supposed to apply for the scholarship, but John didn't.
2. John had the opportunity to leave early, but he stayed.
3. It was a good idea to ask the teacher for help, but John didn't do it.
4. John's school required him to take two English courses.
5. John was allowed to register late.
6. John promised to call his parents yesterday, but then he forgot to do it.
7. John had two job opportunities: one at a bank and one at a department store. He chose the department store.
8. I was sorry that I didn't call John last night.

CHAPTER 9

A2 (p. 192)

Please refer to the book excerpt in the Student Book.

B1: Listening for Form (p. 195)

1. Last year some research was being done on smiling across cultures.
2. I was asked to join the study after it began.
3. A number of questions were being studied at the same time.
4. For example, is the general meaning of a smile always understood?
5. Why is the mouth covered in some cultures?
6. Is it true that smiles are reserved for friends and family in some cultures?
7. The results of this research were reported at a psychology conference.
8. The results are also being published in a popular psychology magazine.

C1: Listening for Meaning and Use (p. 199)

1. Twenty-five students were asked to participate in a research study.
2. Each student took a test.
3. The test was designed to measure cultural attitudes.
4. The instructions were given by a graduate student.
5. Several sentences were read aloud.
6. The students were looking at some pictures at the same time.
7. The students matched the sentences with the pictures.
8. The results were reported by the professor on his website.

D1: Listening for Meaning and Use (p. 203)

1. Visitors are asked not to smoke in this building.
2. French is spoken in Quebec.
3. We called Julie at the hospital yesterday. She was permitted to speak to us briefly.
4. Several people were injured by a falling tree.
5. The book was written in 1966.
6. Your assistance is appreciated.

CHAPTER 10

A2 (p. 212)

Please refer to the newspaper article in the Student Book.

B1: Listening for Form (p. 215)

1. What can be done to control violence among children?
2. The average twelve-year-old has seen thousands of violent incidents on television.
3. Childhood violence has definitely been linked to television and video games.
4. According to experts, children under two years of age shouldn't be allowed to watch television.
5. Older children can be permitted to watch a limited amount of TV.
6. Parents should monitor the programs that their children watch.
7. Parents will protest against TV stations that show violent programs.
8. Will violence be reduced by these actions?

C1: Listening for Meaning and Use (p. 219)

1. Have you ever been blamed by someone for something that you didn't do?
2. I was punished by my fifth-grade teacher for someone else's bad behavior.
3. Later that year, I was sent for by the principal. I was so scared!
4. I was chosen by the school to represent my school at a student conference.
5. I was allowed by the school to miss classes for a whole day.
6. At the conference, we were given lunch by the conference organizers.
7. I wrote an article about the conference. It was published by the publisher in my local newspaper.
8. Not long after, I was interviewed by another newspaper in the next town.

D1: Listening for Meaning and Use (p. 222)

1. Tonight we bring to you the following question: Could the latest school violence have been prevented? Our panel is a group of parents, teachers, and psychologists who have each been personally touched by the issue of school violence in recent months.
2. I'd like to summarize what has been covered so far. First, it is generally assumed that mental processes are accompanied by changes in the brain. Similarly, it is assumed that changes in the brain accompany the encoding, storage, and retrieval of information. In other words, memory is a mental process that is accompanied by changes in the brain.
3. It was a great weekend. The most experienced managers were sent to the new facility in Phoenix, Arizona. We were required to spend two weeks training newcomers, after participating in several workshops on interpersonal relations.
4. Tonight's performance has been canceled due to the weather. Tickets will be refunded at the ticket office, beginning on Monday, January second. Refunds can also be arranged by mail. For further information about mail refunds, press two. Thank you.

5. They're not gonna accept this unless you bring another form of identification with you. Look, it says right here that two forms of identification are required. Take a look at the list of acceptable documents that's given in the manual on page forty-three.
6. A look at the future, brought to you by the United Fabric Guild. In a few years, clothing will be made of antibacterial fabrics. Odors will be eliminated, which means that deodorant will no longer be needed. Also, more industrial materials like Kevlar, Teflon, and Tyvek will be used to make durable, cutting-edge clothing.
7. Remember, BASIC is one of several programming languages that are used for personal computers. Now, learning to understand and use BASIC, or another programming language, can be considered very much like learning a foreign language. BASIC has its own vocabulary and a set of rules that must be followed when using that vocabulary.
8. Several aftershocks were again felt this afternoon by survivors of the latest earthquake to hit the area. No major damage has been reported, although unconfirmed reports of gas leaks in outlying areas are being investigated as we speak.

Informally Speaking (p. 224)

F: Guess what? I'm going to get promoted to district manager.
M: Congratulations!

D3: Understanding Informal Speech (p. 224)

1. Do you think you'll get sent to the convention in Hawaii?
2. I might get promoted soon.
3. John may get transferred to the Boston office.
4. He got accepted by Harvard Business School.
5. Liz got caught breaking the rules.
6. She could get fired.
7. Steve finally got rewarded for all of his extra work.
8. He got nominated for a special award yesterday.

CHAPTER 11

A2 (p. 230)

Please refer to the book excerpt in the Student Book.

B1: Listening for Form (p. 234)

1. I try to relax when I drive.
2. Experts recommend learning simple breathing exercises.
3. Breathing a certain way can calm your mind almost immediately.
4. Most of us don't allow ourselves to breathe deeply and release tension.
5. If you can't seem to relax, simple breathing exercises can help enormously.
6. Anytime you feel stress, remember to breathe in, breathe out, and relax.

C1: Listening for Meaning and Use (p. 240)

1. I stopped helping John.
2. I didn't remember to put gas in the tank.
3. I tried to take fish oil.
4. I regret to tell you that she left.
5. I stopped to buy the newspaper.
6. I'll never forget meeting the President.

D1: Listening for Form (p. 245)

A: You should consider taking a vacation. You could spend some time relaxing.
B: I can't. I'm busy working on a project that's due soon. My boss has told me to finish it as quickly as possible.
A: I know. That's the point. Aren't you sick of working?
B: Well, instead of taking a long vacation, I might be interested in going away for a weekend. But I'd have trouble leaving before noon on Saturday. I save Saturday morning for catching up on my office e-mail.
A: Didn't you promise to relax more?

E1: Listening for Meaning and Use (p. 248)

1. The doctor advised my friend not to work so hard.
2. I asked the doctor to recommend some exercises.
3. She had us call a health club.
4. They didn't mind us calling in the evening.
5. We arranged to speak to the manager.
6. My brother invited us to come over.
7. The roads were wet. I worried about my friend's driving in the rain.
8. Before we left, the manager made us leave a deposit.

CHAPTER 12

A2 (p. 256)

Please refer to the book excerpt in the Student Book.

B1: Listening for Form (p. 260)

Although the common cold is generally not serious, it causes people to be absent from work and go to the doctor more often than other illnesses. The majority of colds come from contact with surfaces that people touch frequently. People transmit the cold viruses on these surfaces to their eyes, noses, and mouths. Once the symptoms appear, there are many treatments for relieving the discomfort. Whatever a person does, unfortunately, a cold will probably still last from six to ten days.

C1: Listening for Meaning and Use (p. 263)

1. I drank orange juice with my breakfast this morning.
2. Apples are supposed to be very healthy.
3. I need a new doctor. Mine has retired.
4. I have a friend who works for Dr. Garcia. I'll ask her if she recommends him.
5. Please have some soup. I made it myself. It'll help your cold.
6. I made an appointment with Dr. Garcia after I spoke to your friend. I'm going tomorrow at three.
7. I'd like to find a book about herbal medicine. Do you know of any?
8. I took cough medicine last night before I went to bed. It didn't help.

D1: Listening for Meaning and Use (p. 267)

1. The salesman showed me a beautiful blue shirt and a plaid tie.
2. My neighbor's daughter was selling candy to make money for her school trip.
3. We'd like to invite a writer to come and speak to our creative writing class.
4. I went to a wedding yesterday.
5. What are they fixing on your car?
6. Is that new CD on the top shelf?
7. Please hold on for a minute.
8. I sent them a check last week, but they didn't receive it.

E1: Listening for Meaning and Use (p. 273)

1. I threw out the carrot. It was rotten.
2. Almonds are a high-fat food that is actually good for the heart.
3. The National Cancer Institute is carrying out research on the effects of garlic for preventing and treating cancer.
4. I cooked food that was good for her cold. I made chicken soup with garlic and pepper in it.
5. The onion has many health benefits, according to the latest research.
6. I had a cold for only a few days this time. I was lucky.
7. My doctor thinks people don't need to take vitamins if they eat properly.
8. A headache can last for a few minutes, hours, or days.

CHAPTER 13

A2 (p. 280)

Please refer to the newspaper article in the Student Book.

B1: Listening for Form (p. 284)

1. I like to wear clothes that express my individuality.
2. The dress code, which is very casual, is being eliminated.
3. I was talking to Ms. Chang, who is the manager.
4. In some banks and law firms, the dress code is still very conservative.
5. Barker Bank, which has a strict dress code, seems out of date.
6. We used to wear clothes that were more formal.
7. At some companies, the men don't have to wear ties anymore.
8. Everyone likes my boss, who dresses very casually.

C1: Listening for Meaning and Use (p. 289)

1. Which one is your boss?
2. What do you think about the dress code?
3. Which computer isn't working?
4. Who's on the phone?
5. Who's going to lunch with you?
6. Who is Juan's neighbor?
7. Which books are yours?
8. What did they say you should wear?

D1: Listening for Meaning and Use (p. 295)

1. My sister, who lives in New York, has two children. She calls me on Saturdays.
2. Have you met her brother who works at the bank? He's not as tall as the younger one.
3. Give me the sheet of paper which has the list of names. It's next to those other papers.
4. The man who is talking is my boss. Do you know the men who are sitting with him?
5. She showed me her necklace, which had beautiful stones. She got it for her birthday.
6. Her grandmother, who lived until eighty, was a teacher.

CHAPTER 14

A2 (p. 302)

Please refer to the magazine article in the Student Book.

B1: Listening for Form (p. 306)

1. The team that played didn't do very well.
2. The equipment which broke is expensive to repair.
3. Did you hear about the team that we beat?
4. We didn't know about the rules they changed.
5. I didn't meet the player they called.
6. The man who called wanted to join the team.

C1: Listening for Meaning and Use (p. 310)

1. A woman I know has become a professional hockey player.
2. She started out on a local boys' hockey team, which she quit to join a girls' team.
3. She had a wonderful coach, who her parents adored too.
4. Two women who I knew in high school became professional athletes.
5. My high school, which didn't have a lot of money, actually had a sports program for girls.
6. Well, the sports they offered girls in my high school weren't that interesting.

D1: Listening for Form (p. 315)

1. Do you know the woman he's married to?
2. The man who he spoke to helped quite a bit.
3. Let's look at the book I brought in.
4. Did you meet the people he works with?
5. Did you see the doctor? I was waiting for her.

E1: Listening for Meaning and Use (p. 318)

1. Q: Didja buy the CD I told you about?
   A: No, not yet.
2. This lecture will explore two issues about which you've already read a great deal, and one more with which you may be unfamiliar.
3. Ladies and gentlemen, there is someone in this room whom we would all like to thank. Let's have a round of applause for Robin Strauss, who has worked tirelessly for the last six years.
4. Scotty, please pick up the magazine you were just looking at.
5. The court has the list of the witnesses whom you will call. Be advised that . . .
6. After you beat the eggs, pour them into the bowl you mixed the dry ingredients in.

CHAPTER 15

A2 (p. 328)
Please refer to the selections in the Student Book.

B1: Listening for Form (p. 332)
1. I wish we could spend more time together.
2. If we were married, our phone expenses would be less.
3. If you finish your term paper by Wednesday, take an early flight on Thursday.
4. If you find a good job, I'll move there.
5. Don't you wish we attended the same university?
6. If our summer plans don't work out, it doesn't matter.
7. Would you be upset if I didn't want a big wedding?
8. If my parents don't approve of our wedding plans, do you want to elope?

Informally Speaking (p. 334)
F1: I need a jacket, but nothing fits me. I wish I was taller.
F2: If it was earlier, we could go to another store. Let's do that tomorrow.

B6: Understanding Informal Speech (p. 334)
1. If I wasn't so tired, I'd go out for a cup of coffee with you.
2. What would you do if it was too late to take the bus?
3. I wish my boss wasn't so unfriendly.
4. If he was ready, we could leave now.
5. She'd tell you if she was mad at you.
6. Don't you wish he was going with us?

C1: Listening for Meaning and Use (p. 337)
1. You have reached A and H Healthcare. If you want to speak to a representative, press one.
2. If I am elected, I'll lower taxes and spend more money on education.
3. If a holiday falls on a Thursday, the company usually **closes** for the weekend.
4. It's 3 A.M. If you don't turn down the music, I'm going to complain to the police.
5. I'll help you this morning if you help me this afternoon.
6. If it snows hard, you should get a ride with Lauren.
7. Generally, the mall is crowded if it's raining.
8. Call me if the flight gets delayed.

D1: Listening for Meaning and Use (p. 341)
1. Would you mind if I came late?
2. What'll you do if the bus arrives late?
3. Would you quit your job if your boss didn't treat you well?
4. If you could have dinner with a famous person, who would you choose?
5. Will you be home later if I call?
6. Would it be OK if I used your phone?

E1: Listening for Meaning and Use (p. 345)
1. I wish I didn't have a cold. I'd go out tonight.
2. I wish this book had pictures. It would be so much easier to follow.
3. If only I had free time, I'd volunteer at the hospital.
4. I wish I didn't have a car. It's so much trouble.
5. I wish he'd get a safety lock for that window.
6. I wish there weren't a limit for carry-on luggage on planes. Then I could take more bags.
7. If only I didn't have a credit card, then I couldn't spend so much money.
8. I wish you would get rid of your guitar.

CHAPTER 16

A2 (p. 352)
Please refer to the magazine article in the Student Book.

B1: Listening for Form (p. 355)
1. A: Do you agree with what I did?
   B: Not really. If it had been me, I wouldn't have interrupted him.
2. A: Would you do anything differently next time?
   B: If I had another chance, I'd prepare more for the interview.
3. A: If it had been you, would you have come so late in the evening?
   B: No, I wouldn't have.
4. A: What do you think about the introductory course?
   B: If I had listened to my roommate, I wouldn't have taken it.
5. A: Have you ever thought about moving?
   B: Yes, if I'd had my way, we would have moved to Seattle.
6. A: You didn't call.
   B: I know. I would have called if it hadn't been so late.

Informally Speaking (p. 357)
M: The waiter overcharged me for lunch today, but I didn't say anything.
F: Well, I woulda shown him the mistake. I sure wouldn't-uv paid the extra money.

B4: Understanding Informal Speech (p. 357)
1. Would you-uv chosen a different career if you hadn't married so young?
2. If I had studied, I might-uv done much better on the quiz.
3. We wouldn't-a been so late if the car had been working.
4. If I hadn't been careful, I could-a had an accident.
5. I would-uv been late if I'd missed the bus.
6. If I hadn't scored, we wouldn't-uv won the game.

C1: Listening for Meaning and Use (p. 360)
1. What would have happened if John F. Kennedy hadn't been shot?
2. Would he have ended the Vietnam War sooner?
3. Would he still be in politics?
4. Would the sixties have been different?
5. Would the students still have rebelled?
6. Would the world be a safer place right now?
7. Would your country be any different?
8. Would there have been a nuclear war?

D1: Listening for Meaning and Use (p. 364)
1. I wish I'd read about World War II before I saw the movie *Saving Private Ryan*.
2. If only I'd been home when the phone rang.
3. If only she'd been elected to the council, then she'd be able to represent us.
4. I wish you had called at the end of your exam.
5. We would've flown home but we couldn't get reservations.

6. If only the tree hadn't fallen on the driveway as I was leaving.
7. Don't you wish you had taken a day off last week instead of today?
8. I wish I had stayed, but I had a headache.

CHAPTER 17

A2 (p. 372)

Please refer to the website article from the Student Book.

B1: Listening for Form (p. 375)

1. Find out what opportunities are out there.
2. If possible, find out who your boss would be.
3. Decide if you would work weekends or not.
4. Demonstrate how you will achieve the company's goals.
5. Figure out whether you want to work for a big or small company.
6. Don't assume that you'll find work immediately.
7. Decide what you want.
8. Consider whether or not you would work part-time.

C1: Listening for Meaning and Use (p. 380)

1. Do you know what time the show starts?
2. I was wondering why John's not taking the job.
3. Do you know what office she works in?
4. Our meeting's been postponed.
5. Please tell me if you got the raise.
6. Do you know whether the mail has come?
7. Can you tell me what time the meeting is?
8. Could you tell me what the most important advice for a job hunter is?

D1: Listening for Meaning and Use (p. 386)

1. Linda is going to meet us tonight.
2. Someone's at the door.
3. He regrets that he left the party.
4. I've decided I'm going to buy more insurance.
5. He admitted he was wrong.
6. I thought she was sleeping when I called.

CHAPTER 18

A2 (p. 392)

Please refer to the magazine article in the Student Book.

B1: Listening for Form (p. 396)

1. I asked Scott what he wanted for his birthday, and he said that he didn't know.
2. I asked if he wanted some books.
3. We said we'd call him back on Monday.
4. He asked if we could call on Tuesday instead.
5. He told us he had a special date on Monday night.
6. That made us curious. We asked him who he was going out with.
7. He politely answered that it was none of our business.
8. We asked him if he had any secrets he wanted to tell us.

C1: Listening for Meaning and Use (p. 401)

1. He asked me if he needed a prescription.
2. I told you that she has a headache.
3. She said she'll call when she gets the results.
4. He asked when the results would come.
5. She said they would come tomorrow.
6. She told me that I'd missed my last appointment.
7. I informed them that my ankle was sprained.
8. He said they'd call back that day.

Student Book Answer Key

CHAPTER 1

A3: After You Read (p. 5)
2. T 3. F 4. F 5. T 6. F

Examining Form (p. 6)
1. Simple Present
   - line 1: 's
   - line 1: is
   - line 9: does
   - line 12: 's
   - line 17: helps
   - line 44: interferes
   - line 20: has
   - line 21: contains
   - line 25: publicizes
   - line 49: are
   - line 26: take
   - line 27: stretch out
   - line 29: predicts
   - line 34: 's
   - line 36: needs
   - line 39: is
   - line 40: get
   - line 43: say
   - line 44: 're
   - line 46: misses
   - line 47: says
   - line 49: 're
   - line 50: 're
   - line 52: is
   - line 53: leads
   - line 54: doesn't stop

   Present Continuous
   - line 2: ('re) plowing
   - line 3: 're fighting
   - line 5: are zooming
   - line 6: is beginning
   - line 11: are beginning
   - line 13: are sleeping
   - line 14: (are) working
   - line 16: are warming up
   - line 32: is getting
   - line 33: is aging
   - line 34: are not getting
   - line 56: 're napping
   - line 58: are trying
   - line 59: 're putting
   - line 60: ('re) pretending

2. Simple Present Negative Statements
   - line 12: 's not
   - line 50: 're not
   - line 52: is not
   - line 54: doesn't stop

   Present Continuous Negative Statements
   - line 34: are not getting

   To make a negative statement in the simple present with forms of *be*, the form to use is *BE + not*. With other verbs, the form to use is *do/does + not + verb*. To make a negative statement in the present continuous, the form to use is *BE + not + verb + -ing*.

3. a. Does the average American sleep six hours a night?
   b. Are Americans sleeping less?

   In sentence a (simple present), you have to add *do/does* before the subject and change the main verb to its base form. In sentence b (present continuous), you have to invert the subject and *be* (auxiliary verb).

B1: Listening for Form (p. 8)
2. c
3. b
4. c
5. a
6. c
7. a
8. b

B2: Working on Verb Forms (p. 9)

	BASE FORM	SIMPLE PRESENT	PRESENT CONTINUOUS
2.	open	open / opens	opening
3.	fix	fix / fixes	fixing
4.	stop	stop / stops	stopping
5.	wake	wake / wakes	waking
6.	say	say / says	saying
7.	rest	rest / rests	resting
8.	dry	dry / dries	drying

B3: Working on Present Continuous Statements and Questions (p. 9)

Conversation 1
2. I'm wearing shoes.

Conversation 2
1. Are you buying a soda?
2. I'm not getting anything.
3. What are you doing?
4. I'm trying to get back my money.

Conversation 3
1. What are you doing?
2. I'm looking for a pencil.
3. Why are you making such a mess?

B4: Working on Simple Present Statements and Questions (p. 10)

A.
2. The earth doesn't revolve around the moon. It revolves around the sun.
3. Palm trees don't grow in cold climates. They grow in warm climates.
4. Bees don't live in ponds. They live in hives.
5. The sun doesn't rise in the north. It rises in the east.
6. Penguins don't live in the desert. They live in the Antarctic.
7. Flowers don't bloom in the winter. They bloom in the summer.
8. Spiders don't have six legs. They have eight legs.

B. Answers will vary. Some examples are:
2. A: What does the earth revolve around?
   B: The earth revolves around the sun.
   A: Does the earth revolve around the moon?
   B: No, it doesn't. It revolves around the sun.
3. A: Where do palm trees grow?
   B: Palm trees grow in warm climates.
   A: Do palm trees grow in warm climates?
   B: Yes, they do.
4. A: Where do bees live?
   B: Bees live in hives.
   A: Do bees live in ponds?
   B: No, they don't. Bees live in hives.
5. A: Where does the sun rise?
   B: The sun rises in the east.
   A: Does the sun rise in the east?
   B: Yes, it does.
6. A: Where do penguins live?
   B: Penguins live in the Antarctic.
   A: Do penguins live in the desert?
   B: No, they don't. They live in the Antarctic.

7. A: When do flowers bloom?
   B: Flowers bloom in the summer.
   A: Do flowers bloom in the summer?
   B: Yes, they do.
8. A: How many legs do spiders have?
   B: They have eight legs.
   A: Do spiders have six legs?
   B: No, they don't. They have eight legs.

B5: Understanding Informal Speech (p. 11)
2. Do you need
3. Are you having
4. Are you doing
5. Do you have
6. Do you like
7. Are you working
8. Do you need

Examining Meaning and Use (p. 12)
1. b   2. a

C1: Listening for Meaning and Use (p. 14)
2. c   4. c   6. b   8. c
3. c   5. a   7. b

C2: Contrasting Activities in Progress with Routine Activities (p. 14)
A. Answers will vary. Some examples are:
A boy is building a sandcastle.
His mother is reading a book.
A man is playing with his dog.
He is throwing a ball to his dog.
The dog is catching the ball.
Two teenage boys are sitting on a towel on the sand.
They are listening to a radio and talking.
One boy is holding a soft drink in his hand and is wearing black sunglasses.
Another boy is talking.
People are playing volleyball on the beach.

B. Answers will vary.

C3: Describing Activities in the Extended Present (p. 15)
Answers will vary.

C4: Contrasting Permanent and Temporary Situations (p. 15)
2. f   3. e   4. a   5. b   6. d

C5: Expressing Complaints (p. 16)
Answers will vary.

C6: Introducing a Topic with the Simple Present (p. 16)
A. Answers will vary.
B. Answers will vary.

Examining Meaning and Use (p. 17)
1. b, d   2. a, c, e

D1: Listening for Meaning and Use (p. 19)

	STATE OR CONDITION	ACTIVITY
2.		✓
3.	✓	
4.	✓	
5.		✓
6.	✓	

D2: Making Critical Remarks with Stative Verbs (p. 19)
Answers will vary. Some examples are:
2. I don't like it. It smells awful.
3. I don't like it. The fabric feels cheap.
4. I'm not sure. They seem small.
5. I don't like it. It sounds terrible.
6. I don't think so. It is expensive.

D3: Choosing the Simple Present or the Present Continuous (p. 20)

Conversation 1
2. Is it
3. depends on
4. guess
5. 's
6. 'm having

Conversation 2
1. hope
2. 'm not interrupting
3. need
4. seems
5. smell

Conversation 3
1. do you dream
2. don't dream
3. has
4. don't remember

Conversation 4
1. are you doing
2. am smelling
3. think
4. does it smell
5. seems

D4: Describing Physical Sensations (p. 21)
Answers will vary. Some examples are:
2. B: My head aches. OR My head is aching.
3. B: My eye burns. OR My eye is burning.
4. B: My ankle hurts. OR My ankle is hurting.
5. B: My stomach feels bad. OR My stomach is feeling bad.
6. B: My arm itches. OR My arm is itching.

D5: Describing Behavior (p. 21)
A. The dogs are sick.
The flowers are purple.
The children are quiet.
The children are sick.
The children are rude.
The children are being quiet.
The children are being rude.

B. Answers will vary. Some examples are:
2. She often helps her friends and family.
3. It is usually very stingy.
4. Usually, they are very noisy.
5. He yells at his employees for no reason.
6. Usually, he is very understanding.
7. Usually, she says hello.

D6: Understanding Informal Speech (p. 22)

2. I hate
3. We just love
4. She really dislikes
5. I love
6. I really like

D7: Writing Descriptions (p. 23)

Answers will vary.

E1: Thinking about Meaning and Use (p. 24)

1. a. No   b. It's not clear   c. Probably not
2. a. No   b. Yes   c. No
3. a. It's not clear   b. Probably not   c. It's not clear
4. a. No   b. No   c. It's not clear
5. a. No   b. Yes   c. No
6. a. No   b. No   c. Probably

E2: Editing (p. 25)

It's mid-afternoon at a busy law firm in Washington, D.C. The telephones ~~is~~ *are* ringing, voice mail ~~piles~~ *is piling* up, and faxes are arriving. But what many of the lawyers ~~are~~ *are* doing? They ~~take~~ *are taking* naps at their desks! As more and more busy professionals ~~works~~ *work* from morning until night, many are ~~sleep~~ *sleeping* in their offices for just 15 or 20 minutes during the afternoon. And they are not embarrassed about it at all. It ~~becomes~~ *is becoming* a new trend, according to a recent survey on napping.

Some people ~~sleeps~~ *sleep* in their chairs, while some ~~are~~ *are* ~~preferring~~ *prefer* the floor or couches. Everyone agrees that a little nap ~~help~~ *helps* them get through their very long workday. Meanwhile, many experts are asking "What ~~means~~ *does* this new trend *mean*?" It's simple, according to the most experienced nappers. They ~~are~~ *are* ~~do~~ *doing* what people in other cultures and climates do every day. And they are pleased that napping finally ~~gets~~ *is getting* more common in the workplace.

CHAPTER 2

A3: After You Read (p. 29)

2. c   3. b   4. b   5. a   6. b

Examining Form (p. 30)

1. Regular Simple Past

line 7: lifted	line 26: occurred
line 8: asked	line 31: faded
line 9: replied	line 31: disappeared
line 13: glanced	line 32: continued
line 14: stared	line 35: seemed
line 15: realized	line 35: rushed
line 20: seemed	line 35: swirled
line 24: impressed	line 36: slammed
line 24: clattered	line 36: leaped
line 25: scattered	

Irregular Simple Past

line 3: were	line 21: was
line 4: saw	line 22: was
line 4: was	line 24: came
line 5: grew	line 24: was
line 7: rang	line 26: were
line 8: did see	line 26: were
line 10: said	line 27: were
line 12: felt	line 29: felt
line 14: thought	line 30: ran
line 14: saw	line 30: got
line 15: was	line 30: saw
line 15: was	line 32: went
line 19: did	line 34: rang
line 21: was	line 37: found

2. Singular Past Continuous

line 12: was standing	line 30: was scraping
line 23: was making	line 33: was talking

Plural Past Continuous

line 17: were sitting	line 27: were enjoying
line 18: were doing	line 28: were enjoying
line 19: were gossiping	line 29: were playing
line 20: were talking	line 29: (were) laughing

3. Before Main Clause

line 19: while they were talking
line 23: When the jolt came
line 29: While they were playing and laughing
line 30: When they got there
line 35: Before the watertight door slammed down

After Main Clause

line 4: when Fleet suddenly saw something directly ahead
line 14: before he realized it was an iceberg
line 26: when the strange vibration occurred
line 33: when the warning bell rang

B1: Listening for Form (p. 32)

2. went   9. failed
3. was working   10. lost
4. were going   11. landed
5. caused   12. declared
6. cut off   13. occurred
7. forced   14. returned
8. was landing

B2: Building Simple Past and Past Continuous Sentences (p. 33)

When did you go online yesterday?
What did you do when the bell rang?
What were you studying this morning?
Did you buy a computer?
Did you go online yesterday?
Who paid cash?
What happened last night?
You paid cash.

B3: Identifying Dependent and Independent Clauses (p. 33)

3. Something vibrated inside the ship.
5. The iceberg hit the ship.
6. Some passengers were getting ready for bed.
8. A group was still playing bridge.

B4: Combining Sentences with Time Clauses (p. 34)

2. While he was reading, he was listening to music.
   He was listening to music while he was reading.
   While he was listening to music, he was reading.
   He was reading while he was listening to music.
3. After he studied hard, he went to law school.
   He went to law school after he studied hard.
4. Before she fell asleep, the doorbell rang.
   The doorbell rang before she fell asleep.
   Before the doorbell rang, she fell asleep.
   She fell asleep before the doorbell rang.
5. When the fire started, we were sleeping.
   We were sleeping when the fire started.
   When we were sleeping, the fire started.
   The fire started when we were sleeping.
6. Before the TV show started, they went to bed.
   They went to bed before the TV show started.
   Before they went to bed, the TV show started.
   The TV show started before they went to bed.
7. While the phone was ringing, they were cooking dinner.
   They were cooking dinner while the phone was ringing.
   While they were cooking dinner, the phone was ringing.
   The phone was ringing while they were cooking dinner.
8. Before the package arrived, she called the post office.
   She called the post office before the package arrived.
   Before she called the post office, the package arrived.
   The package arrived before she called the post office.

B5: Asking and Answering Questions with Time Clauses (p. 34)

Answers will vary.

Examining Meaning and Use (p. 35)

Completed event: 1a and 2a; Unfinished event: 1b and 2b

C1: Listening for Meaning and Use (p. 36)

	ACTIVITY	COMPLETED	MAY CONTINUE
2.	eating dinner	✓	
3.	taking a bath	✓	
4.	painting his kitchen	✓	
5.	baking a cake		✓
6.	writing a letter	✓	

C2: Describing Activities in Progress in the Past (p. 37)

Answers will vary. Some examples are:
A woman was talking on a cell phone.
A man was trying to read a book.
A young man was trying to study.
Someone was using a copier.
Two people were using computers.
Someone was looking for a book.
A library employee was shelving books.
A woman was checking out books.
Someone was returning books.
Someone was asking the reference librarian questions.
A mother was reading to her child.

C3: Contrasting In-Progress and Completed Past Situations (p. 38)

2. were playing
3. were studying
4. was reading
5. was doing
6. I heard
7. were telling
8. went
9. stopped
10. jumped
11. dropped
12. ran
13. sat
14. saw

C4: Describing Background Activities (p. 38)

Answers will vary. Some examples are:
2. We were cooking dinner.
   My roommate was doing her homework.
3. We were watching television.
   The rain was pouring down.
4. I was using my brother's car.
   I was doing my weekly shopping.
5. I was working on an important report.
   I was doing research on the Internet.
6. Smoke was coming out of the cafeteria.
   The students were taking an exam.

B. Answers will vary.

C5: Describing the Habitual Past (p. 39)

2 I used to walk the other way when I saw my friends with their dogs.
7 All of my fears disappeared.
3 I would worry about visiting their homes.
1 I used to be very afraid of dogs.
5 That all changed two years ago when my son brought home a stray puppy.
8 Now I am a dog lover just like my friends.
4 I would shudder with fear when their dogs greeted me at the door.
6 The poor little thing looked so helpless.

C6: Using the Simple Past in Discourse (p. 40)

A. Answers will vary. Some examples are:
2. When I was five, my parents took me to the circus.
3. Last night, I waited in line for an hour to see a movie, and my feet hurt.

B. Answers will vary.

Examining Meaning and Use (p. 41)

1. c   2. a   3. b

D1: Listening for Meaning and Use (p. 43)

2. a   3. b   4. a   5. a   6. b   7. a   8. a

D2: Using Past Time Clauses (p. 43)

Answers will vary. Some examples are:
After the dam collapsed, a train engineer outside of the town tried to warn people that the flood was coming.
While the train engineer sped down the tracks, he blew his train whistle loudly.
After the water crashed into Johnstown at a very high speed, it destroyed everything in its path.
When the water crashed into Johnstown, it wiped out villages, bridges, and freight trains.
Before the force of the water lifted some houses and knocked them into each other, some people were able to escape to the hills right above Johnstown.
After the Johnstown tragedy, more than 200 photographers came to record the story.

D3: Relating Events with Before and After (p. 44)

A. Answers will vary. Some examples are:

Situation 2
Before Jim tripped and fell, he was winning the race.
After Jim tripped and fell, he was unable to finish the race.

Situation 3
Before their parents came home, the boys were running around the house.
After their parents came home, they were watching television.

B. Answers will vary.

D4: Understanding Cause and Effect (p. 45)

Answers will vary. Some examples are:
2. a. effect   b. cause
   After they ran out of gas, they had to call for help.
   When they ran out of gas, they had to call for help.
3. a. cause   b. effect
   After the lightning struck, the lights went out.
   When the lightning struck, the lights went out.
4. a. cause   b. effect
   After they painted their house bright pink, their neighbors refused to talk to them.
   When they painted their house bright pink, their neighbors refused to talk to them.
   a. effect   b. cause
   After their neighbors refused to talk to them, they painted their house bright pink.
   When their neighbors refused to talk to them, they painted their house bright pink.
5. a. effect   b. cause
   After his best suit didn't fit anymore, he went on a strict diet.
   When his best suit didn't fit anymore, he went on a strict diet.
   a. cause   b. effect
   After he went on a strict diet, his best suit didn't fit anymore.
   When he went on a strict diet, his best suit didn't fit anymore.
   (In the first situation, he lost weight because his best suit was too small.
   In the second situation, because he lost weight, his best suit was too big for him.)
6. a. effect   b. cause
   After a mosquito bit her, her arm started to itch.
   When a mosquito bit her, her arm started to itch.
7. a. cause   b. effect
   After the doorbell rang, he answered the door.
   When the doorbell rang, he answered the door.
8. a. cause   b. effect
   After she found the lost jewelry, she got a reward.
   When she found the lost jewelry, she got a reward.

D5: Talking About Interrupted Activities (p. 46)

A. 2. while I was going down the stairs, I tripped on a shoe
3. while I was making coffee, I spilled the whole can of coffee on the floor
4. while I was taking a shower, the phone rang
5. when I stepped out of the shower, I slipped on the wet floor
6. While I was trying to explain, he got mad and hung up
7. While I was typing the paper, the computer system went down
8. when I was riding the elevator to class, it got stuck

B. Answers will vary.

E1: Thinking about Meaning and Use (p. 47)

2. ?   3. T   4. F   5. ?   6. ?

E2: Editing (p. 47)

2. ~~After~~ *Before* he fell asleep, he was reading a book.
3. ~~Were you having~~ *Did you have* your own car in college?
4. No errors.
5. Oh, no! I ~~was dropping~~ *dropped* my earring. I can't find it.
6. No errors.

CHAPTER 3

A3: After You Read (p. 51)

Circle numbers 4, 5, 7, 9, and 12

Examining Form (p. 52)

1. *am/is/are* + *going to* + verb:
   line 20: are going to be   line 41: are going to be
   line 26: 're going to be   line 42: are going to do

   will + verb:
   line 18: will live   line 46: will spend
   line 27: will have   line 51: will die out
   line 36: 'll own   line 52: will become
   line 44: will come   line 54: will make

   will be + verb + *-ing*:
   line 60: will be working
   line 62: will be growing
2. line 22: aren't going away
3. simple present as future

B1: Listening for Form (p. 54)

2. c   4. c   6. d   8. d
3. a   5. c   7. b

B2: Working on the Future Continuous (p. 55)

Answers will vary. Some examples are:
He'll also be writing his English paper.
Abdul will also be cleaning his apartment for his mother's visit.
He'll also be preparing a speech for his debate class.
Abdul will be having dinner with Kelly.

B3: Building Sentences Using Future Forms (p. 55)

I'll be leaving soon.
I'm leaving soon.
I leave tomorrow.
Who is going to leave tomorrow?
Who will leave tomorrow?
Who will be leaving soon?
Her family is going to leave tomorrow.
Her family will leave tomorrow.
Her family will be leaving soon.

B4: Asking *When* Questions About the Future (p. 56)

Answers will vary. Some examples are:

2. A: When are you going to get / are you getting / will you be getting a medical checkup?
   B: Next week.
3. A: When are you going to take / are you taking / will you be taking the day off?
   B: Tomorrow.
4. A: When are you going to clean / are you cleaning / will you be cleaning your apartment?
   B: This afternoon.
5. A: When are you going to finish / are you finishing / will you be finishing your work?
   B: Later today.
6. A: When are you going to go / are you going / will you be going out to dinner?
   B: Tomorrow evening.
7. A: When are you going to do / are you doing / will you be doing your laundry?
   B: This Saturday.
8. A: When are you going to shop / are you shopping / will you be shopping for groceries?
   B: Tonight.

B5: Working on the Simple Present as Future (p. 56)

A. Answers will vary. Some examples are:
Fall vacation begins on October 12.
It ends on October 15.
Thanksgiving break starts on November 22.
It lasts until November 25.
Classes end on December 6.
Final exams start on December 13.
They last until December 20.

B. Answers will vary.

B6: Working on Future Time Clauses (p. 57)

Answers will vary. Some examples are:

2. Before I go shopping, I'll call you.
   Before I go shopping, I'm going to call you.
   Before I call you, I'll go shopping.
   Before I call you, I'm going to go shopping.
3. After the mail arrives, I'll eat breakfast.
   After the mail arrives, I'm going to eat breakfast.
   (Illogical: After I eat breakfast, the mail will arrive.
   After I eat breakfast, the mail is going to arrive.)
4. When he reads the newspaper, he'll fall asleep.
   When he reads the newspaper, he's going to fall asleep.
   (Illogical: When he falls asleep, he'll read the newspaper.
   When he falls asleep, he's going to read the newspaper.)
5. Before he sets the table, he'll cook dinner.
   Before he sets the table, he's going to cook dinner.
   Before he cooks dinner, he'll set the table.
   Before he cooks dinner, he's going to set the table.
6. When I go home, I'll clean my house.
   When I go home, I'm going to clean my house.
   (Illogical: When I clean my house, I'll go home.
   When I clean my house, I'm going to go home.)

Examining Meaning and Use (p. 58)

1. 1b, 1a   2. 2a, 2b

C1: Listening for Meaning and Use (p. 59)

2. a   4. a   6. b   8. a
3. a   5. b   7. b

C2: Expressing Promises, Plans, and Expectations (p. 60)

Answers will vary.

C3: Using Direct and Indirect Requests (p. 60)

A. Answers will vary. Some examples are:

2. A: Will you please drive me to school?
   B: Sure. No problem.
3. A: Will you please lend me your car?
   B: Sorry. I need it tonight.
4. A: Will you please buy me one, too?
   B: Sure. No problem.

B. Answers will vary. Some examples are:

2. A: Will you be driving to school this evening?
   B: Yes. Would you like me to drive you?
   A: Yes. Thank you.
3. A: Will you be using your car later?
   B: Yes, I will.
   A: OK. Never mind.
4. A: Will you be buying concert tickets?
   B: Yes. Would you like me to buy you one, too?
   A: Yes, please.

Examining Meaning and Use (p. 61)

1. a, c   2. b

D1: Listening for Meaning and Use (p. 63)

	SAME	DIFFERENT
2.	✓	
3.		✓
4.		✓
5.	✓	
6.	✓	

D2: Expressing Plans, Scheduled Events, and Predictions (p. 63)

A. Plans or scheduled events:
We're having an exam tomorrow.
We're having an election tomorrow.
We're having a sale tomorrow.
We're going to have a party tomorrow.
We're going to have an exam tomorrow.
We're going to have an election tomorrow.
We're going to have a sale tomorrow.
We have a party tomorrow.
We have an exam tomorrow.
We have an election tomorrow.
We have a sale tomorrow.
Predictions:
We're having a storm tomorrow.
We're going to have a storm tomorrow.

B. Appropriate:
My new job, It, School, Winter vacation
Illogical:
An explosion, A snowstorm

D3: Discussing Plans and Scheduled Events (p. 64)
A. Answers will vary.
B. Answers will vary.

Examining Meaning and Use (p. 65)
1. 1a. 'll snow
   1b. 's (probably) going to snow
   2a. 'll do
   2b. 'm going to do
2. 2a and 2b
3. 1a and 1b

E1: Listening for Meaning and Use (p. 67)
2. b   4. a   6. b   8. b
3. b   5. a   7. a

E2: Restating Formal Announcements (p. 68)
Answer will vary. Some examples are:
2. Context: airport announcement
   Restatement: Flight 276 is going to be arriving at Gate 12.
3. Context: sign in subway
   Restatement: On April 1, the fare is going to increase to $1.75.
4. Context: class schedule
   Restatement: Classes are going to resume on January 22.
5. Context: poetry reading
   Restatement: Tonight we are going to begin with a short poem.

E3: Restating Predictions (p. 68)
2. The driver is going to lose control.
3. Computers will cost much less in a few years.
4. The buzzer is going to sound.
5. In a few years, "smart refrigerators" will tell owners when they need milk.
6. He is going to die.

For numbers 2, 4, and 6, use *be going to* rather than *will* because there is evidence that an event is fairly certain to happen very soon.

E4: Making Quick Decisions and Stating Plans (p. 68)
A. Answers will vary.
B. Answers will vary.

E5: Understanding the Order of Future Events (p. 69)
A.
2. a   3. b   4. b   5. b   6. b
B. Answers will vary.

E6: Verbs Expressing the Future (p. 70)
2. b   4. b   6. a   8. a   10. a
3. a   5. a   7. b   9. a

E7: Repeating Future Forms in Discourse (p. 71)
Answers will vary.

F1: Thinking About Meaning and Use (p. 72)
2. I'll be working.
3. I'm going to carry in the packages.
4. I'll answer it.
5. I'll have a bowl of soup.
6. I'm making a cake later.
7. I'm going to cook pasta.
8. I work Monday and Friday.
9. Maybe I'll do my homework.
10. I did. I'm going to get it.

F2: Editing (p. 73)

One of the most exciting advances in medicine in the next few years is ~~gonna be~~ *going to be* the widespread use of robots in the operating room. Experts predict that "robot assistants" ~~are never replacing~~ *will never/are never going to replace* surgeons. Nevertheless, there is no doubt that robots ~~going to~~ *will/are going to* revolutionize surgery. In just a few years, robots ∧ become the standard in certain *will/are going to* types of heart surgery, eye surgery, hip surgery, and brain surgery. Why ~~this is~~ *is this* going to happen? The answer is simple. No surgeon will ever be able keep his or her hand as steady as the hand of a robot. No surgeon ~~is ever being~~ *is ever going to be/will ever be* able to greatly magnify a microscopic blood vessel with his or her own eyes. These are simple and routine tasks for medical robots.

Some patients are still worried, however. In the words of one patient before hip surgery, "How do I know the robot ~~doesn't~~ *isn't going to/won't* go crazy? Maybe it ~~drills~~ *is going to/will drill* a hole in my head instead of my hip!"

Surgeons are quick to reassure their patients. "That's impossible," says one optimistic surgeon. "I promise that ~~isn't happening~~ *isn't going to/won't happen*. Robots are medical assistants. They'll work when I ~~am going to give~~ *give* them a command, and they'll stop when I ~~will~~ say so. I ∧ be right there the whole time." *am going to/will*

CHAPTER 4

A3: After You Read (p. 79)
2. T
3. F
Scientists think that we haven't discovered everything about the human brain.
4. F
Scientists haven't discovered how to move memories from one person to another person.
5. F
Physicists have observed only about 10% of the universe.
6. T

Examining Form (p. 80)

1. line 19: haven't discovered
   line 30: have estimated
   line 32: 've observed
   line 34: haven't found
   line 39: has evolved
   line 43: have reached
   line 47: 've begun
2. The two forms of *have* are *has* and *have*. Use *has* for third-person singular subjects. For first- and second-person subjects, and for third-person plural subjects, use *have*.
3. Regular Verbs
   line 19: haven't discovered
   line 30: have estimated
   line 32: 've observed
   line 39: has evolved
   line 43: have reached

   Irregular Verbs
   line 34: haven't found
   line 47: 've begun
   The past participle of regular verbs is the same as the simple past form (verb +-*ed*). Irregular verbs have special past participle forms.

B1: Listening for Form (p. 81)

2. They called their senator in Washington.
3. Who's read the book over there?
4. Where's the team playing this week?
5. She's worried about her father.
6. Who's gone fishing?
7. You've bought all of the equipment already.
8. We looked up his telephone number.

B2: Identifying Past Participles (p. 82)

1. cooked   had
   eaten   heard
   forgotten   sung
   found   written
   gotten
2. appeared   happened
   broken   left
   exploded   rained
   fallen   started
   gone   sunk
   allowed   driven
   bought   kept
   cut   spent
   destroyed   taken
   drawn   thrown

B3: Building Present Perfect Sentences (p. 82)

I've been sick.
I've forgotten your umbrella.
She hasn't arrived early.
She hasn't been sick.
She hasn't forgotten your umbrella.
She hasn't bought herself anything.
It hasn't snowed a lot.
It hasn't melted quickly.
Have you arrived early?
Have you been sick?
Have you forgotten your umbrella?

B4: Completing Conversations with the Present Perfect (p. 83)

Conversation 1
2. 've heard
3. has begun

Conversation 2
1. has Tom been
2. 's been
3. have known

Conversation 3
1. haven't sent
2. has happened
3. haven't called
4. written

Conversation 4
1. have we done
2. 've made
3. 've done
4. 've swept
5. has bought
6. haven't taken

B5: Understanding Informal Speech (p. 84)

2. Have you taken
3. Have you been
4. Have you eaten
5. Has she left
6. Have you seen
7. Have you done
8. Has he called

Examining Meaning and Use (p. 85)

1. b   2. a

C1: Listening for Meaning and Use (p. 86)

2. a   3. c   4. c   5. c   6. b

C2: Talking About Life Experiences with *Ever* (p. 86)

A. 2. A: Have you ever bounced a check?
       B: Yes, I have. Have you? OR No, I haven't. Have you?
   3. A: Have you ever lost your wallet?
       B: Yes, I have. Have you? OR No, I haven't. Have you?
   4. A: Have you ever run out of gas?
       B: Yes, I have. Have you? OR No, I haven't. Have you?
   5. A: Have you ever told a lie?
       B: Yes, I have. Have you? OR No, I haven't. Have you?
   6. A: Have you ever met a famous person?
       B: Yes, I have. Have you? OR No, I haven't. Have you?
   7. A: Have you ever seen a comet?
       B: Yes, I have. Have you? OR No, I haven't. Have you?
   8. A: Have you ever ridden a motorcycle?
       B: Yes, I have. Have you? OR No, I haven't. Have you?

B. Answers will vary.

C3: Making Up Reminders with Indefinite Past Time (p. 87)

A. Answers will vary. Some examples are:
   2. go to bed early, choose an interview suit, set the alarm clock
   3. ask the salesperson the price, take it to the mechanic, take it for a test drive
   4. pack the sunscreen, buy snacks, bring a beach umbrella

B. Answers will vary.
C. Answers will vary.

C4: Writing About Accomplishments and Progress (p. 87)

A. Answers will vary.
B. Answers will vary.

Examining Meaning and Use (p. 88)

1. c   2. a and b   3. b

D1: Listening for Meaning and Use (p. 89)

A.

	RECENT PAST TIME	CONTINUING TIME UP TO NOW
2.	✓	
3.		✓
4.		✓
5.	✓	
6.	✓	

B. 2. a   3. b   4. b

D2: Talking About Continuing Time up to Now (p. 90)

Answers will vary, but questions will be as follows:
2. How long have you known how to speak English?
3. How long have you had your driver's license?
4. How long have you owned this book?
5. How long have you been a student?
6. How long have you lived in your apartment/house/dorm?
7. How long have you known the student in this class?
8. How long have you owned your car/ bicycle?
9. How long have you known how to use a computer?
10. How long have you been in this city?

D3: Reaching Conclusions About Recent Past Time (p. 91)

Answers will vary. Some examples are:
1. Recently, she's become more confident, too.
2. (I think) he has just asked her to marry him.
   He's acted nervous lately.
   Recently, he's become very devoted to his girlfriend.
3. (I think) she has just stolen a cookie.
   Lately, she's stolen many cookies from the cookie jar.
   She's recently learned how to climb on the stepstool.
4. (I think) he has just graduated.
   Lately, he's studied hard to get good grades.
   He recently graduated.
5. (I think) he has just burned his meal.
   He's cooked very few meals lately.
   He's recently learned how to cook.
6. (I think) he has just gone shopping.
   Lately, he's done his shopping on Saturday morning.
   Recently, he's bought extra food for his family.

D4: Writing About Recent Past Events (p. 92)

A. 2. has signed antipollution legislation
3. has won $2 million in the lottery
4. has made a rare discovery
5. has received a grant

B. 2. Technology Stock Rise
3. MCJ Moves to Texas
4. State Universities Lose Millions
5. Perez Leaves for China and Japan

Examining Meaning and Use (p. 93)

1. 1a
   In 1a, the speaker still works in Los Angeles, which is indicated by the use of the present perfect verb tense, 've worked and the use of the simple present in *I love my job*. The present perfect can express situations that continue at the present time. In 1b, the speaker no longer works in Los Angeles, which is indicated by the use of the simple past *worked* and *loved*. The simple past can express only situations that are completed and no longer exist.
2. 2a asks about the time of a past event.
   2b does not ask about the time of a past event.

E1: Listening for Meaning and Use (p. 94)

2. a   4. b   6. b   8. a
3. a   5. a   7. b

E2: Choosing the Simple Past or the Present Perfect (p. 95)

2. I bought
3. I moved
4. I've owned
5. I've had
6. It's been
7. Have you called
8. She's worked
9. she graduated
10. I phoned
11. she was
12. Didn't he take
13. he left
14. died
15. He lived
16. They were

E3: Asking for Information (p. 96)

Answers will vary. Some examples are:
3. A: Has the mayor spoken yet?
   B: No, he hasn't. He speaks at twelve.
   A: Did the mayor speak yet?
   B: No, he didn't. He speaks at twelve.
4. A: Has the picnic already started?
   B: Yes, it has. It started at four thirty.
   A: Did the picnic already start?
   B: Yes, it did. It started at four thirty.
5. A: Have the fireworks begun yet?
   B: No, they haven't. They begin in an hour.
   A: Did the fireworks begin yet?
   B: No, they didn't. They begin in an hour.
6. A: Has the three-legged race happened already?
   B: Yes, it has. It happened at two.
   A: Did the three-legged race happen already?
   B: Yes, it did. It happened at two.
7. A: Has the pie-eating contest already ended?
   B: Yes, it has. It ended forty-five minutes ago.
   A: Did the pie-eating contest already end?
   B: Yes, it did. It ended forty-five minutes ago.
8. A: Have The Melodians sung yet?
   B: Yes, they have. They sang an hour ago.
   A: Did The Melodians sing yet?
   B: Yes, they did. They sang an hour ago.
9. A: Has the sing-along taken place already?
   B: No, it hasn't. It takes place at seven thirty.
   A: Did the sing-along take place already?
   B: No, it didn't. It takes place at seven thirty.
10. A: Have the line dancers performed yet?
    B: Yes, they have. They performed at three.
    A: Did the line dancers perform yet?
    B: Yes, they did. They performed at three.

E4: Introducing Topics with the Present Perfect (p. 97)
A. Answers will vary.
B. Answers will vary.

F1: Thinking About Meaning and Use (p. 98)
2. a. T   4. a. T   6. a. F   8. a. T
   b. ?   b. ?   b. T   b. ?
3. a. F   5. a. ?   7. a. F
   b. ?   b. T   b. ?

F2: Editing (p. 99)

Since 1993, the Hubble space telescope has ~~provide~~ *provided* us with extraordinary pictures of the universe. It has shown us new comets and black holes. It ~~is~~ *has* found exploding stars. Astronomers have been amazed that the Hubble space telescope ~~have~~ *has* sent back so many spectacular images. But it hasn't always been this way. The Hubble space telescope ~~was~~ *has* actually been in space since 1990. However, for the first three years, there was a problem with the main mirror. The pictures that it sent back to earth were not at all clear. In 1993, two astronauts ~~have~~ fixed the problem. They took a space walk and dropped a special lens over the mirror. Since then, there ~~was~~ *has been* no problem with the space telescope.

CHAPTER 5

A3: After You Read (p. 103)
2. knits (a pair of mittens)
3. aging
4. similar
5. our genes
6. exercise

Examining Form (p. 104)
1. line 13: have been knitting
   line 18: have been participating
   line 19: has been trying
   line 48: have been studying
   line 51: have been reading
   line 52: (have been) learning
   line 52: (have been) interacting
   line 56: have been getting
2. There are two auxiliaries in each example: *have/has* + *been*. The *-ing* ending is added to the main verb.
3. The two forms of *have* are *has* and *have*. Use *has* for third-person singular subjects. For first- and second-person subjects, and third-person plural subjects, use *have*.

B1: Listening for Form (p. 105)
2. a   3. b   4. b   5. a   6. a

B2: Completing Conversations with the Present Perfect Continuous (p. 106)

Conversation 1
2. haven't been feeling
3. Have you been getting
4. haven't been sleeping

Conversation 2
1. haven't been going
2. 've been helping
3. 've been packing up
4. 's been taking

Conversation 3
1. has been giving
2. haven't been making
3. has been getting

Conversation 4
1. have you been doing
2. 've been exercising
3. haven't been eating

B3: Unscrambling Questions (p. 107)
A. 2. Who have you been writing to lately?
   3. Have you been sleeping well recently?
   4. Have you been working hard this semester?
   5. Have you been exercising enough lately?
   6. What time have you been getting up recently?
   7. What have you been doing in the evening?
   8. Where have you been eating lunch this semester?
B. Answers will vary.

B4: Writing Your Own Sentences (p. 107)
Answers will vary. Some examples are:
2. I haven't been sleeping.
3. They have been talking.
4. Have you been listening to the teacher?

B5: Understanding Informal Speech (p. 108)
2. I have been visiting
3. Have you been feeling
4. I have been having
5. Have you been exercising
6. I have been walking

Examining Meaning and Use (p. 109)
1. b   2. a   3. c

C1: Listening for Meaning and Use (p. 110)

		MAX	HELEN
2.	Who is no longer sick?	✓	
3.	Who still volunteers at a hospital?		✓
4.	Who has been to Chicago more than once this year?	✓	
5.	Who has tried to call Eddie more recently?		✓
6.	Who is playing chess these days?	✓	

C2: Making Apologies and Excuses (p. 110)
Answers will vary. Some examples are:
2. I'm sorry. I've been waiting for the bus.
3. I'm sorry. I've been working late every night this week.
4. I'm sorry. I've been visiting my friends after school.
5. I'm sorry. I've been thinking about something.
6. I'm sorry. I've been forgetting to help out lately.

C3: Reaching Conclusions (p. 111)

Answers will vary. Some examples are:
There's an open bag of potato chips on the coffee table. Someone has been having a snack.
The computer is on. Someone has been using the computer.
There is a book on the sofa. Someone has been reading.
There is a piece of cake and a glass of milk on the table. Someone has been having a snack.
The bed is unmade. Someone has been sleeping in her bed.
The drawers are open. Someone has been going through her drawers.
The shower is dripping. Someone has been taking a shower.

C4: Writing Advertisements (p. 112)

A. Answers will vary. Some examples are:
2. Have you been trying to exercise more?
3. Have you been looking for an apartment?
4. Have you been planning to get away for a vacation?

B. Answers will vary.

Examining Meaning and Use (p. 113)

1. 2a and 2b
2. 1a and 1b
3. Vera has probably finished the book.
In 1a, the activity is continuing up to the present.

D1: Listening for Meaning and Use (p. 114)

	COMPLETED	CONTINUES
2.	✓	
3.		✓
4.		✓
5.	✓	
6.		✓
7.		✓
8.	✓	

D2: Contrasting the Present Perfect and the Present Perfect Continuous (p. 115)

A.
2. have been thinking/have thought
3. have been wondering/wondering
4. have been reading
5. have read
6. have been
7. haven't had
8. have been writing
9. have changed
10. have you been doing
11. Have you been working
12. Have you had
13. have had
14. Have you decided / Did you decide

B. Answers will vary.

D3: Writing a Conversation (p. 116)

Answers will vary.

D4: Connecting the Past and the Present in Discourse (p. 117)

2. since
3. had
4. were
5. been having OR had
6. been getting OR gotten
7. happened OR I thought
8. criticized
9. did they say
10. have been applying OR applied
11. gotten
12. did Eric say
13. been talking
14. reached
15. I've been thinking
16. said
17. been putting it off

E1: Thinking About Meaning and Use (p. 118)

2. a
3. a
4. b
5. b
6. b
7. a
8. a

E2: Editing (p. 119)

Life expectancy is the average number of years that a person will live. Two thousand years ago, the Romans ~~have been living~~ *lived* only an average of 22 years. In other words, they ~~have been having~~ *had* a life expectancy of 22. Since the beginning of the twentieth century, life expectancy around the world has been rising dramatically in many parts of the world. It will certainly continue to go up well into the twenty-first century. The rise in life expectancy ~~has been being~~ *is* due to the fact that people have been taking much better care of themselves. Each generation has experienced better nutrition and medical care than the one before. In 1900, people in the United States ~~have been living~~ *lived* to an average age of 47. All that has changed, however: the life expectancy in 1998 was 77, and it may be even higher today.

CHAPTER 6

A3: After You Read (p. 123)

2. T   3. F   4. T   5. F   6. F

Examining Form (p. 124)

1. line 16: 'd admired
line 17: had been
line 18: 'd lumped
line 20: 'd relied
line 28: 'd attempted
The contracted form of *had* in the past perfect is *'d*.
2. auxiliaries: had, been
main verb: search
The past perfect form is *had* + past participle.
The past perfect continuous form is *had* + *been* + main verb + *-ing*.

B1: Listening for Form (p. 126)

2. 'd been working
3. visited
4. made up
5. wanted
6. became
7. hadn't flown
8. hadn't let
9. didn't care
10. had crossed
11. had been trying
12. had died
13. had been
14. seemed
15. happened
16. flew

B2: Working on Verb Forms (p. 127)

2. We went to school. (simple past)
   We had been going to school. (past perfect continuous)
3. They tried hard. (simple past)
   They had tried hard. (past perfect)
4. I had held his hand. (past perfect)
   I had been holding his hand. (past perfect continuous)
5. You had fun. (simple past)
   You had had fun. (past perfect)
6. He had made a mess. (past perfect)
   He had been making a mess. (past perfect continuous)
7. They thought about it. (simple past)
   They had been thinking about it. (past perfect continuous)
8. We did nothing. (simple past)
   We had done nothing. (past perfect)
9. What had happened? (past perfect)
   What had been happening? (past perfect continuous)
10. It got harder. (simple past)
    It had been getting harder. (past perfect continuous)

B3: Building Sentences (p. 127)

Had you been sick?
Had you had lunch?
She had left.
She had lunch.
She had taken a walk.
She had been working.
She had been left.
She had been sick.
Who had left?
Who had lunch?
Who had taken a walk?
Who had been working?
Who had been left?
Who had been sick?

B4: Asking and Answering Questions (p. 128)

A. 2. A: Before you started this course, had you ever studied English grammar?
3. A: Before you started this course, had you ever spoken on the phone in English?
4. A: Before you started this course, had you ever written any letters in English?
5. A: Before you started this course, had you ever seen any English-language movies?

B. 2. A: Before you started this course, had you been learning any songs in English?
3. A: Before you started this course, had you been practicing English with friends?
4. A: Before you started this course, had you been watching any TV programs in English?
5. A: Before you started this course, had you been listening to English language news broadcasts?

B5: Transforming Sentences (p. 128)

3. She had limped for the last mile.
6. Had anyone looked for us?
7. They had tried to call for help.
8. What had been happening?

Items 2, 4, and 5 cannot change because verbs with stative meanings are not usually used with the past perfect continuous.

B6: Understanding Informal Speech (p. 129)

2. had gone
3. had taught
4. had prepared
5. had, signed up
6. had, been trying

Examining Meaning and Use (p. 130)

1. a. because a tree had fallen across my driveway
   b. after she had enrolled
   c. He'd been on a mountain climbing expedition
   d. Although I'd been terrified,
2. past perfect
3. simple past

C1: Listening for Meaning and Use (p. 132)

2. a   4. b   6. b   8. a
3. a   5. a   7. a

C2: Expressing the Order of Past Events (p. 132)

2. 2, 1
Before he graded the exam, he read the answers carefully.
Before he graded the exam, he had read the answers carefully.
3. 1, 2
They had been married for five years when they got divorced.
4. 1, 2
After the car collided with a truck, someone called the police.
After the car had collided with a truck, someone called the police.
5. 2, 1
Until the doctor said she was very healthy, she was worried.
Until the doctor said she was very healthy, she had been worried.
6. 1, 2
By the time she slept for ten hours, I decided to wake her up.
By the time she had slept for ten hours, I decided to wake her up.

C3: Discussing Previous Accomplishments (p. 133)

1. They hadn't fixed the window yet.
   They hadn't repaired the lock yet.
2. He had already completed the English requirement.
   He had already taken the math courses.
   He hadn't passed the writing test yet.
3. She had already looked at the classified ads.
   She had already gone to an employment agency.
   She hadn't written her résumé yet.

C4: Describing New Experiences (p. 134)

A. Answers will vary. Some examples are:
1. b. They had never bathed a baby before.
   c. They had never fed a baby before.
2. a. She had never lived on her own before.
   b. She had never slept in a dormitory before.
   c. She had never cooked her own meals before.
3. a. He had never used an electronic cash register before.
   b. He had never gotten a paycheck before.
   c. He had never stocked shelves before.
4. a. She had never driven a car before.
   b. She had never been so scared before.
   c. She had never felt so nervous before.

B. Answers will vary.

Examining Meaning and Use (p. 135)

1. a   2. b

D1: Listening for Meaning and Use (p. 137)

	JUST BEFORE	UNCLEAR
2.		✓
3.	✓	
4.	✓	
5.		✓
6.	✓	
7.		✓
8.		✓

D2: Talking About Continuing Past Actions (p. 137)

2. When Brigitte's fiancé joined the company, she had been working at C & M for two years.
   When Brigitte's fiancé joined the company in 1999, she had been working at C & M since 1997.
3. When the electricity went off, the chicken had been baking for fifteen minutes.
   When the electricity went off at 5:45, the chicken had been baking since 5:30.
4. When the phone woke Lisa up, she had been sleeping for three hours.
   When the phone woke Lisa up at 2:00 A.M., she had been sleeping since 11:00 P.M.
5. When Paulo and Celia got married, they had been dating for two years.
   When Paulo and Celia got married in 2000, they had been dating since 1998.
6. When Kate graduated from medical school, she had been studying for six years.
   When Kate graduated from medical school, she had been studying since 1996.
7. When Carlos moved to Paris, he had been living in Mexico City for two years.
   When Carlos moved to Paris in 2000, he had been living in Mexico City since 1998.
8. When Eric gave his first recital, he had been taking piano lessons for six months.
   When Eric gave his first recital in July 2000, he had been taking piano lessons since January of that year.

D3: Expressing Reasons and Results (p. 138)

A. Answers will vary. Some examples are:
2. because she had cheated.
3. because she hadn't liked it.
4. He joined a gym because he had been gaining weight.

B. Answers will vary. Some examples are:
2. We were tired
3. she made a big mistake.
4. Because the traffic had been bad, we were late for our appointment.

D4: Expressing Contrasts (p. 138)

A. Answers will vary. Some examples are:
2. even though she hadn't done her homework.
3. Although they had dressed warmly,
4. Even though he had been making a lot of money,

B. Answers will vary. Some examples are:
2. We had no more food
3. we stopped communicating.
4. I didn't finish the project.

D5: Adding Background Information (p. 139)

A. Answers will vary. Some examples are:
2. I had been up all night packing my belongings. I had been feeling excited to move into my new apartment.
3. It had started to rain. We had been planning to meet our friends for dinner.
4. My furniture had been moved. My window had been opened.

B. Answers will vary.

E1: Thinking About Meaning and Use (p. 140)

2. a. F	4. a. F	6. a. F	8. a. T
b. T	b. T	b. T	b. ?
3. a. F	5. a. ?	7. a. F	
b. T	b. T	b. T	

E2: Editing (p. 141)

In 1953, Edmund Hillary and Tenzing Norkay were the first climbers to reach the top of Mount Everest. Since then, many people ~~had~~ *have* climbed Mount Everest, especially in recent years. Before 1953, no human had ever stood on top of the world's highest peak, although some had tried. George Mallory and Sandy Irvine, for example, ~~had~~ died almost thirty years earlier on a perilous path along the North Ridge.

Since 1953, many more people ~~had~~ *have* [have] set world records. In 1975, Junko Tabei of Japan ~~had become~~ *became* the first woman on a mountaineering team to reach the top. In 1980, Reinhold Messner of Italy ~~had become~~ *became* the first person to make the climb to the top alone, without other people and without oxygen. In 1995, Alison Hargreaves of Scotland ~~had~~ duplicated Messner's triumph. She became the first woman to climb Mount Everest solo and without oxygen.

Each climber faces frigid winds, storms, avalanches, and most dangerous of all, the serious effects of the high altitude on the heart, lungs, and brain. So why *have* many hundreds of people tried to climb Mount Everest in recent years? In 1998, for example, 650 people ~~had~~ tried to reach the top, and on one single day, 12 people actually succeeded. The only way to explain these numbers is to understand that the climb up Mount Everest represents the ultimate challenge of reaching the "top of the world."

CHAPTER 7

A3: After You Read (p. 147)
2. c   3. b   4. a   5. a   6. b

Examining Form (p. 148)
1. line 4: might do
   line 5: might have
   line 17: could be
   line 20: might strengthen
   line 21: may offer
   line 31: could be
   line 32: may be
   line 33: may add
   line 35: might be

2. Modals followed by the main verb *be*
   line 17: could be
   line 31: could be
   line 32: may be
   line 35: might be

   Modals followed by a different main verb
   line 4: might do
   line 5: might have
   line 20: might strengthen
   line 21: may offer
   line 33: may add

B1: Listening for Form (p. 150)
3. may
4. can't
5. might
6. must
7. Could
8. Could
9. has to
10. may
11. could
12. 's got to

B2: Completing Conversations with Modals (p. 151)
Conversation 1
2. can't be

Conversation 2
1. should arrive
2. won't arrive
3. ought to be

Conversation 3
1. has to be
2. couldn't be
3. must be

Conversation 4
1. has got to be
2. should be

B3: Using Short Answers with Modals (p. 152)
Answers will vary. Some examples are:
3. B: It might.
4. B: They must.
5. B: They may not.
6. B: They couldn't.
7. B: They could.
8. B: It might be.

B4: Building Sentences with Modals (p. 152)
John must have a problem.
John might be sleeping.
John might have a problem.
John can't be sleeping.
John can't have a problem.
John has to be sleeping.
John has to have a problem.
It must be sleeping.
It must be true.
It must be a problem.
It must be broken.
It must have broken.
It might be sleeping.
It might be true.
It might be a problem.
It might be broken.
It might have a problem.
It might have broken.
It can't be sleeping.
It can't be true.
It can't be a problem.
It can't be broken.
It can't have a problem.
It can't have broken.
It has to be sleeping.
It has to be true.
It has to be a problem.
It has to be broken.
It has to have a problem.
It has to have broken.

B5: Writing Your Own Sentences with Modals (p. 152)
Answers will vary.

Examining Meaning and Use (p. 153)
1. a, c, f   2. b, d, e

C1: Listening for Meaning and Use (p. 155)

	LESS CERTAINTY	MORE CERTAINTY
2.		✓
3.	✓	
4.		✓
5.		✓
6.		✓
7.		✓
8.	✓	

C2: Expressing Degrees of Certainty (p. 156)
Answers will vary. Some examples are:

Conversation 2
1. should
2. must

Conversation 3
1. has to
2. ought to

Conversation 4
1. has got to
2. could

Conversation 5
1. might
2. must

C3: Guessing with *Could, Might,* and *May* (p. 157)

Answers will vary. Some examples are:
1. They might be looking at the horse race.
   They may be enjoying an outdoor concert.
2. They could be celebrating a pay raise.
   They might be having a birthday celebration.
   They may be throwing old papers away.

C4: Making Guesses and Drawing Conclusions (p. 157)

Answers will vary. Some examples are:
2. There might not be a fire. The fire alarm was ringing all day yesterday.
3. He may be shy around new people. He doesn't seem unhappy.
4. She has to be on a diet. She didn't eat dessert yesterday, either.
5. I must be getting sick. I never sneeze unless I'm sick.
6. She could have a secret admirer. Yesterday, she received a box of chocolate without a card.
7. She may be asleep. She said she didn't sleep well last night.
8. He has got to be exhausted. He has two jobs.

C5: Stating Expectations and Drawing Conclusions (p. 158)

3. Terry must be admitting new patients. OR Terry should be admitting new patients.
4. it must be 4:30. OR it should be 4:30.
5. Terry must be giving patients medicine. OR Terry should be giving patients medicine.
6. Terry must be discharging patients. OR Terry should be discharging patients.
7. Terry must be meeting with night nurses. OR Terry should be meeting with night nurses.
8. it must be 10:00. OR it should be 10:00.
9. it must be 2:45. OR it should be 2:45.
10. Terry must be attending a meeting. OR Terry should be attending a meeting.

C6: Expressing Understanding (p. 159)

Answers will vary. Some examples are:
2. You must be hungry. OR You must feel starved.
3. You must be nervous. OR You must feel anxious.
4. You must be relieved. OR You must feel glad.
5. You must be excited. OR You must feel happy.
6. You must be angry. OR You must feel mad.
7. You must be disappointed. OR You must feel unhappy.
8. You must be upset. OR You must feel sad.

C7: Expressing Strong Certainty and Disbelief (p. 159)

A. Answers will vary.
B. Answers will vary.

Examining Meaning and Use (p. 160)

1. a, c   2. b, d   3. a, c

D1: Listening for Meaning and Use (p. 162)

	LESS CERTAINTY	MORE CERTAINTY
2.		✓
3.		✓
4.	✓	
5.		✓
6.		✓
7.	✓	
8.		✓

D2: Expressing Degrees of Certainty (p. 162)

Answers will vary. Some examples are:
2. We may come later.
3. The flight will arrive at 8:10.
4. It could rain this afternoon.
5. It shouldn't be cold tonight.
6. He ought to get the job.
7. Genetically engineered dogs and cats may become common.
8. He might be taking the express train this evening.
9. The class will meet on Thursdays next semester.
10. She should be in Miami for the winter.

D3: Making Predictions About the Weather (p. 163)

Answers will vary. Some examples are:
Tomorrow:
Tomorrow may be cloudy.
There might be sleet in the afternoon.
It should rain overnight.
Saturday:
There will be rain and strong winds on Saturday morning.
It should clear in the afternoon, but it may rain on Saturday evening.
There could be flooding.
Sunday:
There will be sunshine on Sunday morning.
It could snow in the evening.
It probably won't snow after midnight.

D4: Making Predictions About Your Lifetime (p. 164)

A. Answers will vary. Some examples are:
3. might
4. won't
5. could
6. might
7. could
8. may not
9. will
10. will not

B. Answers will vary.
C. Answers will vary.

E1: Thinking About Meaning and Use (p. 165)

2. c   4. c   6. a   8. a
3. a   5. b   7. b

E2: Editing (p. 165)

Epilepsy is an illness that causes people to have brain seizures. ~~Might~~ Could a dog help a person with epilepsy? Scientists believe that dogs ~~should~~ could warn their owners before a seizure occurs and researchers think there ~~maybe~~ may be an explanation. They believe that a dog may ~~smelling~~ smell the chemical changes that usually happen in a person's body before a seizure. Some dogs have success rates of over 90 percent. Since this rate is higher than chance, researchers think ~~there's to be~~ there must be something going on.

CHAPTER 8

A3: After You Read (p. 169)
2. ✓ 3. ✓ 4. 5. ✓ 6.

Examining Form (p. 170)
1. line 8: has to have been
   line 19: could have happened
   line 23: could have launched
   line 23: could have fallen
   line 24: (could have) managed
   line 31: could have helped
   line 39: may have provided
   line 43: could have generated
   line 45: must have acted
   line 48: must have rotated
   line 56: could have taken off
   line 62: could have helped
   line 63: might have developed

2. Past Modals with Singular Subjects
   line 8: has to have been
   line 19: could have happened
   line 23: could have launched
   line 23: could have fallen
   line 24: (could have) managed
   line 31: could have helped
   line 39: may have provided
   line 43: could have generated
   line 48: must have rotated
   line 56: could have taken off
   line 63: might have developed

   Past Modals with Plural Subjects
   line 45: must have acted
   line 62: could have helped
   There is no difference in form between past modals with singular subjects and past modals with plural subjects. Past modals have only one form with all subjects.

3. The auxiliary *have* follows the modals. The form of the main verbs is the past participle.

B1: Listening for Form (p. 172)
2. shouldn't have
3. may have
4. could have
5. couldn't have
6. should have
7. must have
8. shouldn't have

B2: Completing Conversations (p. 173)

Conversation 1
2. might not have liked
3. must have been

Conversation 2
1. shouldn't have driven
2. should have taken

Conversation 3
1. couldn't have left
2. might have forgotten

Conversation 4
1. must have had
2. should have stopped by
3. could have heard

Conversation 5
1. might have left
2. couldn't have
3. must have dropped
4. might have locked

B3: Asking and Answering Questions with Past Modals (p. 174)
Answers will vary. Some examples are:
3. A: Could prehistoric birds have had wings?
   B: Yes, they must have.
4. A: Could prehistoric birds have jumped from trees?
   B: No, they couldn't have.
5. A: Could prehistoric birds have run fast?
   B: Yes, they could have.
6. A: Could prehistoric birds have lived on the ground?
   B: No, they couldn't have.
7. A: Could prehistoric birds have eaten smaller animals?
   B: Yes, they could have.
8. A: Could prehistoric birds have eaten seeds?
   B: Yes, they must have.

B4: Forming Past Modals (p. 174)
2. The report should have been available on April 12.
3. He ought to have studied more for the test.
4. I could have worked harder.
5. She has to have been home.
6. I should have done things differently. I should have exercised more. I know I could have found the time.
7. I should have relaxed more. Perhaps I could have learned yoga.
8. I shouldn't have worried so much. Worrying couldn't have been good for my health.

B5: Understanding Informal Speech (p. 175)
2. could have
3. might not have
4. must have
5. should have
6. must have
7. could have
8. might have

Examining Meaning and Use (p. 176)
1. a, d   2. b, c

C1: Listening for Meaning and Use (p. 177)

	LESS CERTAINTY	MORE CERTAINTY
2.		✓
3.		✓
4.		✓
5.	✓	
6.	✓	
7.	✓	
8.		✓

C2: Understanding Degrees of Certainty (p. 178)

Answers will vary. Some examples are:
2. A: He couldn't have built a fire.
   B: He might have built a fire.
3. A: He could have frozen to death.
   B: He must have frozen to death.
4. A: He must have lived in a valley.
   B: He may not have lived in a valley.
5. A: He might not have been older than 25.
   B: He couldn't have been older than 25.

C3: Making Guesses and Drawing Conclusions (p. 178)

Answers will vary.

C4: Expressing Impossibility and Disbelief (p. 179)

Answers will vary. Some examples are:
2. B: He couldn't have sent me a letter. He died a very long time ago.
3. B: It couldn't have run out of gas. I don't have a car.
4. B: I couldn't have grown three inches taller this week. I haven't grown in years.
5. B: I couldn't have lost a million dollars yesterday. I've never had a million dollars.
6. B: I couldn't have swum the English Channel last week. I don't know how to swim.

C5: Writing About Impossibility and Disbelief (p. 179)

A. Answers will vary.
B. Answers will vary.

Examining Meaning and Use (p. 180)

1. b, c   2. a   3. c

D1: Listening for Meaning and Use (p. 182)

2. a   4. b   6. b   8. a
3. b   5. b   7. b

D2: Contrasting *Could* and *Could Have* (p. 182)

2. could have ridden
3. could see
4. could have taken
5. could have called

D3: Talking About Past Opportunities (p. 183)

A. Answers will vary. Some examples are:

Situation 1
2. He could have gone to medical school.
3. He could have taught science in a high school.
4. He could have directed a research program.

Situation 2
1. He could have become a cook in a restaurant.
2. He could have opened a restaurant.
3. He could have worked in a hotel.
4. He could have started his own business.

Situation 3
1. She could have been a fiction writer.
2. She could have gone to law school.
3. She could have worked for a newspaper.
4. She could have become a teacher.

Situation 4
1. He could have become an art teacher.
2. He could have gotten a job in advertising.
3. He could have done graphic design.
4. He could have opened an art gallery.

B. Answers will vary.
C. Answers will vary.

D4: Talking About Advice in the Past (p. 184)

Answers will vary. Some examples are:

Situation 1
2. A: Should he have brought an expensive gift?
   B: No, he shouldn't have. His friend didn't expect an expensive gift.
3. A: Should he have brought a bottle of wine?
   B: Yes, he could have. Wine is a common gift.
4. A: Should he have brought five friends?
   B: No, he shouldn't have. There was not enough food for his friends, too.

Situation 2
1. A: Should he have waited for the host?
   B: Yes, he should have. It is rude to eat before the host.
2. A: Should he have eaten more slowly?
   B: Yes, he could have. He might not be hungry anymore.
3. A: Should he have asked for more?
   B: No, he shouldn't have. He should have waited for his friend to offer him more.
4. A: Should he have waited for someone to offer him more?
   B: Yes, he should have. It's polite to wait until you are offered more.

Situation 3
1. A: Should he have whistled?
   B: No, he shouldn't have. It's not polite to whistle at waiters.
2. A: Should he have snapped his fingers?
   B: No, he shouldn't have. It is rude to snap your fingers.
3. A: Should he have clapped loudly?
   B: No, he shouldn't have. It's not common to clap loudly in a restaurant.
4. A: Should he have raised his hand when the waiter was looking at him?
   B: Yes, he could have. That is a polite way to get the waiter's attention.

Situation 4
1. A: Should he have ignored it?
   B: No, he shouldn't have. He should have brought it to the waiter's attention.
2. A: Should he have told the waiter?
   B: Yes, he should have. The waiter could have corrected the mistake.
3. A: Should he have called the manager immediately?
   B: No, he shouldn't have. He should have talked to the waiter first.
4. A: Should he have shouted at the waiter?
   B: No, he shouldn't have. It may not have been the waiter's mistake.

D5: Expressing Regret (p. 185)

Answers will vary. Some examples are:
2. I should have paid more attention to the rice. I shouldn't have left it on the stove.

3. I should have closed the car windows. I shouldn't have left them open during the rainstorm.
4. I should have insured my aunt's birthday gift. I shouldn't have been in such a hurry.
5. I should have applied for a summer job. I shouldn't have waited so long.
6. I should have obeyed the speed limit. I shouldn't have driven so fast.

D6: Writing About Regrets (p. 185)
A. Answers will vary.
B. Answers will vary.

E1: Thinking About Meaning and Use (p. 186)
2. a. T   4. a. T   6. a. F   8. a. F
   b. T   b. F   b. T   b. T
3. a. F   5. a. T   7. a. T
   b. T   b. T   b. F

E2: Editing (p. 187)
2. When ~~he could~~ *could he* have called?
3. He might *have* been late.
4. I ~~ought to~~ *have* visited him at the hospital.
5. ~~May~~ *Could* he have taken the train instead of the bus?
6. She must have *had* a cold yesterday.
7. I ~~should~~ *shouldn't* have asked him. I'm sorry that I did.
8. He should have ~~taking~~ *taken* the exam.
9. You could ~~of~~ *have* called me.
10. She ~~have~~ *had* to have arrived yesterday.
11. The letter might *have* arrived this afternoon.
12. He must *have* had a cold yesterday.

CHAPTER 9

A3: After You Read (p. 193)
2. b   3. a   4. b   5. a   6. a

Examining Form (p. 194)
1. Singular Simple Present Passive
   line 15: is (universally) recognized
   line 24: is (generally) recognized
   line 27: Is (ever) produced

   Plural Simple Present Passive
   line 11: are signaled
   line 27: are ever produced
   line 28: are induced
   line 29: are induced
   line 32: are not understood

2. Singular Simple Past Passive
   line 18: was found
   line 22: was shown

   Plural Simple Past Passive
   line 21: were permitted

3. Present Continuous Passive
   line 24: are being studied

   Past Continuous Passive
   line 14: were being shown
   line 23: were being expressed

B1: Listening for Form (p. 195)
2. was asked   6. are reserved
3. were being studied 7. were reported
4. is, understood   8. are, being published
5. is, covered

B2: Asking and Answering Questions with Simple Present Passives (p. 196)
2. is picked up
3. is recycled
4. are the recycled items collected
5. are collected
6. are taken away
7. is done
8. is sold

B3: Working on Simple Past Passives (p. 196)
2. were melted   6. were removed
3. were cooled   7. was poured
4. were heated   8. was formed
5. were built

B4: Working on Present and Past Continuous Passives (p. 197)
A. 2. are being made
3. are being painted
4. is being replaced
5. are being built
6. is being upgraded
7. is being added
8. are being installed

B. 2. were being made
3. were being painted
4. was being replaced
5. were being built
6. was being upgraded
7. was being added
8. were being installed

B5: Working on Passive Questions (p. 197)
A. 2. How many computers are not being replaced?
3. Which software program is being installed?
4. How much money is being spent?
5. Are more employees being hired?
6. Is new furniture being purchased?
7. Is the old equipment being thrown away?
8. Are the hours of operation being expanded?

B. 2. How many computers were not being replaced?
3. Which software program was being installed?
4. How much money was being spent?

C. 6. Was new furniture purchased last semester?
7. Was old equipment thrown away last semester?
8. Were the hours of operation expanded last semester?

Examining Meaning and Use (p. 198)
1. They have about the same meaning.
2. 1a and 2a
3. 1b and 2b

C1: Listening for Meaning and Use (p. 199)

	ACTIVE	PASSIVE
2.	✓	
3.		✓
4.		✓
5.		✓
6.		✓
7.	✓	
8.		✓

C2: Using Agents and Receivers (p. 200)
3. The window was broken by the child.
4. The concert was attended by many people.
5. She made the cake.
6. We canceled the appointment.
7. The car was repaired by two mechanics.

C3: Focusing on Receivers (p. 200)
1. b. the bride and groom were being photographed.
   c. drinks were being served.
   d. Answers will vary.
2. a. the wine was being chilled.
   b. the salad was being made.
   c. the table was being set.
   d. Answers will vary.
3. a. one person was being lifted into an ambulance.
   b. a man was being given oxygen.
   c. two witnesses were being questioned.

Answers will vary.

C4: Choosing Verbs with Active or Passive Forms (p. 201)
2. A new theory about facial expressions was proposed by a psychologist.
3. This sentence cannot change into the passive form because *emerge* is an intransitive verb. Intransitive verbs have no passive form.
4. The new theory was being considered by the research team.
5. This sentence cannot change into the passive form because *have* is a transitive nonpassive verb. Many transitive verbs with nonpassive meanings, such as *have*, do not have passive forms.
6. Each participant is being paid by the psychology department.
7. This sentence cannot change into the passive form because *arrive* is an intransitive verb. Intransitive verbs have no passive form.
8. More equipment for data analysis is still needed by the researchers.

Examining Meaning and Use (p. 202)
1. 1b   2. 2a

D1: Listening for Meaning and Use (p. 203)
2. a   3. b   4. a   5. a   6. b

D2: Describing Results (p. 204)
Answers will vary. Some examples are:
1. b. was blocked.
   c. were injured.
   d. was trapped.
   e. was actually untouched.
   f. were shattered.
2. a. was closed.
   b. was canceled.
   c. were given.
   d. were forced to stay home.
3. a. were put away.
   b. were vacuumed.
   c. was dusted.
   d. were cleaned.
   e. was swept.

D3: Omitting Agents (p. 205)
2. The prices at the farmer's market are always being reduced. (b)
3. Applications for summer employment are being accepted at the supermarket. (b)
4. Our new carpet was ruined when a pipe burst in our house. (b)
5. The report was lost sometime during the week. (d)
6. At that moment, the door was being unlocked. (a)
7. Attention, please. Tickets for the 5:00 PM show are now being sold. (c)
8. Many books about health and nutrition are being written. (b)
9. Last year, undergraduates were required to take a minimum of four courses per semester. (b)
10. Portuguese and a number of other languages are spoken in Brazil. (b)

D4: Writing Definitions (p. 205)
A. Answers will vary. Some examples are:
2. Labor Day is an American holiday that is celebrated in September.
3. The tuxedo is a garment that is worn by a groom.
4. Farsi is a language that is spoken in Iran.
5. Wine is an alcoholic beverage that is made from grapes.
6. Rice is a food that is eaten by people all over the world.

B. Answers will vary.

D5: Keeping the Focus (p. 206)
A. 2. b   4. a   6. b   8. a
   3. a   5. b   7. a

B. Answers will vary. Some examples are:
2. They must be prescribed by a physician.
   They may be harmful to your health.
3. It is not difficult to learn.
   Romance languages also include Italian and Spanish.
4. It is now recorded on compact discs.
   They are collectors' items now.
5. They can understand a lot about a person that way.
   Our expressions tell what we are thinking.
6. It is more common than meat.
   A staple is a food that is eaten at almost every meal.

C. Answers will vary.

E1: Thinking About Meaning and Use (p. 208)

2. b   4. b   6. b   8. a
3. a   5. b   7. b

E2: Editing (p. 209)

It is ~~claiming~~ *claimed* by psychologists that everyone lies at some time or other. Moreover, many people can lie without showing it in their facial expressions or body language. For this reason, lie detector tests are frequently ~~use~~ *used* in police investigations. The use of such tests to detect lies is many hundreds of years old.

For example, it is ~~believe~~ *believed* that in China suspected liars were forced to chew rice powder and then spit it out. If the powder was dry, the suspect ~~is~~ *was* considered guilty. In Spain, another variation for lie detection *was* used. The suspect ~~was being required~~ *was required* to swallow a slice of bread and cheese. It was believed that if the bread stuck inside the suspect's mouth, then he or she was lying. Psychologists report that these strange methods actually show a basic principle that is ~~know~~ *known* about lying: Anxiety that is related to lying is linked to lack of saliva, or dry mouth.

Modern lie detectors, which are ~~calling~~ *called* polygraphs, are used to indicate changes in heart rate, blood pressure, breathing rate, and perspiration while a person is ~~be~~ *being* examined. Questions about the validity of the polygraph, however, are frequently ~~raising~~ *raised*. Consequently, results from polygraphs are often thrown out in legal cases.

CHAPTER 10

A3: After You Read (p. 213)

1. b, c, d   2. a, c, d   3. a, b

Examining Form (p. 214)

1. Modal Passive
   headline: should be punished
   line 8: can be punished
   line 22: can be ordered
   line 24: may be required
   line 31: can be imprisoned
   line 34: could be fined
   line 35: (could be) jailed
   The three parts of the modal passive are: modal + *be* + past participle.

2. Future Passive
   line 38: will be considered
   line 39: will not be enforced
   The three parts of the future passive are: *will* + *be* + past participle. Another way to form it is: *be going to* + past participle.

3. The three parts of the present perfect passive are: *has/have* + *been* + past participle.

B1: Listening for Form (p. 215)

	ACTIVE	PASSIVE
2.	✓	
3.		✓
4.		✓
5.		✓
6.	✓	
7.	✓	
8.		✓

B2: Working on Future and Modal Passives (p. 216)

A. 2. will be posted
3. will not be announced
4. will be canceled
1. will be shipped
2. will be added
3. will be credited
4. will be refunded

B. 2. cannot be refilled
3. should be kept
4. may be stored
1. needs to be listed
2. has to be reported
3. must be accompanied
4. should be sent

B3: Working on Present Perfect Passives (p. 217)

2. These products have been manufactured by the company for three years.
3. This book has been translated into many languages.
4. The senator has been called dishonest.
5. The recipes have been created by a famous chef.
6. A new prescription has been recommended by the doctor.

B4: Asking and Answering Passive Questions (p. 217)

A. 2. A: Should bicyclists be allowed on busy streets?
   B: Yes, they should. OR No, they shouldn't.
3. A: Should violent scenes be banned from television?
   B: Yes, they should. OR No, it shouldn't.
4. A: Should guns be sold in stores?
   B: Yes, they should. OR No, they shouldn't.
5. A: Should men be given parental leave for childcare?
   B: Yes, they should. OR No, they shouldn't.
6. A: Should women be paid the same wages as men?
   B: Yes, they should. OR No, they shouldn't.
7. A: Should parents be punished for their children's crimes?
   B: Yes, they should. OR No, they shouldn't.
8. A: Should animals be used for medical research?
   B: Yes, they should. OR No, they shouldn't.

B. Answers will vary.

Examining Meaning and Use (p. 218)

1. Agents:
   1a: the instructor
   1b: a team of experts
   2a: Gregory Marks
   2b: the author
2. The agents in 1b and 2a give important or unexpected information.
   The agents in 1a and 2b seem unnecessary.

C1: Listening for Meaning and Use (p. 219)

	NECESSARY AGENT	UNNECESSARY AGENT
2.		✓
3.	✓	
4.		✓
5.		✓
6.		✓
7.		✓
8.	✓	

C2: Including or Omitting Agents (p. 219)

3. Many car accidents in this community have been caused by drunk drivers.
   (The agent is included because it completes the meaning of the sentence.)
4. Children shouldn't be allowed to watch too much television.
   (The agent is omitted because it is obvious.)
5. Lawmakers will pass a gun control law soon.
   (The agent is omitted because it is obvious.)
6. The British government was led by Winston Churchill in World War II.
   (The agent is included because it contains important information.)
7. Will parents of juvenile offenders be punished?
   (The agent is omitted because it is obvious.)
8. This incredible story was written by a young child.
   (The agent is included because it is surprising.)

C3: Including or Omitting Agents (p. 220)

At the hospital:
3. He'll be told whether it is broken.
4. If his arm is broken, he'll be sent back to the emergency room.
5. First his arm will be put in the proper position.
6. Then a cotton sleeve will be put over his arm, and it will be wrapped with wet bandages.
7. After it sets, he'll be told how to care for the cast.

At school:
1. Please listen carefully. The instructions are going to be read only once.
2. Each student will be given a test booklet and a pencil.
3. The students will be asked to turn to the first page.
4. Then they will be shown a set of pictures.
5. They will be told to check the correct answer in the booklet.
6. After the last picture, the booklets will be collected.
7. Finally, the students will be dismissed.

Examining Meaning and Use (p. 221)

1. a. We use sulfur dioxide to produce sulfuric acid.
   b. As a special benefit to on-line customers, we will ship orders free of charge.
   c. You must insure your vehicle. You must present proof of insurance.
2. Passive sentences sound more formal and impersonal because the focus is on the results or the receiver of the action and not on the agent.
3. Sentence *a* would be used in academic discourse such as a textbook; sentence *b* would be used in public discourse such as an advertisement; and sentence *c* would be used in public discourse such as a rule.

D1: Listening for Meaning and Use (p. 222)

A.

	ACADEMIC DISCOURSE	PUBLIC DISCOURSE	PERSONAL DISCOURSE
2.	✓		
3.		✓	
4.		✓	
5.			✓
6.		✓	
7.	✓		
8.		✓	

B. Answers will vary.

D2: Understanding Newspaper Headlines (p. 223)

A. 2. A new cancer treatment has been discovered.
      A new cancer treatment was discovered.
   3. The president's trip has been delayed by the weather.
      The president's trip was delayed by the weather.
   4. A site has been selected for the recycling plant.
      A site was selected for the recycling plant.
   5. The restaurant has been closed by the Health Department.
      The restaurant was closed by the Health Department.
   6. A golfer has been struck by lightning.
      A golfer was struck by lightning.

B. In newspaper headlines, the passive is used to convey an objective or impersonal tone. The passive often sounds more formal, factual, or authoritative. In some sentences, the agent was included because it provided information necessary to complete the meaning or because it was important information.

D3: Understanding Informal Speech (p. 224)

2. might be promoted
3. may be transferred
4. was accepted
5. was caught
6. could be fired
7. was rewarded
8. was nominated

D4: Writing Rules (p. 225)

A.
1. Membership passes must be shown at the gate.
2. Guest passes can be purchased at the main office.
3. The number of guests may be limited on weekends.
4. Children under 12 are not admitted unless an adult accompanies them. OR ... unless they are accompanied by an adult.
5. Small children must be supervised at all times.
6. A shower must be taken before entering the pool.
7. The lifeguard must be obeyed at all times.
8. Diving is permitted in designated areas only.
9. Smoking, gum chewing, and glass bottles are prohibited.
10. Food may be eaten in the picnic area only.

B. Answers will vary.

E1: Thinking About Meaning and Use (p. 226)

2. b   4. b   6. a   8. a
3. b   5. b   7. b

E2: Editing (p. 227)

2. The letter ought to *be* delivered in the afternoon.
3. The bell will be *rung* (rang) several times.
4. A young man has *been* put in prison for 20 years. That's terrible!
5. The mail has *been* sent to the wrong address.
6. Will a new road *be built* (build) soon, or will the old one be repaired?
7. It will *not be* (be not) needed any longer.
8. All applications must *be* (get) accompanied by a check.

CHAPTER 11

A3: After You Read (p. 231)

2. F   3. T   4. T   5. F   6. T

Examining Form (p. 232)

1. Gerund as Subject
   line 6: driving   line 16: His weaving
   line 14: driving   line 16: (His) putting

2. Gerund Following a Verb
   line 10: weaving   line 22: using

3. Infinitive Directly Following a Verb
   line 22: to relax

4. It is in subject position.

B1: Listening for Form (p. 234)

	GERUND	INFINITIVE
2.	✓	
3.	✓	
4.		✓
5.		✓
6.		✓

B2: Rephrasing Subject Gerunds as *It* ... + Infinitive (p. 234)

2. It's not a good idea to study all night.
3. It takes too much time to walk to work.
4. It is important to get exercise.
5. It costs a lot of money to own a house.
6. It can be useful to know a foreign language.

B3: Working on Subject Gerunds and *It* ... + Infinitive (p. 235)

A. Answers will vary.
B. Answers will vary.

B4: Building Sentences with Gerunds and Infinitives (p. 235)

He told me to speak Spanish.
She expects me to go more slowly.
She expects me to speak Spanish.
She expects to go more slowly.
She expects to speak Spanish.
He learned to go more slowly.
He learned to speak Spanish.
They advised me to go more slowly.
They advised me to speak Spanish.
They advised leaving.
They advised taking a driving class.
Don't delay leaving.
Don't delay taking a driving class.

B5: Distinguishing Gerunds and Infinitives After Verbs (p. 235)

2. seeing it?   7. to see it.
3. seeing it.   8. to see it.
4. to see it.   9. seeing it.
5. seeing it.   10. to see it.
6. to see it.

B6: Using Short Answers to Questions with Infinitives (p. 236)

2. B: don't expect to
3. B: would like to
4. B: doesn't want to
5. B: plan to
6. B: needs to

B7: Asking Information Questions with Gerunds and Infinitives (p. 237)

A. Answers will vary. Some examples are:

2. A: What do you enjoy doing on Sundays?
   B: Reading the paper. What about you?
   A: I enjoy cooking (on Sundays).
3. A: What do you suggest doing after dinner?
   B: Watching television. What about you?
   A: I suggest taking a walk (after dinner).
4. A: What would you like to do on your birthday?
   B: Go to a movie. What about you?
   A: I would like to go to a club (on my birthday).
5. A: What do you want to do during your vacation?
   B: Relax. What about you?
   A: I want to go to the beach (during my vacation).
6. A: What do you avoid doing on the weekend?
   B: Working. What about you?
   A: I avoid getting up early (on the weekend).

7. A: What do you hope to do next summer?
   B: Go to Europe. What about you?
   A: I hope to buy a new car (next summer).
8. A: What do you dislike doing in the morning?
   B: Eating breakfast. What about you?
   A: I dislike waking up early (in the morning).

B. Answers will vary.

B8: Asking *Yes/No* Questions with Gerunds and Infinitives (p. 237)

Answers will vary. Some examples are:
2. A: Do you suggest staying home or going out tonight?
   B: Going out.
3. A: Do you hope to live in a big city or a small town?
   B: A big city.
4. A: Do you need to study a lot or a little?
   B: A lot.
5. A: Do you recommend eating breakfast or skipping breakfast?
   B: Eating breakfast.
6. A: Do you want to stay in your apartment or find a new apartment?
   B: Find a new apartment.

Examining Meaning and Use (p. 238)

Same meaning: 2a and 2b; Different meaning: 1a and 1b

C1: Listening for Meaning and Use (p. 240)

2. b   3. a   4. b   5. a   6. b

C2: Rephrasing Gerunds and Infinitives (p. 240)

2. A: I hate driving in traffic.
   B: Then you should continue taking the bus home.
3. A: It started raining a few minutes ago.
   B: Then let's wait here. I don't like walking in the rain.
4. A: I hate to wait in line.
   B: So do I. That's why I prefer shopping late at night.

C3: Making Suggestions (p. 241)

Answers will vary.

C4: Expressing Feelings and Preferences (p. 242)

A. 1. 2. getting up
        3. to worry / worrying
        4. to do
    2. 1. shopping
        2. to watch / watching
        3. to buy
        4. to fight / fighting
        5. to go
        6. going
        7. to have / having
    3. 1. to feel
        2. to find / finding
        3. to avoid
        4. cooking

B. Answers will vary.

Examining Form (p. 243)

1. In sentence b, the gerund follows a verb phrase ending in a noun. In sentence c, the gerund follows a phrasal verb. In sentence a, the gerund follows a preposition.
2. Sentence d has a phrase containing an infinitive (*to reach* their distinctions). The infinitive follows an adjective (anxious).

D1: Listening for Form (p. 245)

2. relaxing   7. going
3. working   8. leaving
4. to finish   9. catching up
5. working   10. to relax
6. taking

D2: Using Gerunds After Prepositional Phrases (p. 245)

Answers will vary. Some examples are:
2. After finding a job, make sure to start a savings account.
3. Instead of cooking dinner, let's go out to eat.
4. Besides doing the laundry, I need to go to the grocery store.
5. By reducing stress, you will be a healthier person.
6. In addition to cleaning your apartment, you need to get your car fixed.
7. Before using a computer, make sure you know how to type.
8. After looking for an apartment, you'll need to buy furniture.

D3: Choosing Between Gerunds and Infinitives (p. 246)

A. Answers will vary. Some examples are:
2. A: What are you good at?
   B: I'm good at cooking chicken. What about you?
   A: I'm good at playing the guitar.
3. A: What are you eager to do?
   B: I'm eager to finish college. What about you?
   A: I'm eager to visit my family in two weeks.
4. A: What are you afraid of doing?
   B: I'm afraid of riding in elevators. What about you?
   A: I'm afraid of meeting new people.
5. A: What are you ready to do right now?
   B: I'm ready to go to a movie. What about you?
   A: I'm ready to eat dinner.
6. A: What are you accustomed to doing?
   B: I'm accustomed to eating dessert every night. What about you?
   A: I'm accustomed to spending Sundays with my family.
7. A: What are you determined to do before you are 50?
   B: I'm determined to skydive before I'm 50. What about you?
   A: I'm determined to travel around the world before I'm 50.
8. A: What are you looking forward to doing next year?
   B: I'm looking forward to studying in Japan next year. What about you?
   A: I'm looking forward to going to college next year.

D4: Working on Purpose Infinitives (p. 246)

A. Answers will vary. Some examples are:
2. to pick up my clothes.
3. to fill a prescription.
4. to return a book.
5. to fill up the gas tank.

B. Answers will vary.

Examining Meaning and Use (p. 247)

1. In 1a, Jane is driving. In 1b, Tom is driving.
2. In 2a, Sam might come early. In 2b, Susan might come early.

E1: Listening for Meaning and Use (p. 248)

2. b	4. a	6. b	8. b
3. b	5. a	7. a	

E2: Expressing Intentions and Desires (p. 249)

Answers will vary. Some examples are:
3. Situation A: to be the next president of the United States.
   Situation B: to be unemployed for a few months.
4. Situation A: you to give me advice.
   Situation B: you to help me.
5. Situation A: raising enough money for my campaign.
   Situation B: disappointing my family.
6. Situation A: everyone to vote.
   Situation B: you to find out the truth.
7. Situation A: to tell you why I'll make the best candidate.
   Situation B: to apologize for my mistakes.
8. Situation A: campaigning every weekend.
   Situation B: explaining my side of the story.

E3: Talking About Teaching (p. 249)

A. Answers will vary.
B. Answers will vary.

F1: Thinking About Meaning and Use (p. 250)

2. F	4. F	6. F	8. T	10. F
3. T	5. T	7. T	9. T	

F2: Editing (p. 251)

Unfortunately, it is very common ^to encounter aggressive drivers every day.

They are usually trying to ~~getting~~ get somewhere in a hurry. ~~Their~~ Them speeding can cause them ^to follow too closely or ^to change lanes frequently without signaling.

In order ^to avoid becoming an aggressive driver, there are a number of rules ~~following~~ to follow. First, allow enough time to ~~reaching~~ reach your destination. Second, change your schedule to keep from ~~drive~~ driving during rush hours. Third, call ahead ~~for~~ to explain if you are going to be late. Then you can relax.

If you see an aggressive driver, try ^to get out of the way safely. Never challenge an aggressive driver by ~~speed~~ speeding up or attempting to hold your position in your lane. Don't let others make you ~~driving~~ drive dangerously. You need ^to be in control at all times.

CHAPTER 12

A3: After You Read (p. 257)

2. F Chicken soup makes you feel better both emotionally and physically.
3. T
4. F Dr. Sackner showed that chicken soup was better at fighting congestion than hot or cold water.
5. F Chicken soup is good for colds, but Dr. Ziment thinks spicy foods are even better.
6. T

Examining Form (p. 258)

1. line 22: literature   line 25: chemical
   line 23: centuries   line 26: soup
   line 23: drugs   line 27: drug
   line 24: Chicken

2. Adjective + Noun
   line 22: early, medical literature

   Article + Noun
   line 23: the drugs   line 26: the soup

   Article + Adjective + Noun
   line 25: a certain chemical   line 27: a common drug

3. line 23: centuries   line 24: Chicken

4. Singular   Plural
   line 22: literature   line 23: centuries
   line 24: Chicken   line 23: drugs
   line 25: chemical
   line 26: soup
   line 27: drug

B1: Listening for Form (p. 260)

2. Ø	5. Ø	8. Ø	11. the	14. a
3. Ø	6. The	9. Ø	12. the	
4. the	7. Ø	10. the	13. a	

B2: Identifying Indefinite and Definite Articles (p. 260)

Have you ever eaten coconut? You probably have, but you may not be very familiar with coco palms [I]. Coconuts [I] come from coco palms [I], which are trees [I] that grow in tropical regions [I]. Coco palms [I] are very unusual because all of the parts [D] of the tree [D] have a commercial value [I]. For example, coconuts [I] are an important food [I] in tropical regions [I], and coconut milk [I], which comes from inside the coconut [D], is a nutritious drink [I]. Coconut oil [I], the most valuable product [D] of all, also comes from coconuts [I]. Some of the other parts [D] of the tree [D] that are eaten include the buds [D] and young stems [D]. Besides food [I], the tree [D] is also used for manufacturing commercial products [I]. The leaves [D] are used for making fans [I] and baskets [I], and the fibers [D] from the husks [D] and trunks [D] are made into mats [I], cord [I], and rope [I]. Even the hard shells [D] and the husks [D] are used to make fuel [I], and the trunks [D] are used for timber [I].

B3: Building Sentences with Indefinite and Definite Articles (p. 261)

I ate some rice.
I ate some vegetables.
I ate rice.
I ate vegetables.
I ate the rice.
I ate the vegetables.
They had a pencil.
They had an idea.
They had some rice.
They had some fun.
They had some vegetables.
They had rice.
They had fun.
They had vegetables.
They had the pencil.
They had the rice.
They had the vegetables.
They had the idea.

B4: Transforming Sentences (p. 261)

A. 2. Take some peaches. / Take the peaches.
3. This is an herb.
4. A child gets more colds than an adult.
5. We need a magazine with more information.
6. I watched some movies last night.

B. 2. Take a sheet of paper and a pen.
3. Did you eat the cookies or cake?
4. I'm taking medication and eating yogurt twice a day.
5. Did you see the movie last week?
6. I went to the store yesterday.

Examining Meaning and Use (p. 262)

1. 1a
2. 2b refers to a small quantity of the underlined noun. 2a classifies the underlined noun.

C1: Listening for Meaning and Use (p. 263)

		SPECIFIC	NOT SPECIFIC
2.	apples		✓
3.	a new doctor		✓
4.	a friend	✓	
5.	some soup	✓	
6.	an appointment	✓	
7.	a book		✓
8.	cough medicine	✓	

C2: Introducing New Information (p. 264)

A. Answers will vary. Some examples are:
2. B: I bought a loaf of bread, some eggs, and a watermelon.
3. B: I take a suitcase, some clothes, and an iron.
4. B: I want some new clothes, a watch, and some CDs.
5. B: I keep chewing gum, a comb, and a pen in my pockets.
6. B: You can buy tools, nails, and lightbulbs at a hardware store.

C3: Classifying Nouns (p. 264)

A. Answers will vary.
B. Answers will vary.

Examining Meaning and Use (p. 265)

1. b   2. a   3. c

D1: Listening for Meaning and Use (p. 267)

2. a   4. a   6. a   8. a
3. a   5. b   7. b

D2: Choosing Definite or Indefinite Articles (p. 267)

1. 2. a   4. 1. the
   2. 1. The   2. an
   2. a   3. the
   3. an   5. 1. the
   4. a   2. the
3. 1. an
   2. the

D3: Using *Another* and *The Other* (p. 268)

Answers will vary.

D4: Making Inferences Based on General Knowledge (p. 268)

Answers will vary. Some examples are:
2. The waiter gave a detailed description of the lunch specials.
3. The mechanic said that it would be very expensive to fix the problem.
4. The teller forgot to give me a receipt.
5. The author did an excellent job of creating suspense.
6. The receptionist said that I could make an appointment for next week.

D5: Connecting Information (p. 269)

A. 5. He cut the wire and jumped from the window into a creek.
3. No one knows exactly where he found the ladder.
1. Another prisoner has escaped from the local prison.
4. He was able to reach a high window covered with wire.
6. He swam across the creek, climbed over a wall, stole a car, and drove away.
2. Sometime during the night, the prisoner climbed up a ladder.

B. Answers will vary.

D6: Talking About Familiar Nouns (p. 270)

Answers will vary. Some examples are:
2. I went to the First National bank before I came to class.
3. I bought the *Daily News* before I came to class.
4. The mayor who was just elected is going to speak on television tonight.
5. I didn't feel well yesterday, so I went to the doctor who you recommended to me.

D7: Understanding Shared Information (p. 270)

A. Answers will vary. Some examples are:
2. One man is selling his car. The other man wants to buy the car. They are discussing the price.
3. The couple wants to buy their first home. The woman just found out that the bank will give them a loan to buy a house.
4. The three women attended a concert recently. One of the women took photographs. They want to look at the pictures together.
5. The woman is talking to her roommate who was supposed to pay the telephone bill. He forgot, and now the payment will be late.
6. The two men are brothers. One of them has just gotten season tickets for their favorite basketball team.

B. Answers will vary.

Examining Meaning and Use (p. 271)
1. 1b, 2a, 3b, 4a
2. 1a, 2b, 3a, 4b

E1: Listening for Meaning and Use (p. 273)

		GENERIC	SPECIFIC
2.	almonds	✓	
3.	garlic	✓	
4.	food		✓
5.	the onion	✓	
6.	a cold		✓
7.	vitamins	✓	
8.	a headache	✓	

E2: Defining Nouns with *A/An* (p. 273)
Answers will vary. Some examples are:
2. An iris is a tall yellow or purple flower.
3. An elm is a tall tree with large leaves.
4. A pineapple is a tropical fruit.
5. A crib is a bed for babies.
6. An octopus is an eight-legged sea-creature.
7. A calculator is a small mathematical device.
8. A screwdriver is a tool with a narrow blade for turning screws.

E3: Rephrasing Formal Generic Sentences (p. 274)
A. Kangaroos are Australian animals with very distinctive physical features. They have large back legs that are used for hopping very fast, and they have very large tails that help them maintain their balance. Female kangaroos carry their young around in special pockets of skin on their stomachs that are called pouches.

B. Answers will vary.

E4: Choosing Between Generic and Specific Nouns (p. 274)
A. 1. 2. a
2. 1. A
   2. a
3. 1. Ø
   2. The
4. 1. Ø
   2. The
   3. a
5. 1. Ø
   2. Ø
6. 1. Ø
   2. a

B. Answers will vary.

F1: Thinking About Meaning and Use (p. 276)
2. a. T   5. a. F   8. a. T
   b. F   b. T   b. F
3. a. T   6. a. T
   b. T   b. T
4. a. T   7. a. T
   b. F   b. F

F2: Editing (p. 277)
2. When you get to my house, you don't have to ring ^the doorbell. Just walk in.
3. We have plenty of sandwiches. Please take ~~the~~ another one.
4. My grandparents were ~~some~~ immigrants. They came to this country in 1920.
5. She graduated with a major in ~~the~~ mathematics and physics.
6. ~~The~~ life is not always easy.
7. Calcium is ^a mineral.
8. Please pass the rice and ~~the~~ salt.
9. The book I bought was on sale.
10. Let's sit in ^the last row so that we can leave quickly when the play is over.

CHAPTER 13

A3: After You Read (p. 281)
2. T
3. F The company got a new contract advertising pâté.
4. F The Pollaks think that the business world has gotten too casual.
5. T
6. F Formal Fridays can be a little confusing to outsiders.

Examining Form (p. 282)
1. line 31: that had read about Formal Fridays
   line 32: who wears gowns and tuxedos
   line 36: that has gotten too casual
   line 45: who was dressed in a tuxedo
   line 46: who was wearing a glittery black dress
   line 56: who was wearing a tuxedo

2. Relative Pronoun   Noun/Noun Phrase
   line 31: that   a person
   line 32: who   anyone
   line 36: that   a business world
   line 45: who   Sal Giacchi
   line 46: who   Betty Uhler
   line 56: who   a Pollack employee

3. Nonrestrictive
   line 45: who was dressed in a tuxedo
   line 46: who was wearing a glittery black dress

   Restrictive
   line 31: that had read about Formal Fridays
   line 32: who wears gowns and tuxedos
   line 36: that has gotten too casual
   line 56: who was wearing a tuxedo

B1: Listening for Form (p. 284)
2. a   4. a   6. b   8. b
3. a   5. b   7. b

B2: Identifying Relative Clauses (p. 285)

Paul: Do you mean my new blue shirt, <u>which is at the cleaners?</u>
Rita: Oh. Well, what about the shirts <u>that are hanging on the bedroom door?</u>
Paul: Hmm...should I wear the white one or the one <u>that has pinstripes?</u>
Rita: Wear the one <u>that feels more comfortable.</u> What time is the interview?
Paul: The boss's secretary, <u>who called to confirm yesterday,</u> said 10:15, although the manager <u>who originally contacted me</u> said 10:30. I'd better be there at 10:15.
Rita: By the way, was the booklet <u>that came from the Department of Labor</u> helpful?
Paul: Yes, especially part 3, <u>which had a lot of practical advice.</u>
Rita: Is the position <u>that's open</u> a new one?
Paul: No. I know the person <u>who has it now.</u> She's leaving to work in the Boston branch, <u>which opens after the first of the year.</u>

B3: Building Sentences with Subject Relative Pronouns (p. 285)

We like the man who works in the bakery.
We like Gary, who works in the bakery.
We like the new phone cards, which are affordable.
We like cars that are affordable.
We like cars which are affordable.

B4: Working on Placement of Relative Clauses (p. 286)

A. 2. Some employers won't hire applicants who dress too casually.
3. Employees who oppose dress codes believe that clothing is a form of free expression.
4. Some companies restrict clothing that has sports logos on it.
5. A company dress code may not allow women to wear skirts that are very short.

B. 2. What do you think about rule number 3, which restricts very tight clothing?
3. My nephew Dan, who works for a high-tech company, often wears very unusual clothing.
4. My boss, who has been here only for a year, is trying to enforce a new dress code.
5. Casual dress, which is hard to define, has become the new standard in many companies.

B5: Working on Verb Agreement in Relative Clauses (p. 286)

1. 2. who / that asks
2. 1. which was
   2. that / which looks
3. 1. who lives
   2. who own / that
4. 1. who / that treats
   2. who has
5. 1. who finished
   2. who / that were
6. 1. which has
   2. that / which are

B6: Combining Sentences with Who, That, or Which (p. 287)

2. The professor who / that teaches Russian called me.
3. My sister has a cat that / which has three kittens.
4. Did you buy the socks that / which were on sale?
5. The little girl who / that hurt her knee was crying.
6. They gave us an exam that / which lasted an hour.
7. I spoke to two women who / that saw the accident.
8. The child who / that was sick went home.

Examining Meaning and Use (p. 288)

1. 1b   2. 2b

C1: Listening for Meaning and Use (p. 289)

2. a   4. a   6. a   8. b
3. a   5. b   7. a

C2: Identifying Nouns (p. 290)

Answers will vary. Some examples are:
2. My car is the one that has a dog inside it.
3. My boots are the ones that have a zipper.
4. My raincoat is the one that has a scarf in the pocket.
5. My backpack is the one that has a water bottle in the pocket.
6. My keys are the ones that are on a soccer ball key ring.

C3: Identifying and Defining with Subject Relative Pronouns (p. 291)

Answers will vary. Some examples are:
1. b. She is famous for painting flowers that were colorful.
2. a. Gene therapy is a new branch of genetic engineering that may someday help prevent cancer.
   b. Cancer is a serious medical condition that causes tumors to grow in the body.
3. a. Martin Luther King, Jr. was an African American who led the civil rights movement in the 1960s.
   b. Passive resistance is a nonviolent method of protest that was previously used by Mahatma Gandhi in the 1940s.
4. a. A phobia is an exaggerated fear that can prevent a person from leading a normal life.
   b. People who have a fear of being in open places suffer from agoraphobia. People who have a fear of being in closed places suffer from claustrophobia.

C4: Defining Words with Relative Clauses (p. 291)

Answers will vary. Some examples are:
2. A neurologist is a doctor who treats diseases of the nervous system.
3. A pediatrician is a doctor who treats children.
4. A dentist is a doctor who treats teeth.
5. A cardiologist is a doctor who treats heart problems.
6. A podiatrist is a doctor who treats foot problems.

C5: Distinguishing Between Two Nouns (p. 292)

Answers will vary. Some examples are:
1. The shoes that were made in Brazil.
2. The boy who is wearing shorts./The boy wearing shorts. The boy who is throwing a/the ball./The boy throwing a/the ball.
3. The woman who is on the phone./The woman on the phone.
The woman who is using the computer./The woman using the computer.

4. The man who is drinking a soda./The man drinking a soda.
   The man who is reading a magazine./The man reading a magazine.
5. The hat that is hanging on the wall./The one hanging on the wall.
   The hat that is on the shelf./The one on the shelf.
6. The tea mix that has sugar./The tea mix with sugar.
   The tea mix that doesn't have sugar./The tea mix without sugar.

C6: Connecting Ideas with Relative Clauses (p. 293)

A. Answers will vary. Some examples are:
School dress codes are becoming popular again, although this doesn't necessarily mean that students have to wear uniforms. A school dress code is a set of rules that restricts certain types of clothing. Some dress codes prohibit certain T-shirts which have offensive writing or pictures on them. Other dress codes prohibit certain types of pants or shirts that are very baggy or tight. Many others prohibit certain types of skirts and dresses that are several inches above the knee. Some dress codes go even further. They don't allow sports clothing that has logos on it.

B. Answers will vary.

Examining Meaning and Use (p. 294)

1. a (necessary information); b (not essential information)
2. b

D1: Listening for Meaning and Use (p. 295)

2. b   3. b   4. b   5. b   6. a

D2: Adding Extra Information (p. 296)

A. Answers will vary. Some examples are:
2. I once visited the Vatican, which is in Rome.
3. I've never met Mr. Williams, who is the president of the company.
4. I'd like to meet Bill Gates, who is an extremely successful businessman.

B. Answers will vary. Some examples are:
2. My best friend, who is the best student in her class, studies every night.
3. My birthday, which is in November, is very important to me.
4. My home, which is on the top floor of my building, has a great view of the city.

D3: Choosing Restrictive or Nonrestrictive Relative Clauses (p. 296)

2. restrictive
3. nonrestrictive — We live in the South, which is very warm and humid.
4. nonrestrictive — My father, who loves to play golf, lives next to a golf course. OR My father, who lives next to a golf course, loves to play golf.
5. restrictive
6. restrictive
7. nonrestrictive — I've invited my friend Jane, who works in the legal division at your company.
8. nonrestrictive — Pollution, which is still a major problem, was a political issue in the last election.

D4: Describing a Person (p. 297)

Answers will vary. Some examples are:
2. My uncle who owns a hardware store has three sons. His youngest son, who is a great baseball player, is my age.
3. My friend who is a medical student is always studying. Her boyfriend, who lives in the same apartment building, never sees her.
4. The teacher that we had for biology last year is no longer at our school. Her husband, who is an army officer, was transferred overseas.
5. My neighbor who lives across the street just bought a new car. His son, who helps all the neighbors, is washing it now.
6. My classmate who sits next to me always helps me with my homework. His friend, who has a computer, lets us use it to type our essays.

E1: Thinking About Meaning and Use (p. 298)

1. b. F	4. a. T	6. a. T	8. a. T
2. a. T	b. T	b. F	b. T
b. F	5. a. T	7. a. T	
3. a. F	b. F	b. F	
b. T			

E2: Editing (p. 299)

What kind of clothing should people ~~which~~ *who* visit a place of worship wear? Is it acceptable to wear jeans to mosques, churches, or synagogues? Should a worshiper wear something that is sporty and comfortable or something ~~what~~ *that/which* is more dressy? These are questions ~~who~~ *that/which* concern many religious leaders these days.

Opinions are strongly divided about the type of clothing ‸*that/which* is appropriate for worship. According to some religious leaders, people ~~which~~ *who/that* come to pray should wear clothing that ~~show~~ *shows* respect and admiration for their religion. They shouldn't be wearing clothes that ~~is~~ *are* for jogging, shopping, or attending a ball game. On the other hand, there are many religious leaders ‸*who/that* don't care about such material issues. They believe that religion, which is a spiritual matter, isn't concerned with clothing. They welcome everyone who ~~attend~~ *attends* religious services.

Most people think that the issue actually goes beyond clothing. More formal clothing usually accompanies an atmosphere which ‸*is* more traditional and serious. Informal clothing, on the other hand, is more acceptable in religious services that they are more contemporary and informal.

CHAPTER 14

A3: After You Read (p. 303)
2. b   3. a   4. c   5. c   6. b

Examining Form (p. 304)

1. | Object Relative Pronoun | Noun/Noun Phrase |
    |---|---|
    | line 1: which | Women's World Cup |
    | line 6: who | Mia Hamm |
    | line 9: that | passion |
    | line 16: which | Title IX |
    | line 18: that | role models |
    | line 24: which | Mia Hamm Foundation |
    | line 30: that | things |

2. The object relative pronoun missing from each clause is *which/that*.

B1: Listening for Form (p. 306)
2. b   3. a   4. b   5. a   6. b

B2: Examining Relative Clauses with Object Relative Pronouns (p. 306)

Kay Valera used to be a "soccer mom." She sat on the sidelines while she watched her children play soccer. But now the 40-year-old mom has become a soccer player in a (women's league) which she joined last spring. One of the (things) that she has learned is how challenging it is to play a sport that requires players to think, kick, and run at the same time. As she plays, she recalls all the (advice) that she has given her kids. Everything that looked so easy from the sidelines is now so challenging.

Many kids and dads come to the games to cheer on the moms. And what happens when mom makes a mistake or her team loses? The kids can be very encouraging, but they also love to discuss the (mistakes) that mom made and the (moves) that she should have made. They might say, "Don't feel bad, you did your best, but you know that (kick) that you tried in midfield, well . . ."

B3: Using Object Relative Pronouns (p. 307)
2. Marcus, (who) we saw on Tuesday, (doesn't) work with us.
3. The bike (that / which / Ø) they bought (is) missing.
4. Ellen, (who) works with me, (is) always late for work.
5. The people (that / who / Ø) she (visits) live nearby.
6. The teacher (that / who / Ø) I like (is) not here today.

B4: Combining Sentences Using Relative Clauses (p. 308)
Answers will vary. Some examples are:
2. Here is a photo of your grandfather who I still miss so much.
3. Our dog Teddy, who we loved a lot, is in this picture.
4. The dress which I wore to my wedding is in this box.
5. I'll never forget the guests who I invited to my wedding.
6. I remember my high school teacher Miss Pullman who I liked so much.
7. Here is a poem that I wrote in her class.
8. This is an award that I received for my poem.

B5: Asking and Answering Questions with Object Relative Pronouns (p. 308)
Answers will vary. Some examples are:
2. A: What is a game that you liked to play as a child?
   B: Hide-and-seek is a game that I liked to play as a child.
3. A: Who is the relative that you look like most?
   B: The relative that I look like most is my aunt.
4. A: Who is the person that you call when you're in trouble?
   B: The person that I call when I'm in trouble is my best friend.
5. A: What is a food you have never tasted?
   B: Fried chicken is a food I have never tasted.
6. A: Who is a teacher you will always remember?
   B: My second grade teacher is a teacher I will always remember.
7. A: What is a book which you like to read over and over again?
   B: A book which I like to read over and over again is *The Great Gatsby*.
8. A: What is a thing that you can't live without?
   B: Sunshine is a thing that I can't live without.

Examining Meaning and Use (p. 309)
1. 1a. The (coat) that costs $200 is on sale now.
   1b. The (coat) you wanted is on sale now.
   2a. (Megan Quann), who was only 16, was on the Olympic swimming team.
   2b. (Megan Quann), who I know, was on the Olympic swimming team.
2. In 1a and 1b, the relative clauses help identify the noun.
   In 2a and 2b, the relative clauses add extra information about the noun.

C1: Listening for Meaning and Use (p. 310)
2. b   3. a   4. a   5. b   6. a

C2: Identifying Nouns (p. 311)
A. Answers will vary. Some examples are:
2. that likes to garden.
3. who enjoys reading the newspaper.
4. which challenges me.
5. that has a swimming pool.
6. who goes dancing every Friday night.
7. that offer discount prices.
8. who knows how to have fun.

B. Answers will vary.

C3: Adding Extra Information (p. 311)
A. Answers will vary. Some examples are:
3. The Olympics occur every four years.
4. The New York Yankees have a lot of fans.
5. Wayne Gretzky is a famous hockey player.

B. Answers will vary.

C4: Expressing Your Opinion (p. 312)

Answers will vary. Some examples are:
2. I like teachers who are patient. I don't like teachers that give too much homework.
3. I like clothes that are fashionable. I don't like clothes which are expensive.
4. I like newspapers that have important news. I don't like newspapers which only report gossip.
5. I like friends who are loyal. I don't like friends that are late.
6. I like TV shows which are based on real life. I don't like TV shows that are silly.
7. I like foods that are light and healthy. I don't like foods which are heavy and greasy.
8. I like music that is soothing and relaxing. I don't like music that is too loud.
9. I like books which are interesting. I don't like books that are boring.
10. I like pets that are easy to take care of. I don't like pets which require too much attention.

Examining Form (p. 313)

1. a. We saw the movie that everyone is talking (about).
   b. We saw the movie (about) which everyone is talking.
2. In sentence a, the preposition occurs at the end of the relative clause.
   In sentence b, the preposition occurs at the beginning of the relative clause.
   In sentence a, that is used. (You can also use which or Ø here.)
   In sentence b, which is used. (You can only use which here.)

D1: Listening for Form (p. 315)

2. b   3. a   4. a   5. b

D2: Building Relative Clauses Ending in Prepositions (p. 315)

1. A man who/whom/that/ Ø I always talk to at the supermarket called me last night.
   A man who/whom/that/ Ø I went to high school with called me last night.
   A man who/whom/that/ Ø I used to live next door to called me last night.
2. The movie that/which/ Ø we went to last night was great.
   The movie that/which/ Ø you told us about was great.
   The movie that/which/ Ø I didn't want to go to was great.
   The movie that/which/ Ø you reported on in class was great.
3. Do you know the doctor who/whom/that/ Ø Young-soo lives across from?
   Do you know the doctor who/whom/that/ Ø Eva fell in love with?
   Do you know the doctor who/whom/that/ Ø Luisa works for?
   Do you know the doctor who/whom/that/ Ø I was waiting for?
4. Have you read the book that/which/ Ø the whole class is interested in?
   Have you read the book that/which/ Ø the teacher looked for last week?
   Have you read the book that/which/ Ø Julie wrote about?
   Have you read the book that/which/ Ø I brought in?
5. Today we're going to read the story that/which/ Ø you heard a lot about.
   Today we're going to read the story that/which/ Ø you listened to on tape.
   Today we're going to read the story that/which/ Ø I was working on.
   Today we're going to read the story that/which/ Ø the lecturer talked about.

D3: Working on Relative Clauses Ending in Prepositions (p. 316)

A. Answers will vary. Some examples are:
2. that/which/ Ø she grew up in.
3. that/which/ Ø Stefan is sitting on.
4. who/that/ Ø she spoke to on Tuesday.
5. that/which/ Ø he hasn't heard about.
6. that/which/ Ø she listened to last night.
7. who/that/ Ø he didn't talk to right after the game.
8. that/which/ Ø I'm interested in.

B. Answers will vary. Some examples are:
2. You ask her the name of the town in which she grew up.
3. A salesman recommends the one on which Stefan is sitting.
4. Today she asked for the nurse to whom she spoke on Tuesday.

Examining Meaning and Use (p. 317)

Sentence b sounds the most formal.

E1: Listening for Meaning and Use (p. 318)

	FORMAL	INFORMAL	CONTEXT
2.	✓		an academic lecture
3.	✓		an awards reception or ceremony
4.		✓	a mother talking to her son
5.	✓		a courtroom
6.		✓	a cooking lesson

E2: Rephrasing Formal Relative Clauses (p. 318)

Application for Travel Insurance
2. List the city that/which/ Ø you'll depart from and the city that/which/ Ø you'll return to.
3. List the name of the tour operator who/that/ Ø you'll be traveling with
4. List the hotel that/which/ Ø you'll be staying in.
5. List the code numbers of any extra tours that/which/ Ø you've registered for.

Job Application
1. Name two colleagues who/that/ Ø you've worked closely with.
2. Name one supervisor who/that/ Ø you've worked for in the last year.
3. List two different projects that/which/ Ø you've worked on.
4. Name two decisions that/which/ Ø you've played an important role in.
5. Name the job that/which/ Ø you'd like to apply for.

E3: Reducing Relative Clauses Ending in Prepositions (p. 319)
Answers will vary.

E4: Writing an E-mail Message (p. 320)
Answers will vary.

E5: Using *Where, When,* and Object Relative Pronouns (p. 320)
A. 2. where / in which
3. where / in which
4. when / that / Ø / during which
5. that / which
6. where / in which
7. which
8. when / that / Ø

B. Answers will vary.

C. Answers will vary.

F1: Thinking About Meaning and Use (p. 322)
1. b. T
2. a. F
   b.
3. a. T
   b. F
4. a. F
   b. T
5. a. F
   b. F
6. a. T
   b. F
7. a. T
   b. F
8. a. T
   b. T

F2: Editing (p. 323)

Sisleide Lima do Amor, ~~which~~ *who* soccer fans know as Sissi, was not discouraged as a child by the boys who wouldn't let her play the game ~~with~~ which she loved most. Eventually, she got her way on the streets of Salvador, Brazil, because the soccer ball that the boys wanted to play with ~~it~~ was hers. Still, she often ran home with her ball after she grew frustrated with the negative attitudes that the boys displayed. Sissi had learned to play soccer by practicing with all kinds of objects ~~what~~ *that* she found around the house. These included rolled-up socks, oranges, bottle caps, and the heads of dolls that her parents had given her ~~them~~. It was her father who finally decided that she needed a soccer ball to keep her from destroying her dolls.

Sissi showed her admiration for Brazil's male soccer heroes by choosing the jersey number ~~who~~ *that/which/Ø* Romario wears and by shaving her head to resemble the style ~~in~~ which Ronaldo has made famous. During the Women's World Cup, Sissi displayed the type of skill fans will long remember. Left-footed Sissi scored seven goals for her team, including a goal that she kicked in with her weaker right foot. According to Sissi, her seventh goal is the one about which she keeps thinking ~~about~~ / the one ~~about~~ which she keeps thinking about. During a 3-3 tie, she kicked the ball into a spot the goalkeeper couldn't reach ~~it~~, and her team's 4-3 victory put them into the semifinals. Most fans would agree that it is Sissi's style of playing that has given her the kind of world recognition ~~who~~ *that/which/Ø* she deserves.

CHAPTER 15

A3: After You Read (p. 329)
2. a   3. c   4. b

Examining Form (p. 330)
1. *Selection 1*
   If there is beauty in the person
   If there is harmony in the house
   If there is order in the nation
2. *Selection 2*
   if I had it to do over again (line 13)
   If I had my life to live over (line 15)
   Selection 3
   if it were over tomorrow
   The verb form in each main clause is *would* + verb.
3. *Selection 4*
   Wish is in the present tense. The verb form used in each clause that follows *wish* is the past form.

B1: Listening for Form (p. 332)
2. b   4. a   6. b   8. a
3. b   5. a   7. a

B2: Working on Real and Unreal Conditionals (p. 332)
A. Answers will vary.
B. Answers will vary.

B3: Building Conditional and Wish Sentences (p. 332)
If I were ready, I'd leave.
If she is sick, call for help.
If she is sick, he'll take over.
If she is sick, you could come later.
If they were driving, I'd leave.
If they were driving, you could come later.
I wish I were ready.
I wish they were driving.

B4: Working on *Wish* Sentences and Unreal Conditionals (p. 333)
A. 1. 2. did / 'd
       3. would buy
    2. 1. weren't
       2. were
       3. would get / 'd get
       4. could leave
    3. 1. had
       2. had
       3. would have / 'd have
    4. 1. could
       2. didn't have
       3. would stay / 'd stay

B. Answers will vary.

B5: Completing Real and Unreal Conditionals (p. 333)

A. Answers will vary. Some examples are:
2. I call and let the doctor know.
3. I would stay home.
4. I forget someone's name.
5. I could find a better one.
6. I have enough money.

B. Answers will vary.

B6: Understanding Informal Speech (p. 334)

2. were too late
3. weren't so unfriendly
4. were ready
5. were mad
6. were going

Examining Meaning and Use (p. 335)

Sentence b is a promise.
Sentence a is a statement of fact.
Sentence d is a warning.
Sentence c is an instruction.

C1: Listening for Meaning and Use (p. 337)

	FACTS OR GENERAL TRUTHS	ADVICE, WARNINGS, INSTRUCTIONS	PROMISES
2.			✓
3.	✓		
4.		✓	
5.			✓
6.		✓	
7.	✓		
8.		✓	

C2: Describing Factual Conditions (p. 337)

Answers will vary. Some examples are:
If you're between 7 and 15, it costs $30 to buy a half-season pass.
If you're 16 or older, it costs $75 to buy a full-season pass.
If you're 16 or older, it costs $45 to buy a half-season pass.
If you have children 6 and under, they ski free when accompanied by an adult ticket holder.
If you're a member, you get two free days of skiing: once before December 23 and once after March 6. One guest is allowed each time.
If you're a member, you get a 50% discount on lift tickets on Membership Appreciation Days.
If you're a member, you get a free lift ticket for one guest per member on Membership Appreciation Days.

C3: Making Promises (p. 338)

Answers will vary. Some examples are:
2. If I am elected mayor, I will improve education.
3. If you vote for me, I will build new schools.
4. If I become mayor, I will reduce crime.
5. If I am elected mayor, I will hire more police.
6. If you vote for me, I will expand health care.
7. If I become mayor, I will open more hospitals.
8. If I am elected mayor, I will cut taxes.
9. If you vote for me, I will employ more women.
10. If I become mayor, I will employ more minorities.

C4: Rephrasing Advice with Conditional Sentences (p. 338)

Answers will vary. Some examples are:
2. If you study hard, you won't fail the test.
If you don't want to fail the test, (you should) study hard.
3. If you make calls at night, your telephone bill won't be so high.
If you don't want a high telephone bill, (you should) make calls at night.
4. If you don't eat so much, you won't get indigestion.
If you don't want indigestion, you shouldn't eat so much.
If you don't want indigestion, don't eat so much.
5. If you read a book for a while, you'll fall asleep easily.
If you want to fall asleep easily, (you should) read a book for a while.
6. If you call the doctor, you'll get some good advice.
If you want some good advice, (you should) call the doctor.

C5: Giving Warnings with *If* and *Unless* Clauses (p. 339)

A. Answers will vary. Some examples are:
2. You'll be unhealthy
3. you won't get enough sleep
4. you won't have strong bones
5. you will gain weight

B. Answers will vary. Some examples are:
2. you don't watch your step
3. you read without the light
4. you go outside with wet hair
5. you play with matches

C. Answers will vary.

Examining Meaning and Use (p. 340)

1. 1a expresses something that is more likely to happen.
   1b expresses something that is probably imaginary.
2. 2b sounds more direct.
   2a sounds more indirect.

D1: Listening for Meaning and Use (p. 341)

2. b   3. a   4. b   5. b   6. b

D2: Asking Questions About Unusual Situations (p. 342)

A. Answers will vary. Some examples are:
2. you met the president?
3. you won a million dollars?
4. you had a free plane ticket?
5. you had a big party?
6. you got sick?

B. Answers will vary.

D3: Giving Advice with *If I Were You* (p. 342)

Answers will vary. Some examples are:
2. If I were you, I'd find a new apartment.
   If I were you, I wouldn't pay rent.
3. If I were you, I'd cancel one of them so your friends don't get angry.
   If I were you, I wouldn't be so quick to say "yes" next time.
4. If I were you, I'd change my phone number.
   If I were you, I wouldn't list my number in the phone book.
5. If I were you, I'd try to be nice to him anyway.
   If I were you, I wouldn't put up with it.
6. If I were you, I'd call the police to explain.
   If I were you, I wouldn't pay the ticket.
7. If I were you, I'd take a computer class.
   If I were you, I wouldn't buy a computer yet.
8. If I were you, I'd hire an English tutor.
   If I were you, I wouldn't turn in assignments late.

D4: Asking Permission (p. 343)

Answers will vary. Some examples are:
2. A: Would you mind if I listened to the news?
   B: No, not at all.
3. A: Would it bother you if I opened the window?
   B: No, I'm hot, too.
4. A: Would it be OK if I borrowed your book?
   B: Sure, I just finished reading it.

D5: Using Conditionals with Many Results (p. 343)

A. Answers will vary.
B. Answers will vary.

Examining Meaning and Use (p. 344)

1. 1b is a wish about the present moment. 1a is a wish about the future.
2. 2a expresses a complaint. 2b expresses a regret.

E1: Listening for Meaning and Use (p. 345)

		EXISTS	DOESN'T EXIST
2.	pictures		✓
3.	free time		✓
4.	a car	✓	
5.	a safety lock		✓
6.	a limit	✓	
7.	a credit card	✓	
8.	your guitar	✓	

E2: Making Wishes About the Present (p. 346)

Answers will vary. Some examples are:
2. I wish I made more money. If I made more money, I'd buy a car.
3. I wish I could change classes. If I changed classes, I'd take something more interesting.
4. I wish I weren't so busy. If I weren't so busy, I could spend more time with my friends.
5. I wish I didn't live in a big city. If I didn't live in a big city, I'd spend more time outside.
6. I wish I didn't drive to work. If I didn't drive to work, I'd be much more relaxed.
7. I wish I could get more exercise. If I exercised more, I'd be healthier.
8. I wish I had my cell phone. If I had it with me, I could call for help.

E3: Making Wishes About the Future (p. 346)

Answers will vary. Some examples are:
2. I wish you would eat healthier food!
3. If only you would go out with me tonight!
4. I wish you would relax!
5. I wish you would stay here until the weather improves!
6. If only you would finish college!

E4: Complaining with *Wish* and *If Only* Sentences (p. 347)

Answers will vary. Some examples are:
2. If only he wouldn't use up all the hot water in the shower!
3. I wish he wouldn't stay in the bathroom so long.
4. If only he would write down phone messages!
5. I wish he would clean up the kitchen.
6. I wish he wouldn't talk on the phone for hours.

E5: Expressing Regret with *Wish* Sentences (p. 347)

Answers will vary. Some examples are:
2. I did, but I sold the last one ten minutes ago.
3. I could, but I was absent yesterday.
4. I did, but I have to work.
5. there were, but you just ate the last one.
6. it were, but it's colder than it was yesterday.

F1: Thinking About Meaning and Use (p. 348)

1. b. T	4. a. T	6. a. F	8. a. F
2. a. F	b. F	b. T	b. F
b. F	5. a. T	7. a. F	
3. a. T	b. T	b. T	
b. T			

F2: Editing (p. 349)

What ~~you would~~ *would you* do if there were an earthquake in your area? Would you know what to do? Some people are too frightened to find out about safety precautions. They wish they ~~live~~ *lived* somewhere else. If you could, ~~won~~ *wouldn't* you rather find out what to do in advance? Here is some advice about what to do before, during, and after an earthquake.

1. If you don't have a box of emergency equipment and supplies, you will need to prepare one in advance.
2. If you ~~would~~ *are* indoors during an earthquake, you should stay away from windows, bookcases, and shelves.
3. If it ~~were~~ *is* possible, you should turn off the gas, water, and electricity.
4. If you ~~will be~~ *are* able, stand in a doorway or get under a sturdy desk or table.

5. After the earthquake, don't walk around unless you are
~~not~~ wearing shoes to protect your feet from broken glass.
Don't wait. Don't wish you ~~are~~ *were* prepared. Be prepared!

CHAPTER 16

A3: After You Read (p. 353)
2.
3. ✓
4. ✓
5.

Examining Form (p. 354)
1. line 12: . . . what would have happened if there had been no Bering Strait or English Channel or no Franklin Delano Roosevelt.
line 18: What would have happened if, in February 1933, Giuseppe Zangara's hand had not been pushed aside in Miami and his bullet had killed Franklin Roosevelt rather than the mayor of Chicago?
line 51: If Cleopatra had been less attractive, Marc Antony would have kept his mind on the affairs of the state and not been eliminated from the race for Roman emperor.
line 62: If Marc Antony had done that, it would have hastened the rise of Christianity and the fall of the Roman Empire by a hundred years.
line 69: If Joseph Ginoux, a café owner in Arles, had allowed Vincent van Gogh to pay for his lodgings in paintings instead of evicting him, then Vincent would have had some peace and security.
2. The past perfect verb form is used in each *if* clause. *Would have* + past participle is used in each main clause.

B1: Listening for Form (p. 355)
2. a   3. b   4. b   5. a   6. b

B2: Completing Past Conditional Sentences (p. 356)
A. Answers will vary. Some examples are:
2. I would have chosen my friends more carefully.
3. I would have studied law.
4. I wouldn't have succeeded in school.
5. I would have traveled all over Asia.
6. I would have experienced a different way of life.
7. I wouldn't have come to the United States.
8. I wouldn't have seen my classmates.

B. Answers will vary.

B3: Working on Past Conditionals (p. 356)
Answers will vary.

B4: Understanding Informal Speech (p. 357)
2. might have done
3. wouldn't have been
4. could have had
5. would have been
6. wouldn't have won

B5: Working on Past Wishes (p. 358)
A. 1. 3. wishes
   4. had gone

2. 1. wishes
   2. had seen
   3. wish
   4. had shown
3. 1. Do you ever wish
   2. had learned
   3. wish
   4. had been

B. 2. he had
3. we had
4. they hadn't
5. she could have

Examining Meaning and Use (p. 359)
1. Sentence a refers to a situation that was not true in the past. (In fact, she wasn't a better student, so she didn't graduate on time.)
2. Sentence b refers to a situation that is not true in the present. (In fact, she isn't a better student, so she won't graduate on time.)

C1: Listening for Meaning and Use (p. 360)
2. b   4. a   6. a   8. a
3. a   5. a   7. b

C2: Giving Indirect Advice (p. 361)
Answers will vary. Some examples are:
2. B: (If I'd been you,) I would have asked what the money was for.
3. B: (If I'd been you,) I would have complained to the manager.
4. B: (If I'd been you,) I would have asked the questions again.
5. B: (If I'd been you,) I would have asked my boss why I didn't get the raise.
6. B: (If I'd been you,) I would have demanded to speak to the supervisor.

C3: Distinguishing Fact and Fiction (p. 361)
2. Facts: 1. Napoleon's armies didn't have proper nails for horseshoes.
            2. They didn't conquer Russia.
   Paraphrase: Napoleon's armies would have conquered Russia, but they didn't have proper nails for horseshoes.
3. Facts: 1. *Apollo* 13 had an explosion during its flight.
            2. It didn't land on the moon.
   Paraphrase: *Apollo* 13 would have landed on the moon, but it had an explosion during its flight.
4. Facts: 1. Mozart died young.
            2. He didn't finish his famous piece *Requiem*.
   Paraphrase: Mozart would have finished his famous piece *Requiem*, but he died so young.
5. Facts: 1. I was worried about the "Y2K" problem.
            2. I didn't enjoy my celebration on December 31, 1999.
   Paraphrase: I would have enjoyed my celebration on December 31, 1999, but I was worried about the "Y2K" problem.

C4: Describing the Ifs of History (p. 362)
Answers will vary.

Examining Meaning and Use (p. 363)
1. Present situations: 1a and 2a
   Past situations: 1b and 2b
2. 2a and 2b

D1: Listening for Meaning and Use (p. 364)
2. a
3. a
4. b
5. b
6. a
7. b
8. b

D2: Expressing Regret (p. 364)
Answers will vary. Some examples are:
2. I wish I hadn't raised my voice.
   If only I hadn't gotten angry.
3. I wish I'd told him how I felt.
   If only I'd explained my feelings.
4. I wish I'd called my doctor before I missed so many classes.
   If only I'd called my doctor as soon as I started to feel sick.
5. I wish someone had called to remind me.
   If only I'd remembered his birthday.
6. I wish I hadn't accepted the first offer so quickly.
   If only the other company had called me first.

D3: Expressing Regret or Dissatisfaction (p. 365)
A. Answers will vary. Some examples are:
3. B: I wish he hadn't.
4. B: If only it hadn't.
5. B: I wish it hadn't been.
6. B: If only I had.
7. B: I wish it hadn't.
8. B: If only they had.

B. Answers will vary.

D4: Explaining Wishes (p. 365)
A. Answers will vary.
B. Answers will vary.

E1: Thinking About Meaning and Use (p. 366)
1. b. T
2. a. T
   b. F
3. a. F
   b. T
4. a. F
   b. T
5. a. T
   b. T
6. a. F
   b. T
7. a. T
   b. T
8. a. T
   b. T

E2: Editing (p. 367)

Historians love to think about the dramatic "what-ifs" of history. They have even given the name "counterfactual history" to this pursuit. How would history ~~had~~ *have* changed if some key event had been different? What would the consequences ~~been~~ *have* been if the weather ~~has~~ *had* been different in a certain battle? What would ~~had~~ *have* happened if a famous person had lived instead of died? These are the sorts of questions that are asked in two recent books that imagine how history might ~~been~~ *have* been under different circumstances: *What If?*, edited by R. Cowley and S. Ambrose; and *Virtual History*, edited by N. Ferguson.

Don't just wish ~~you've~~ *you'd* been alive in a different era. Go back and explore what could have, should have, or might have happened at various times in history. You won't be sorry. You'll wish ~~you'll~~ *you'd* gone back sooner!

CHAPTER 17

A3: After You Read (p. 373)
2.
3.
4. ✓
5. ✓

Examining Form (p. 374)
1. a.
   line 5: how bad your job has to be
   line 21: what opportunities are out there
   line 22: what kinds of skills and experience are required to get those jobs
   line 23: how much these positions pay
   line 30: which areas you need more experience in
   line 31: which skills you need to improve
   line 32: what opportunities are available
   line 32: what the salaries are
   line 35: what you learn during your job hunt to improve your current position
   b.
   line 2: whether you want a new job
   line 13: whether he should continue at his present job or start to look for a new one
   line 26: if you would actually end up switching jobs
   line 38: if you can work on different types of projects to expand your opportunities
   c.
   line 10: that his managers treated him with respect
   line 12: that his managers recognized his efforts or his new skills
   line 16: that job hunting and working to improve his current job are opposites
   line 34: that you are not making enough money
   line 36: that you should present your boss with the results of your salary research and a list of your accomplishments, and then ask for a raise
2. Answers will vary. Some examples are:
   a. *Wh-* clause: opportunities are
   b. *Whether/if* clause: you want
   c. *That* clause: you are not making
   The noun clauses listed above are all in statement word order (subject, verb, object).

B1: Listening for Form (p. 375)

	WH-CLAUSE	IF/WHETHER CLAUSE	THAT CLAUSE
2.	✓		
3.		✓	
4.	✓		
5.		✓	
6.			✓
7.	✓		
8.		✓	

B2: Identifying Noun Clauses (p. 376)

Many employment counselors (believe) that your résumé is a kind of personal advertisement. It (summarizes) what you have accomplished and (describes) what kind of work you want. Hopefully, it (tells) why *you* should be hired. A good résumé doesn't always (determine) whether you will get an interview, but a bad one will certainly eliminate your chances.

Résumés are only one tool that you need to use in your employment search. Many employers don't even use them; employers often (decide) whether they should hire you based on other information. Nevertheless, most employment counselors (believe) that it is worthwhile to write a good résumé. It helps you get organized. Most importantly, it helps you (figure out) what kind of job you really want and whether or not you have the qualifications.

B3: Working on *Wh-* Clauses (p. 376)

2. 1. the mail didn't come
   2. happened
   3. the post office closes
3. 1. the chemistry exam will be / is going to be / is
   2. it will start / is going to start / starts
   3. it will last / is going to last / lasts
4. 1. this costs
   2. he is

B4: Working on *If/Whether* Clauses (p. 377)

Answers will vary. Some examples are:
2. 1. it is going to rain today.
3. 1. these avocados are on sale?
   2. they are
4. 1. there are any seats for the concert on May 7.
   2. there are any seats available for the eighth?
5. 1. there is a telephone
   2. there is
6. 1. it is going to be warm
   2. it is (going to be)

B5: Unscrambling Sentences with *That* Clauses (p. 378)

2. They predict it will happen soon.
3. I guess that I need some help.
4. I remembered that my rent is due tomorrow.
5. He proved he could do it.

B6: Completing Noun Clauses (p. 378)

A. 2. how long you worked there?
3. if you liked your job.
4. what your greatest strength is?
5. why you are changing jobs?

B. Answers will vary.

Examining Meaning and Use (p. 379)

1. Noun Clause:
   what I need
   everything on your list
   whether I did or not
   if it's in the car
   Verb:
   decide
   get
   know
   wonder
   Decide, *know*, and *wonder* express mental activities.
2. 2b

C1: Listening for Meaning and Use (p. 380)

2. a
3. b
4. b
5. b
6. a
7. b
8. a

C2: Expressing Uncertainty (p. 381)

Answers will vary. Some examples are:
2. I can't remember what time it occurred.
3. I have no idea what it looked like.
4. I'm not certain how many people there were.
5. I'm not certain what the license plate number was.
6. I don't know how fast it was going.
7. I can't remember what color it was.
8. I'm not sure what he looked like.

C3: Adding *If/Whether* Clauses to Expressions of Uncertainty (p. 382)

A. Answers will vary. Some examples are:
1. b. whether or not she will have to work late.
   c. if her boss will like her.
2. a. if they will ask him a lot of questions.
   b. whether he should bring a gift or not.
   c. If they will approve of him.

B. Answers will vary.

C4: Asking Indirect Questions with *If/Whether* Clauses (p. 383)

Answers will vary. Some examples are:
2. Do you have any idea if the library is closed during vacation?
3. Could you please tell me if the teacher is going to show a film today?
4. Do you know whether the assignment is due tomorrow?
5. Do you have any idea whether the new language lab is open yet?
6. Could you please tell me if I missed anything important yesterday?

C5: Asking Indirect Questions with *Wh-* Clauses (p. 383)

Answers will vary. Some examples are:
1. b. A: Excuse me. Could you please tell me where the baggage claim is?
      B: It's upstairs to the right.
2. a. A: Excuse me. Could you please tell me what time it is?
      B: Sure. It's 3:15.
   b. A: Excuse me. I was wondering if you know where the bus schedule is.
      B: It's next to the bus stop.
3. a. A: Excuse me. Do you have any idea what the price of this shirt is?
      B: It's $37.50.
   b. A: Excuse me. Could you tell me what size these pants are?
      B: They're medium.
4. a. A: Excuse me. Could you tell me where the manager is?
      B: He's in the produce department.
   b. A: Excuse me. I was wondering how much this broccoli is.
      B: It's $1.49 a pound.
5. a. A: Excuse me. Do you know where the history department is?
      B: I think it's on the second floor in Room 217.
   b. A: Excuse me. Could you tell me where I can pay my tuition bill?
      B: You can pay it at the bursar's office.

Examining Meaning and Use (p. 384)

1. 2a and 2b
2. 1a and 1b have different meanings because they have different tenses in their noun clauses. When the mental activity verb is in the present tense, such as *know* in 1a and 1b, the verb in the following noun clause can be in the present, past, or future. The meaning of the sentence depends on which tense is used.

D1: Listening for Meaning and Use (p. 386)

2. a   3. a   4. b   5. b   6. a

D2: Thinking About Tense Agreement with *That* Clauses (p. 386)

A. 2. they'll accept, they accept, they accepted
   3. wouldn't be
   4. had won
   5. needs, needed, will need
   6. will start, starts, started

B. Answers will vary.

D3: Giving Opinions Using *That* Clauses (p. 386)

A. Answers will vary. Some examples are:
   2. I agree that most people are basically honest. It's common for people to tell the truth rather than a lie.
   3. I don't believe that marriage contracts are a good idea. I think that it makes marriage less romantic.
   4. I agree that you can't really change someone. I think if you try, you will just be disappointed.
   5. I feel that all children should leave home at 18. I think parents should only be responsible for the first 18 years of their children's lives.
   6. I agree that we learn from our mistakes. I think the most valuable lessons are learned from making mistakes.

B. Answers will vary.

D4: Expressing Opinions About Work (p. 387)

A. Answers will vary.
B. Answers will vary.

E1: Thinking About Meaning and Use (p. 388)

2. ?   4. F   6. T   8. ?
3. T   5. ?   7. F

E2: Editing (p. 389)

2. I asked her if I could borrow her pen.
3. I thought that she was sleeping when I called.
4. I can't remember who called.
5. Do you know if you are coming with us?
6. I didn't realize that she was absent.
7. She thought that he would come later.
8. Do you know if or not he's staying?/Do you know whether or not he's staying?
9. I need John's phone number, but I don't know where the phone book is.
10. Frederica didn't understand what the teacher was saying.

CHAPTER 18

A3: After You Read (p. 393)

2.
3. ✓
4.
5.
6. ✓

Examining Form (p. 394)

1. **Reporting Verbs**
   line 9: were asked
   line 14: were asked
   line 20: reported
   line 32: ask

2. *wh-* clause: what health problems they had discussed with each patient
   that clause: that they had such problems
   if/whether clause: if they understand
   infinitive clause: to fill out a detailed questionnaire

3. **Reported Speech Clause**   **Reporting Verbs**
   line 12: to list their most serious health problems   asked
   line 19: that cholesterol was a major concern   reported
   line 22: (that) their patients were suffering from obesity, high blood pressure, or certain health problems   said

line 24: that they had an obesity problem	report
line 25: (that) they had high blood pressure	say
line 26: that there was concern about their heart	said
line 28: that patients often misunderstood their doctors	concludes
line 29: that doctors may be missing the most important concerns of their patients	proposes

B1: Listening for Form (p. 396)

2. a   3. b   4. b   5. a   6. b
7. a   8. b

B2: Identifying Reported Speech (p. 396)

1. A: You're kidding. Julia <u>said</u> the same thing happened to her on Tuesday. I <u>wonder</u> whether we should complain to Allison. She hired him.
   B: I'm not sure if we should say anything yet. I <u>asked</u> Tom what he thought. He said that we should wait one more week.
2. A: Did you hear the news? Channel 7 <u>reported</u> that the superintendent just resigned.
   B: I know. I <u>wonder</u> if something happened. Everyone <u>says</u> he was pleased with the way things were going.
   A: Yesterday's news <u>mentioned</u> that he hadn't been feeling well lately. Maybe it's something serious and his doctor told him to resign.
3. A: Did you speak to the travel agent?
   B: Yes. I <u>asked</u> whether I needed to change the flight. He <u>admitted</u> that he'd made a mistake, but he said that he would take care of it. He <u>assured</u> me that everything would work out.
   A: Let's hope so. I <u>told</u> you to be careful during the holiday season. They're so busy that they often make mistakes.

Other reporting verbs:
wonder   report   mention   admit   assure

B3: Building Sentences with *Tell*, *Say*, and *Ask* (p. 397)

He asked them if it was raining.
He asked them if I had called earlier.
He asked if it was raining.
He asked if I had called earlier.
He asked to leave early.
I said that it was raining.
I said that I had called earlier.
I said to leave early.
She told them (that) it was raining.
She told them (that) I had called earlier.
She told them to leave early.

B4: Restating Questions with Reported Speech (p. 398)

A. Answers will vary. Some examples are:
2. What do you like to do?
3. Where do you work?
4. How old are you?
5. How long have you studied English?
6. What are your hobbies?

B. Answers will vary. Some examples are:
2. They also ask me what I like to do.
3. They usually want to know where I work.
4. They sometimes want to know how old I am.
5. Someone typically asks how long I've studied English.
6. Some people even ask what my hobbies are.

B5: Reporting Statements, Questions, and Imperatives (p. 398)

Answers will vary. Some examples are:
2. The patient asked if she could have a copy of the test results.
   The doctor told her (that) the lab is sending one.
3. The patient asked how often she should take the medicine.
   The doctor told her not to take it more than three times a day.
4. The patient asked if she needed to come back.
   The doctor said (that) it wouldn't be necessary unless there was a problem.
5. The patient said (that) she needed to be better by the weekend.
   The doctor asked her why.
6. The patient said (that) she was going out of town for a few days.
   The doctor told her she would be fine and that she should get lots of sleep.

Examining Meaning and Use (p. 399)

1. a and c   2. b

C1: Listening for Meaning and Use (p. 401)

2. a   4. b   6. a   8. b
3. b   5. b   7. b

C2: Understanding Reporting Verbs (p. 402)

2. informed   5. asked   8. promised
3. confessed 6. replied 9. told
4. explained 7. advised 10. admitted

C3: Reporting Messages (p. 403)

Answers will vary. Some examples are:
1. b. Joe's Repair Shop called on Monday. They asked you to call them back before 6:00 P.M.
2. a. Bob called on Tuesday. He said that he would call back later.
   b. Richard Smith called on Tuesday. He explained that he wanted/wants to talk to you about an insurance policy. He said that his number is 555-1221.
3. a. Rosa called on Wednesday. She said that she was just calling to say hello.
   b. Stuart Lee called on Wednesday. He remarked that he had been calling for several days. He asked if anything is/was wrong. He requested that you call him back soon.
4. a. Eric Martin called today. He asked where you are/were. He said that he has/had some questions.
   b. Gibson's called today. They said (that) they will/would be able to deliver the desk you ordered on Monday, March 27.
   c. Tanya called today. She said that she was sorry she hasn't/hadn't called. She said that she should have called sooner.

C4: Reporting a News Item (p. 404)

A. Answers will vary. Some examples are:
This report states that schools have begun to put "communication skills" into the curriculum.
A spokesman for the Medical Association said that the time has come to focus more on doctor-patient communication.
The latest Smith Public Opinion Poll reports that the best doctors talk with their patients.
The poll also indicates that the best doctors encourage questions, explain procedures, and discuss alternatives.
The poll reports that the best doctors also know how to listen and sometimes even use humor.
This reports says that as a result, first-year medical students are spending more time speaking and listening in retirement homes, homeless shelters, soup kitchens, and other community agencies.
The report indicates that first-year medical students are also in the classroom discussing what kinds of communication skills they need to treat these patients, and that they are also learning how to interact with patients in a variety of situations.
The situation is in the present; therefore, the tenses are in the present.

B. Answers will vary.

C5: Reporting Advice (p. 405)

A.
1. she go to an employment agency.
   she should go to an employment agency.
2. (that) she think about getting another degree.
   that she should think about getting another degree.
   her to find out about different types of graduate programs.
   (that) she find out about different types of graduate programs.
3. (that) she quit her job and have a baby
   that she should quit her job and have a baby.
   (that) she should try to teach part-time instead of full-time.
4. (that) she not quit but just take a leave of absence for a year.
   that she shouldn't quit but just take a leave of absence for a year.
   her to ask for a raise before she does anything else.
   (that) she ask for a raise before she does anything else.
   that she should ask for a raise before she does anything else.
5. she ask to teach a different grade next year.
   that she ask to teach a different grade next year.
   that she should ask to teach a different grade next year.
   to do whatever makes her happy.
   that she should do whatever makes her happy.

B. Answers will vary.
C. Answers will vary.

D1: Thinking About Meaning and Use (p. 407)

1. b. T
2. a. F
   b. ?
3. a. T
   b. T
4. a. ?
   b. T
5. a. ?
   b. T
6. a. ?
   b. T
7. a. ?
   b. T
8. a. T
   b. F

D2: Editing (p. 408)

Linguist Deborah Tannen claims ✗ men and women have different conversational styles. She argues that the differences can cause miscommunication between the sexes. Here's a typical example of what Professor Tannen means.

A married couple met at the end of the day. They greeted each other, and he asked her how ~~had~~ [had] her day been. She replied that she ~~has~~ [had had] a very busy day. She explained [to] him that she had attended several different meetings, and she had seen four clients. She described how she had felt and what ~~had she~~ [she had] been thinking. After that, she eagerly turned to her husband and asked how ~~your~~ [his] day had been. He replied that it had been the same as usual. She looked disappointed, but quickly forgot about it until later that evening when they met friends for dinner. During the meal, her husband told the group that something extraordinary had happened to him ~~today~~ [that day]. He went on to explain the amusing details. Everyone laughed except his wife. She felt quite frustrated and confused. She didn't understand why he hadn't told her the story earlier in the evening.

According to Tannen, the answer relates to the difference in conversational styles between men and women. She ~~tells~~ [says] that women use conversation to establish closeness in a relationship, but men consider conversation to be more of a public activity. Men use it to establish their status in a group. Do you agree with this distinction? Do you know men or women like this?